A Graphic Novel Memoir

# HAPPINESS WILL FOLLOW ™

## Mike Hawthorne

Published by
ARCHAIA ™

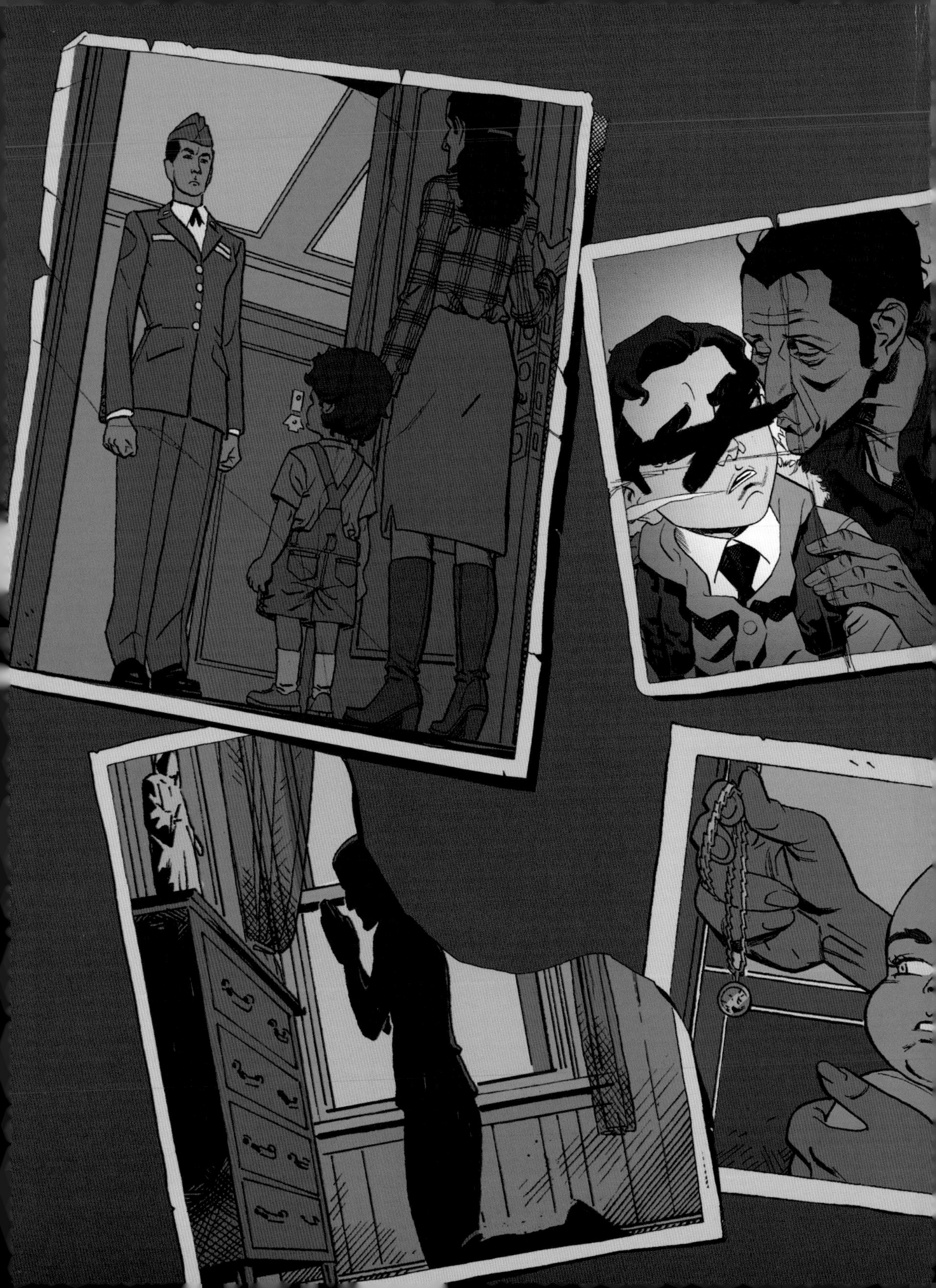

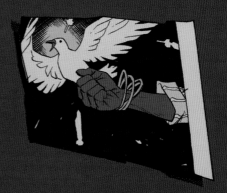

# HAPPINESS WILL FOLLOW.™

## A Graphic Novel Memoir

Written & Illustrated by **Mike Hawthorne**

Colored by **Sam Bowen** & **Ari Pluchinsky**

Lettered by **Clem Robins**

**ARCHAIA**™
Los Angeles, California

Designer **Scott Newman**

Assistant Editor **Allyson Gronowitz**

Editor **Sierra Hahn**

Special thanks to **Bryce Carlson**.

*The Velveteen Rabbit* by Margery Williams is quoted on page 128 of this graphic novel.

**ARCHAIA**™

**HAPPINESS WILL FOLLOW, July 2020.** Published by Archaia, a division of Boom Entertainment, Inc. Happiness Will Follow: A Graphic Novel Memoir is ™ & © 2020 Mike Hawthorne. All rights reserved. Archaia™ and the Archaia logo are trademarks of Boom Entertainment, Inc., registered in various countries and categories. BOOM! Studios does not read or accept unsolicited submissions of ideas, stories, or artwork.

BOOM! Studios, 5670 Wilshire Boulevard, Suite 400, Los Angeles, CA 90036-5679. Printed in China. First Printing.

ISBN: 978-1-68415-545-3, eISBN: 978-1-64144-711-9

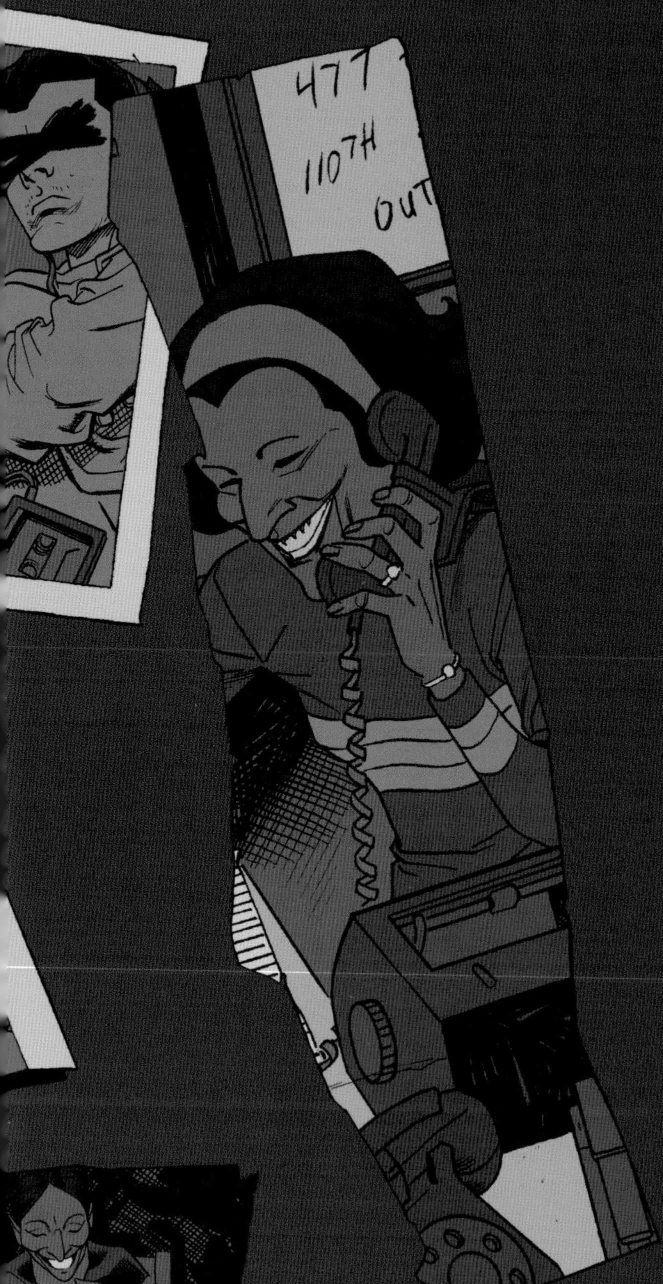

477
110TH
OUT


Dedicated to **Blanca**.

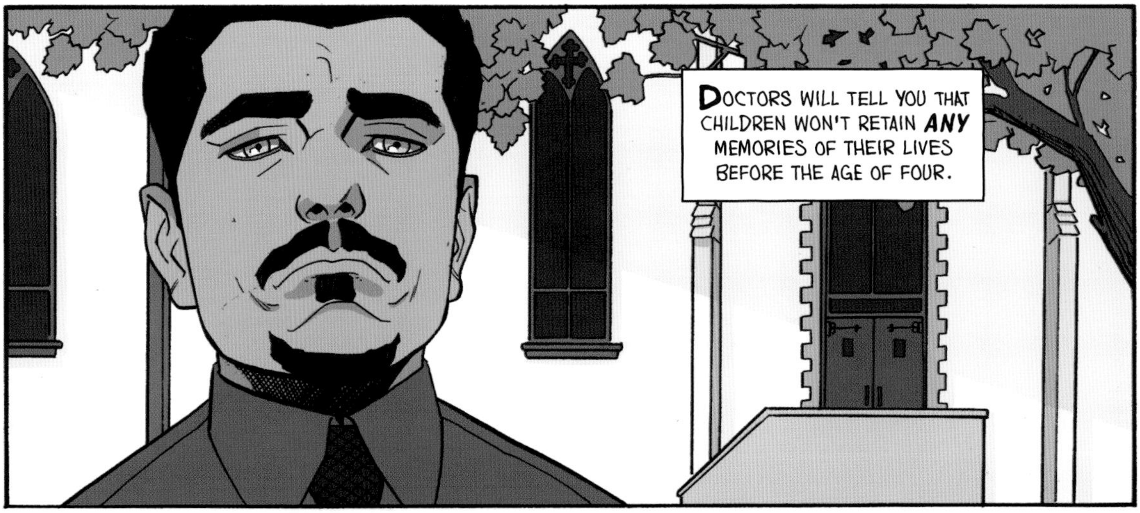
DOCTORS WILL TELL YOU THAT CHILDREN WON'T RETAIN ANY MEMORIES OF THEIR LIVES BEFORE THE AGE OF FOUR.

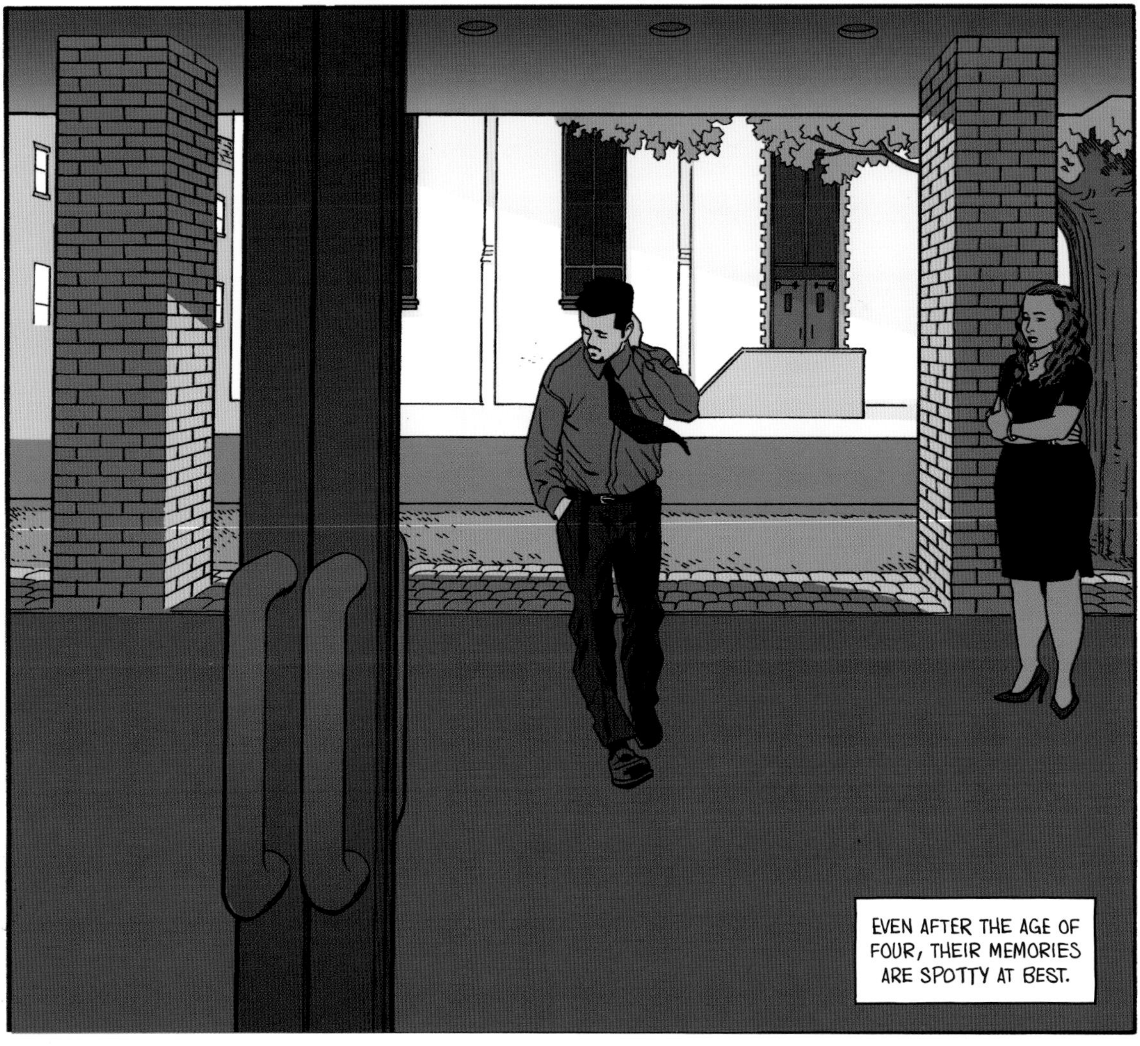
EVEN AFTER THE AGE OF FOUR, THEIR MEMORIES ARE SPOTTY AT BEST.

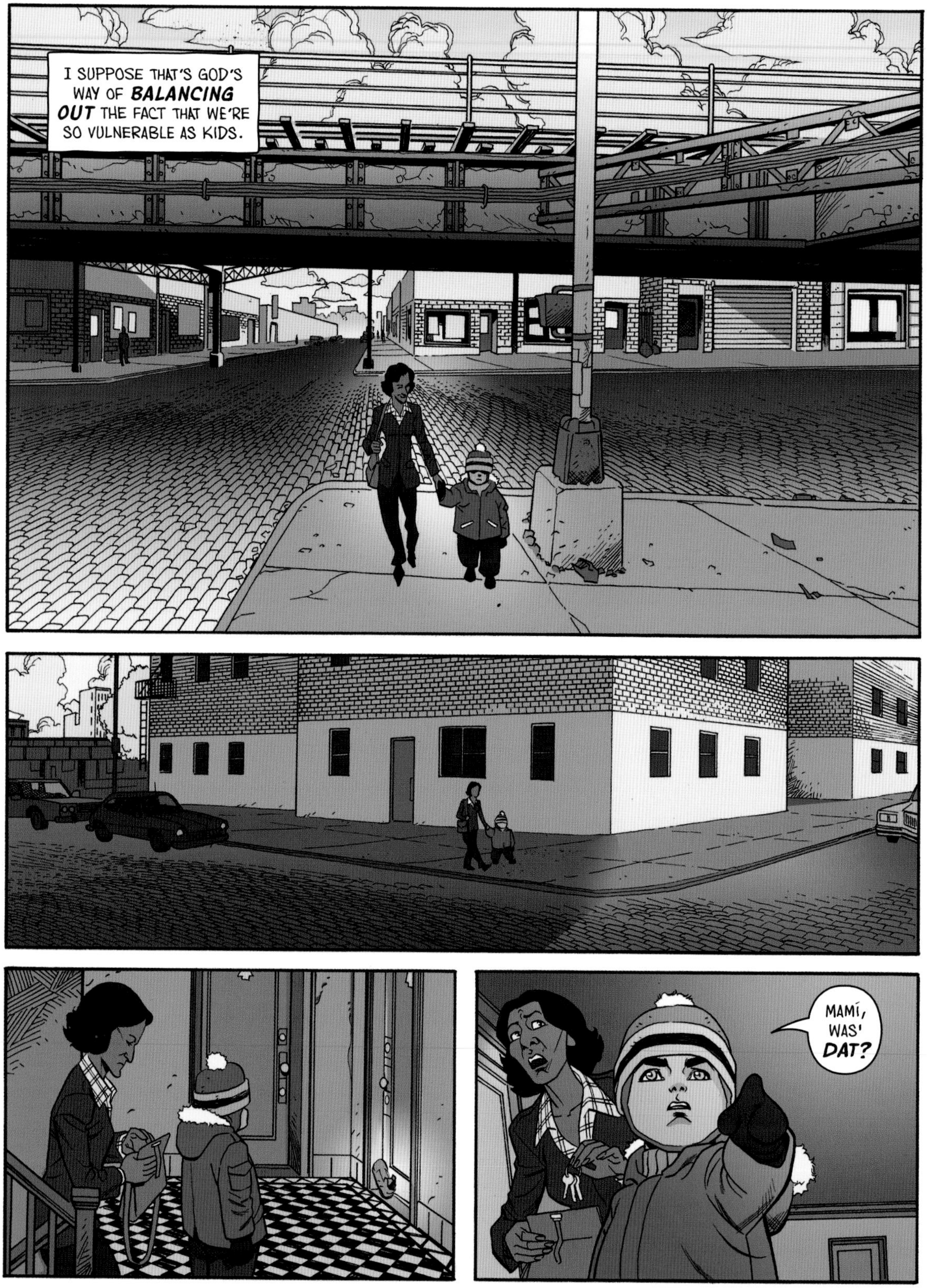
I SUPPOSE THAT'S GOD'S WAY OF BALANCING OUT THE FACT THAT WE'RE SO VULNERABLE AS KIDS.
MAMÍ, WAS' DAT?

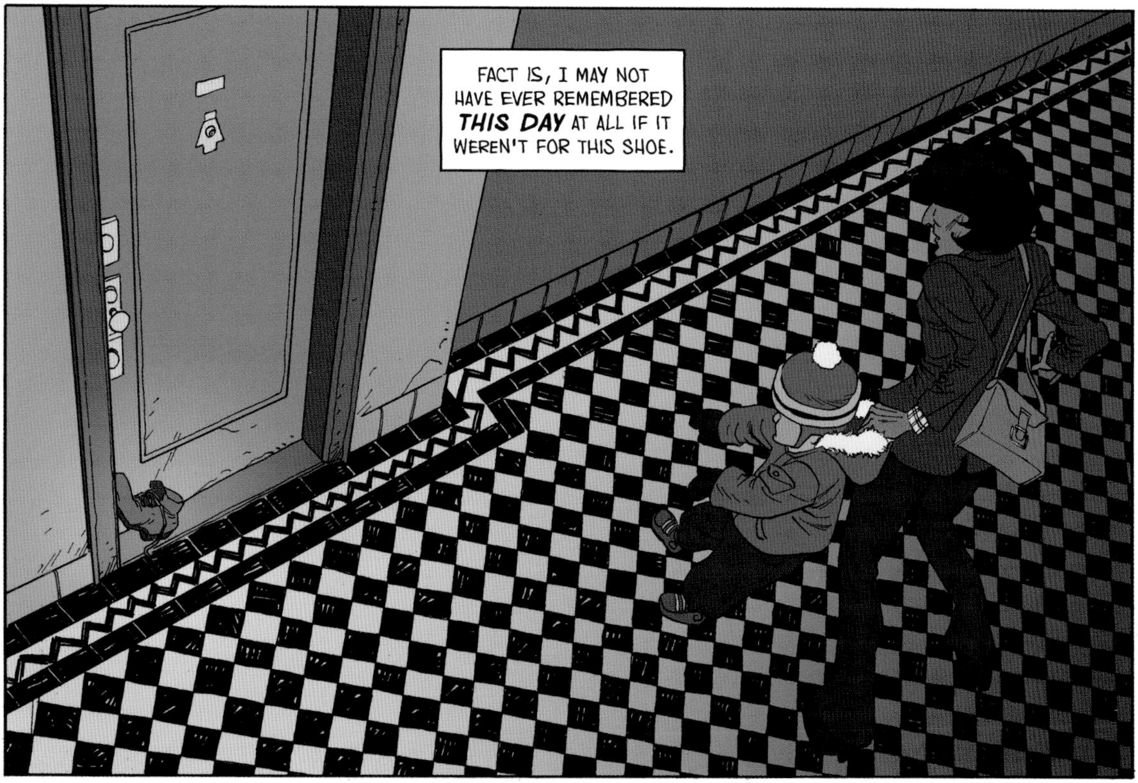
FACT IS, I MAY NOT HAVE EVER REMEMBERED THIS DAY AT ALL IF IT WEREN'T FOR THIS SHOE.

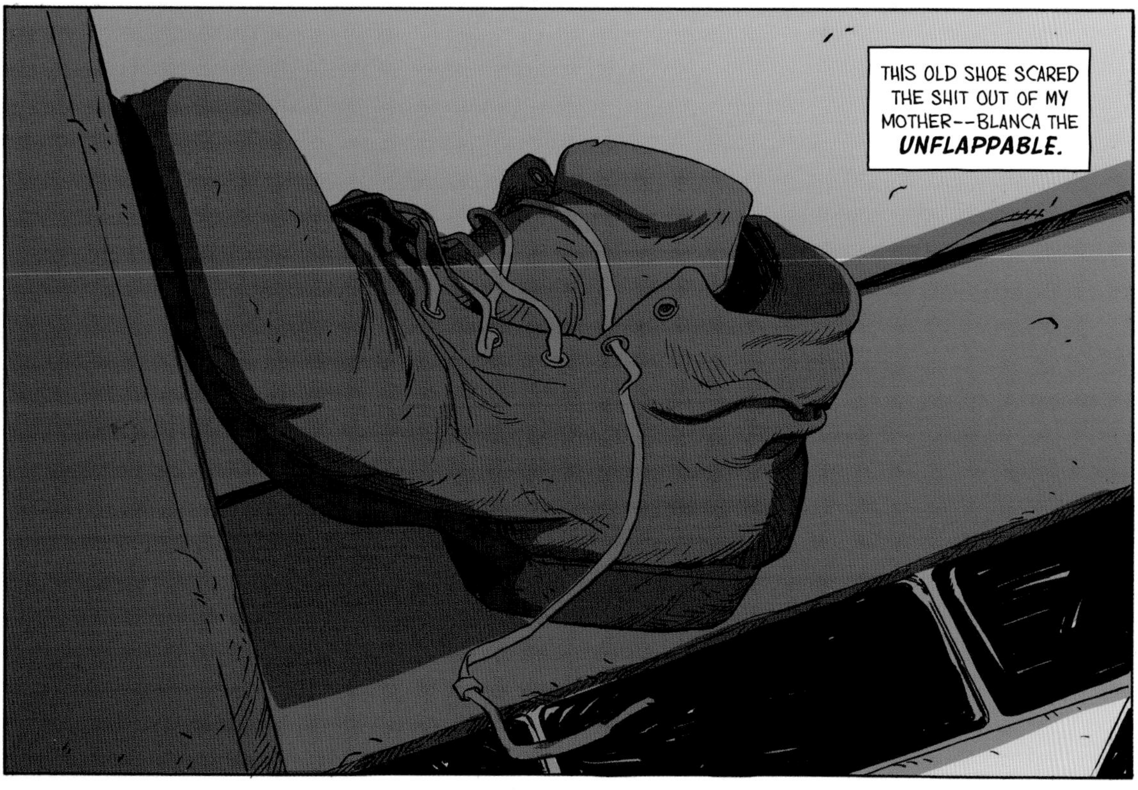
THIS OLD SHOE SCARED THE SHIT OUT OF MY MOTHER--BLANCA THE UNFLAPPABLE.

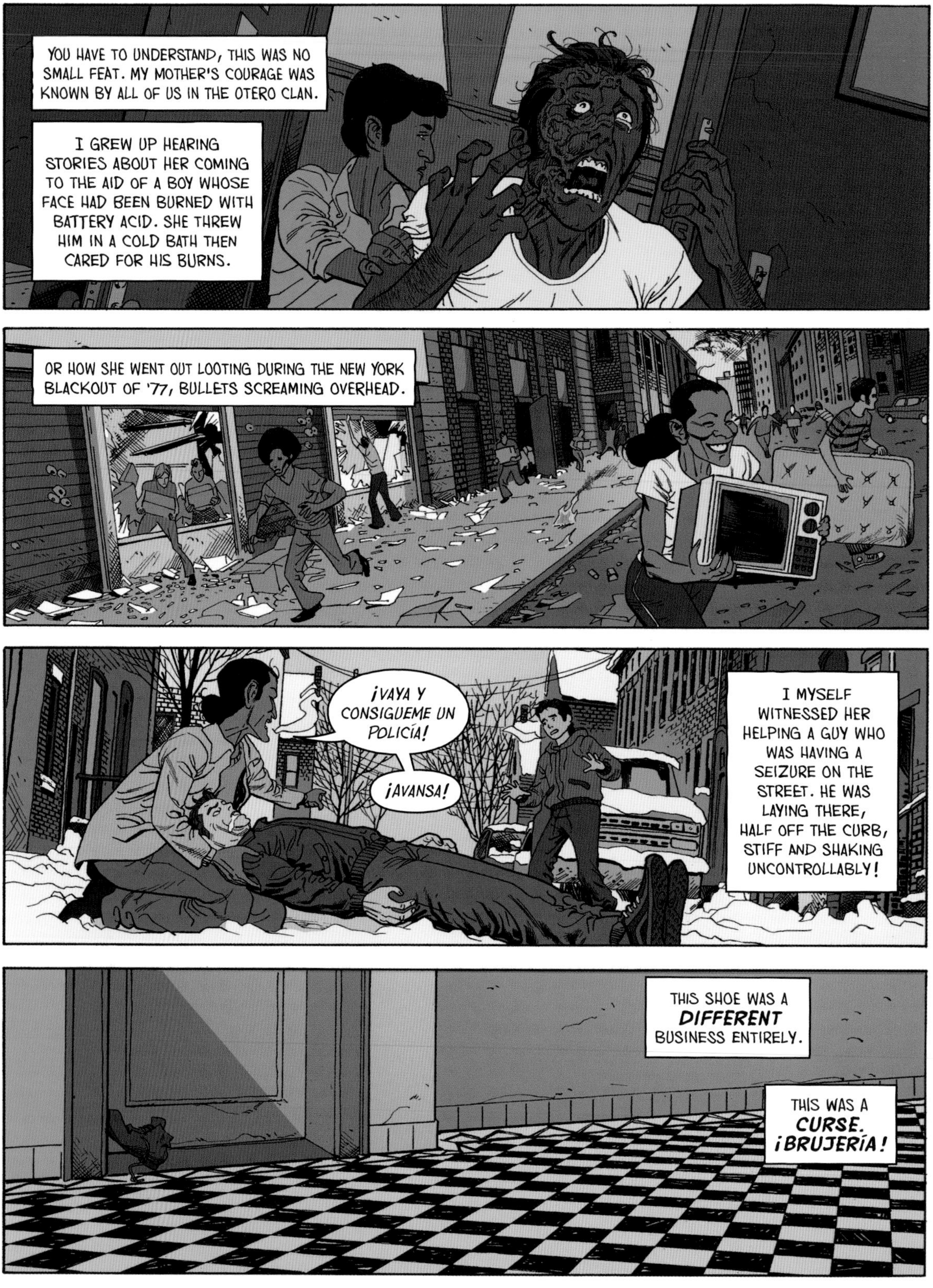
YOU HAVE TO UNDERSTAND, THIS WAS NO SMALL FEAT. MY MOTHER'S COURAGE WAS KNOWN BY ALL OF US IN THE OTERO CLAN.
I GREW UP HEARING STORIES ABOUT HER COMING TO THE AID OF A BOY WHOSE FACE HAD BEEN BURNED WITH BATTERY ACID. SHE THREW HIM IN A COLD BATH THEN CARED FOR HIS BURNS.
OR HOW SHE WENT OUT LOOTING DURING THE NEW YORK BLACKOUT OF '77, BULLETS SCREAMING OVERHEAD.
¡VAYA Y CONSIGUEME UN POLICÍA!
¡AVANSA!
I MYSELF WITNESSED HER HELPING A GUY WHO WAS HAVING A SEIZURE ON THE STREET. HE WAS LAYING THERE, HALF OFF THE CURB, STIFF AND SHAKING UNCONTROLLABLY!
THIS SHOE WAS A **DIFFERENT** BUSINESS ENTIRELY.
THIS WAS A **CURSE. ¡BRUJERÍA!**

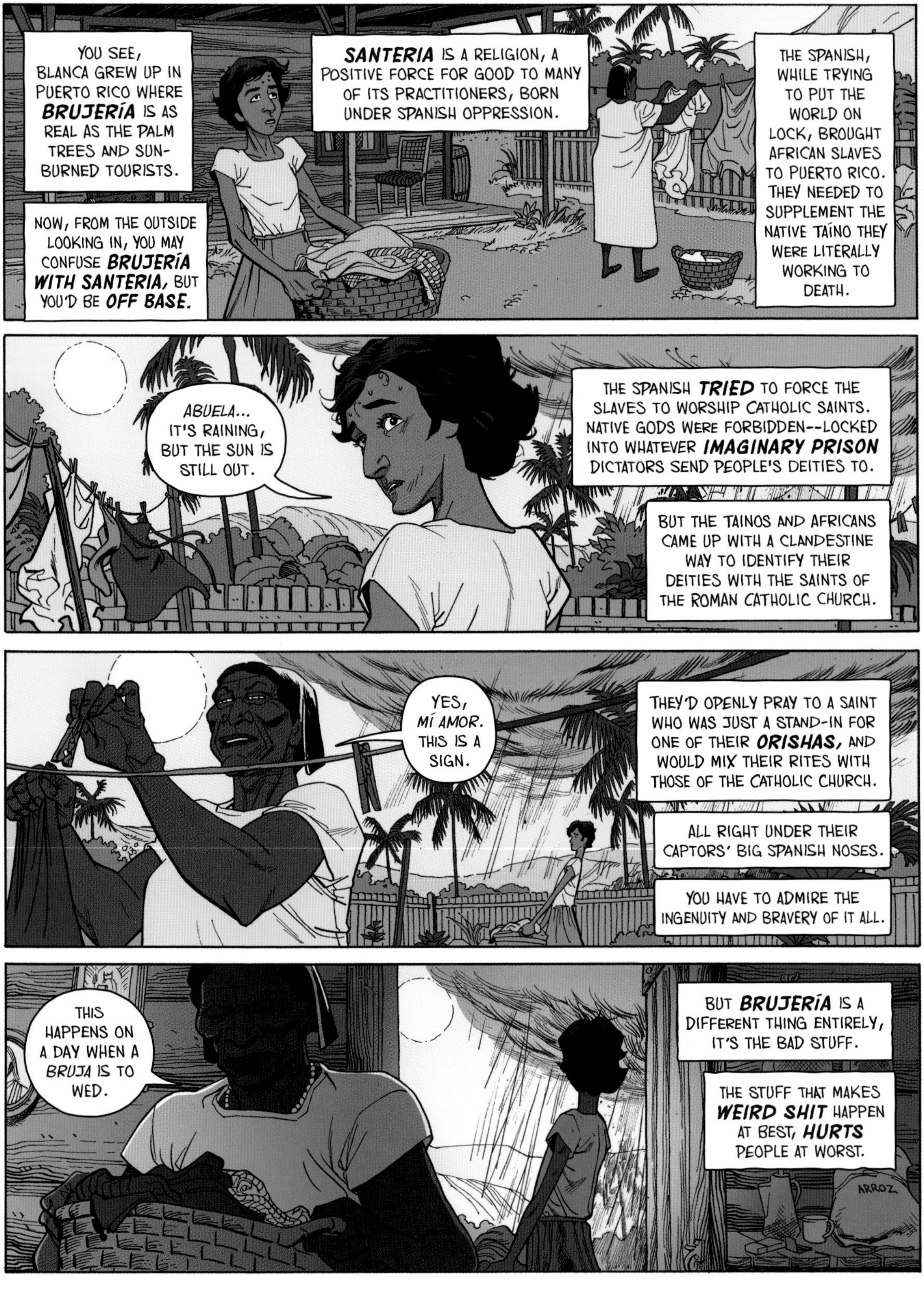
YOU SEE, BLANCA GREW UP IN PUERTO RICO WHERE BRUJERÍA IS AS REAL AS THE PALM TREES AND SUN-BURNED TOURISTS.
NOW, FROM THE OUTSIDE LOOKING IN, YOU MAY CONFUSE BRUJERÍA WITH SANTERIA, BUT YOU'D BE OFF BASE.
SANTERIA IS A RELIGION, A POSITIVE FORCE FOR GOOD TO MANY OF ITS PRACTITIONERS, BORN UNDER SPANISH OPPRESSION.
THE SPANISH, WHILE TRYING TO PUT THE WORLD ON LOCK, BROUGHT AFRICAN SLAVES TO PUERTO RICO. THEY NEEDED TO SUPPLEMENT THE NATIVE TAÍNO THEY WERE LITERALLY WORKING TO DEATH.
ABUELA... IT'S RAINING, BUT THE SUN IS STILL OUT.
THE SPANISH TRIED TO FORCE THE SLAVES TO WORSHIP CATHOLIC SAINTS. NATIVE GODS WERE FORBIDDEN--LOCKED INTO WHATEVER IMAGINARY PRISON DICTATORS SEND PEOPLE'S DEITIES TO.
BUT THE TAINOS AND AFRICANS CAME UP WITH A CLANDESTINE WAY TO IDENTIFY THEIR DEITIES WITH THE SAINTS OF THE ROMAN CATHOLIC CHURCH.
YES, MÍ AMOR. THIS IS A SIGN.
THEY'D OPENLY PRAY TO A SAINT WHO WAS JUST A STAND-IN FOR ONE OF THEIR ORISHAS, AND WOULD MIX THEIR RITES WITH THOSE OF THE CATHOLIC CHURCH.
ALL RIGHT UNDER THEIR CAPTORS' BIG SPANISH NOSES.
YOU HAVE TO ADMIRE THE INGENUITY AND BRAVERY OF IT ALL.
THIS HAPPENS ON A DAY WHEN A BRUJA IS TO WED.
BUT BRUJERÍA IS A DIFFERENT THING ENTIRELY, IT'S THE BAD STUFF.
THE STUFF THAT MAKES WEIRD SHIT HAPPEN AT BEST, HURTS PEOPLE AT WORST.
ARROZ

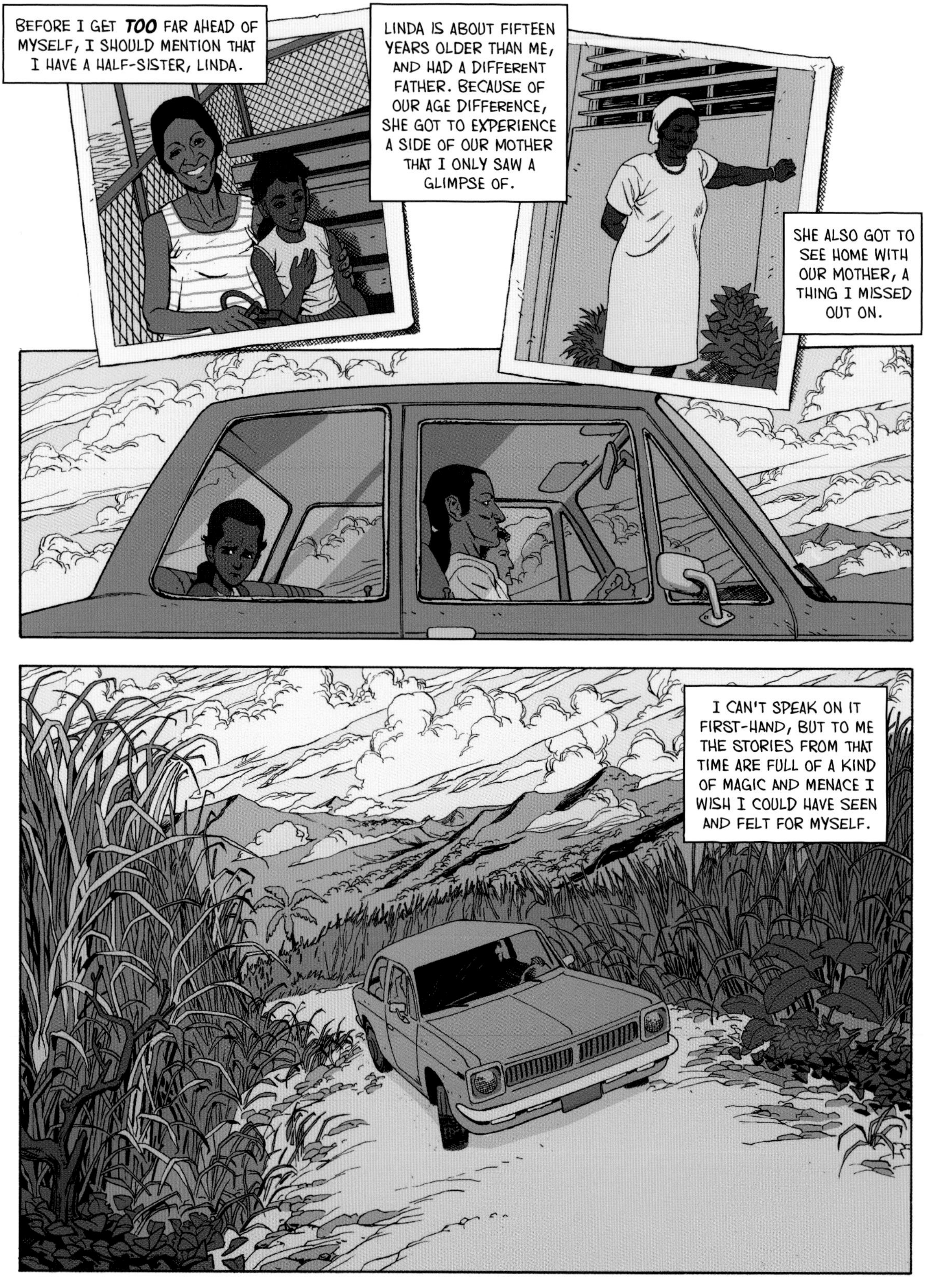
BEFORE I GET TOO FAR AHEAD OF MYSELF, I SHOULD MENTION THAT I HAVE A HALF-SISTER, LINDA.
LINDA IS ABOUT FIFTEEN YEARS OLDER THAN ME, AND HAD A DIFFERENT FATHER. BECAUSE OF OUR AGE DIFFERENCE, SHE GOT TO EXPERIENCE A SIDE OF OUR MOTHER THAT I ONLY SAW A GLIMPSE OF.
SHE ALSO GOT TO SEE HOME WITH OUR MOTHER, A THING I MISSED OUT ON.
I CAN'T SPEAK ON IT FIRST-HAND, BUT TO ME THE STORIES FROM THAT TIME ARE FULL OF A KIND OF MAGIC AND MENACE I WISH I COULD HAVE SEEN AND FELT FOR MYSELF.

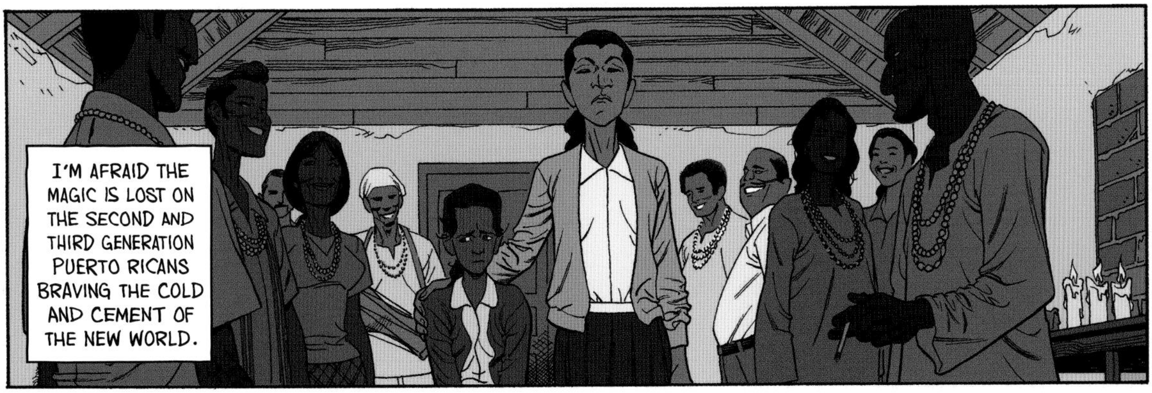
I'M AFRAID THE MAGIC IS LOST ON THE SECOND AND THIRD GENERATION PUERTO RICANS BRAVING THE COLD AND CEMENT OF THE NEW WORLD.

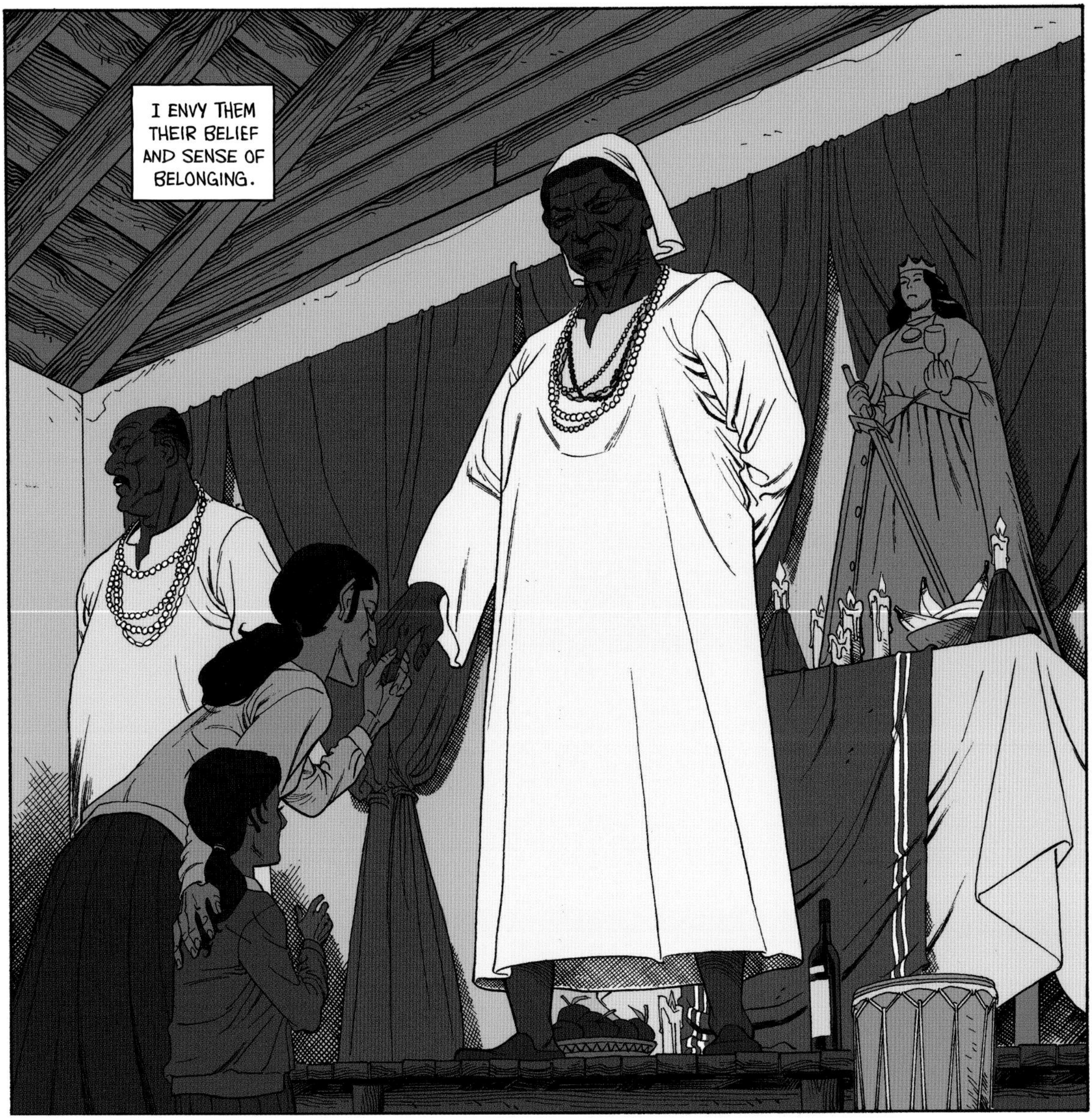
I ENVY THEM THEIR BELIEF AND SENSE OF BELONGING.

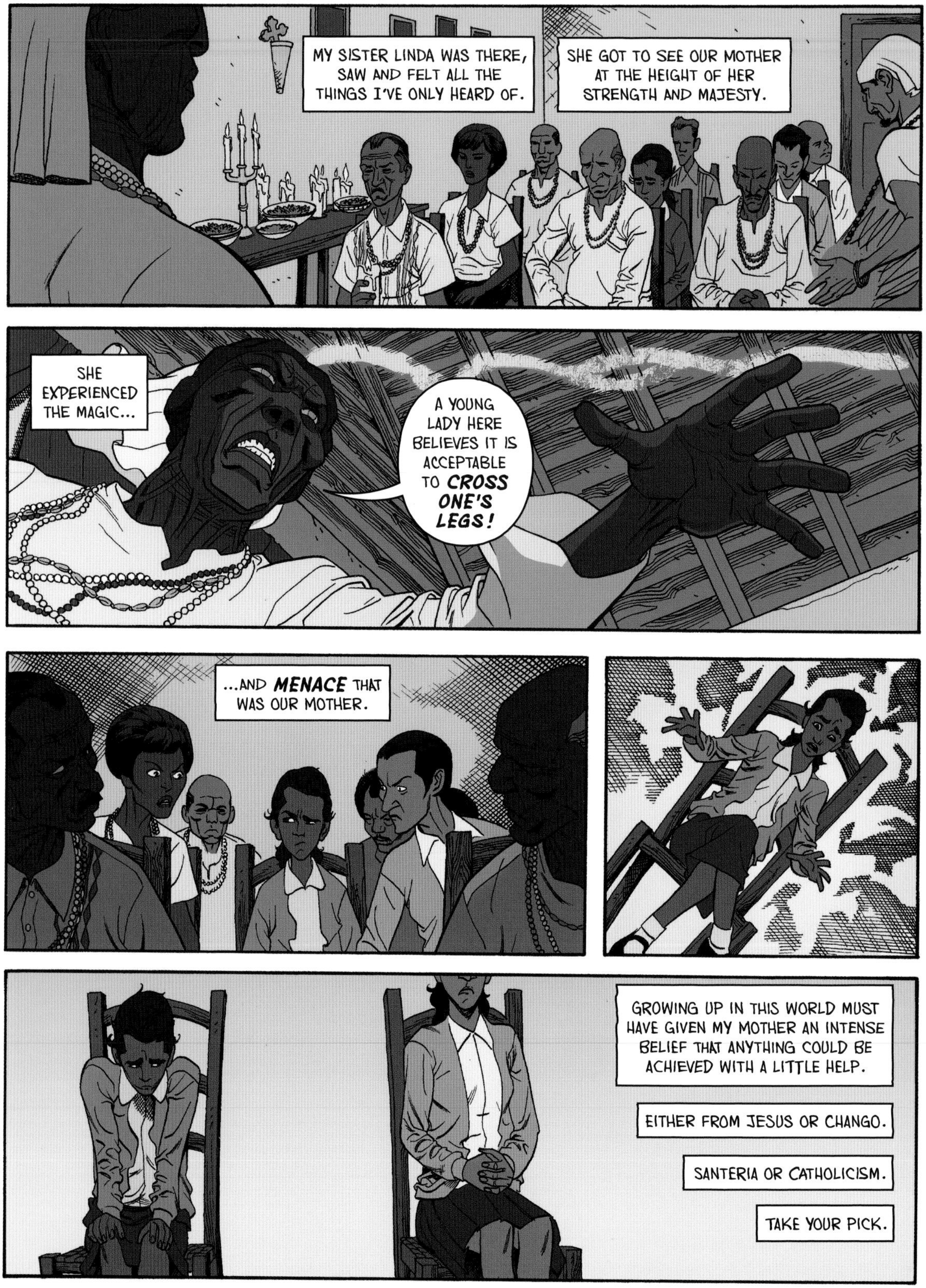
MY SISTER LINDA WAS THERE, SAW AND FELT ALL THE THINGS I'VE ONLY HEARD OF.
SHE GOT TO SEE OUR MOTHER AT THE HEIGHT OF HER STRENGTH AND MAJESTY.
SHE EXPERIENCED THE MAGIC...
A YOUNG LADY HERE BELIEVES IT IS ACCEPTABLE TO CROSS ONE'S LEGS!
...AND MENACE THAT WAS OUR MOTHER.
GROWING UP IN THIS WORLD MUST HAVE GIVEN MY MOTHER AN INTENSE BELIEF THAT ANYTHING COULD BE ACHIEVED WITH A LITTLE HELP.
EITHER FROM JESUS OR CHANGO.
SANTERIA OR CATHOLICISM.
TAKE YOUR PICK.

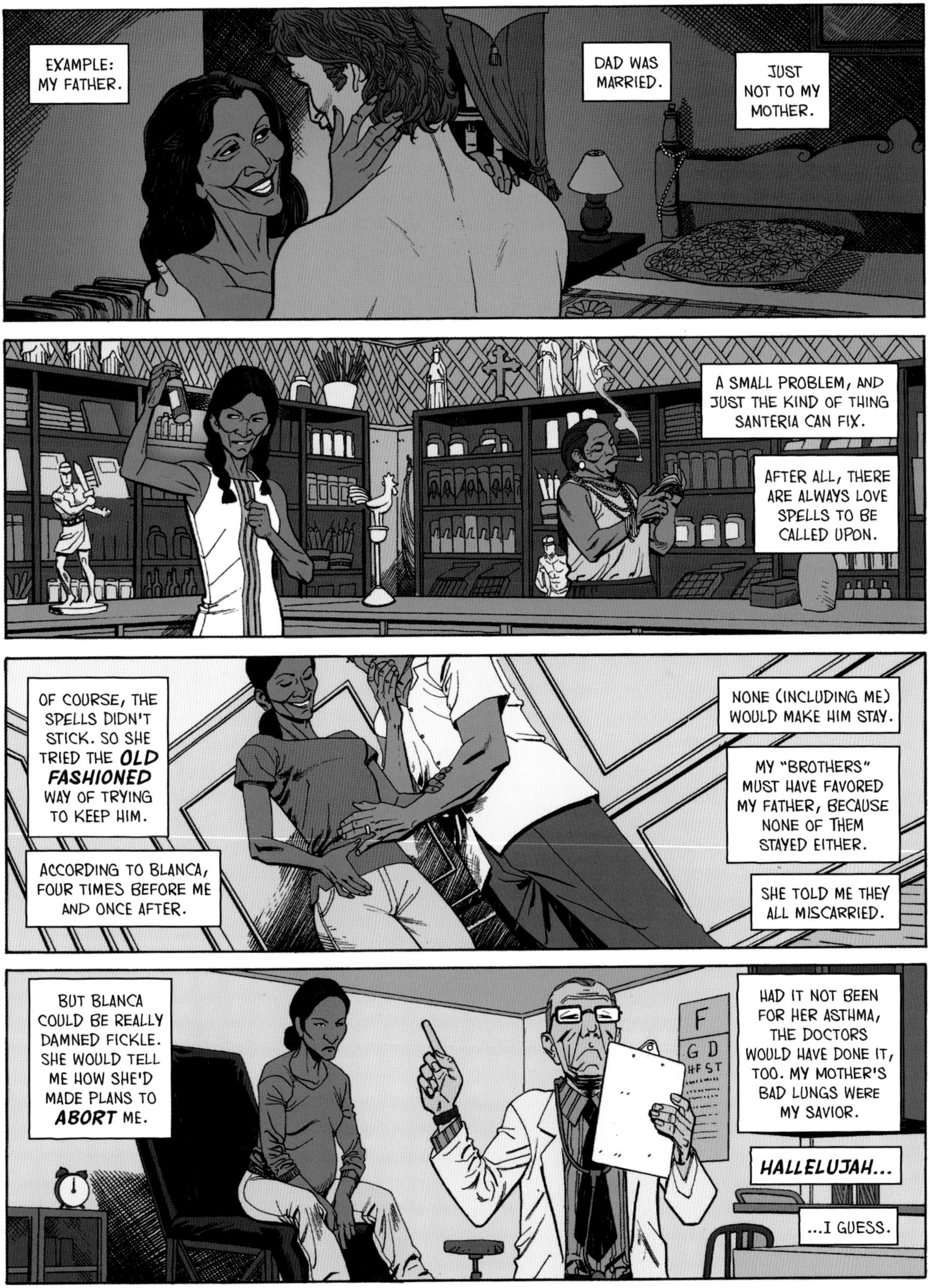
EXAMPLE: MY FATHER.
DAD WAS MARRIED.
JUST NOT TO MY MOTHER.
A SMALL PROBLEM, AND JUST THE KIND OF THING SANTERIA CAN FIX.
AFTER ALL, THERE ARE ALWAYS LOVE SPELLS TO BE CALLED UPON.
OF COURSE, THE SPELLS DIDN'T STICK. SO SHE TRIED THE OLD FASHIONED WAY OF TRYING TO KEEP HIM.
ACCORDING TO BLANCA, FOUR TIMES BEFORE ME AND ONCE AFTER.
NONE (INCLUDING ME) WOULD MAKE HIM STAY.
MY "BROTHERS" MUST HAVE FAVORED MY FATHER, BECAUSE NONE OF THEM STAYED EITHER.
SHE TOLD ME THEY ALL MISCARRIED.
BUT BLANCA COULD BE REALLY DAMNED FICKLE. SHE WOULD TELL ME HOW SHE'D MADE PLANS TO ABORT ME.
F
G D
H F S T
HAD IT NOT BEEN FOR HER ASTHMA, THE DOCTORS WOULD HAVE DONE IT, TOO. MY MOTHER'S BAD LUNGS WERE MY SAVIOR.
HALLELUJAH...
...I GUESS.

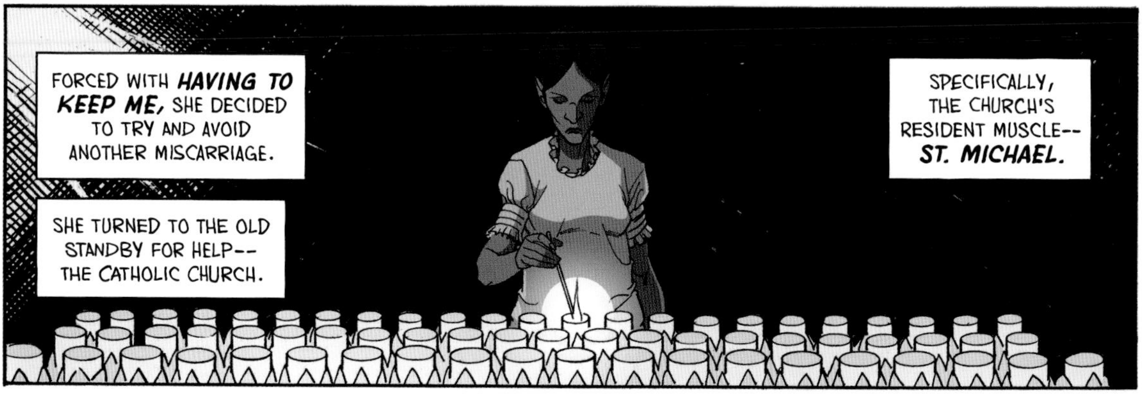
FORCED WITH **HAVING TO KEEP ME,** SHE DECIDED TO TRY AND AVOID ANOTHER MISCARRIAGE.
SHE TURNED TO THE OLD STANDBY FOR HELP-- THE CATHOLIC CHURCH.
SPECIFICALLY, THE CHURCH'S RESIDENT MUSCLE-- **ST. MICHAEL.**

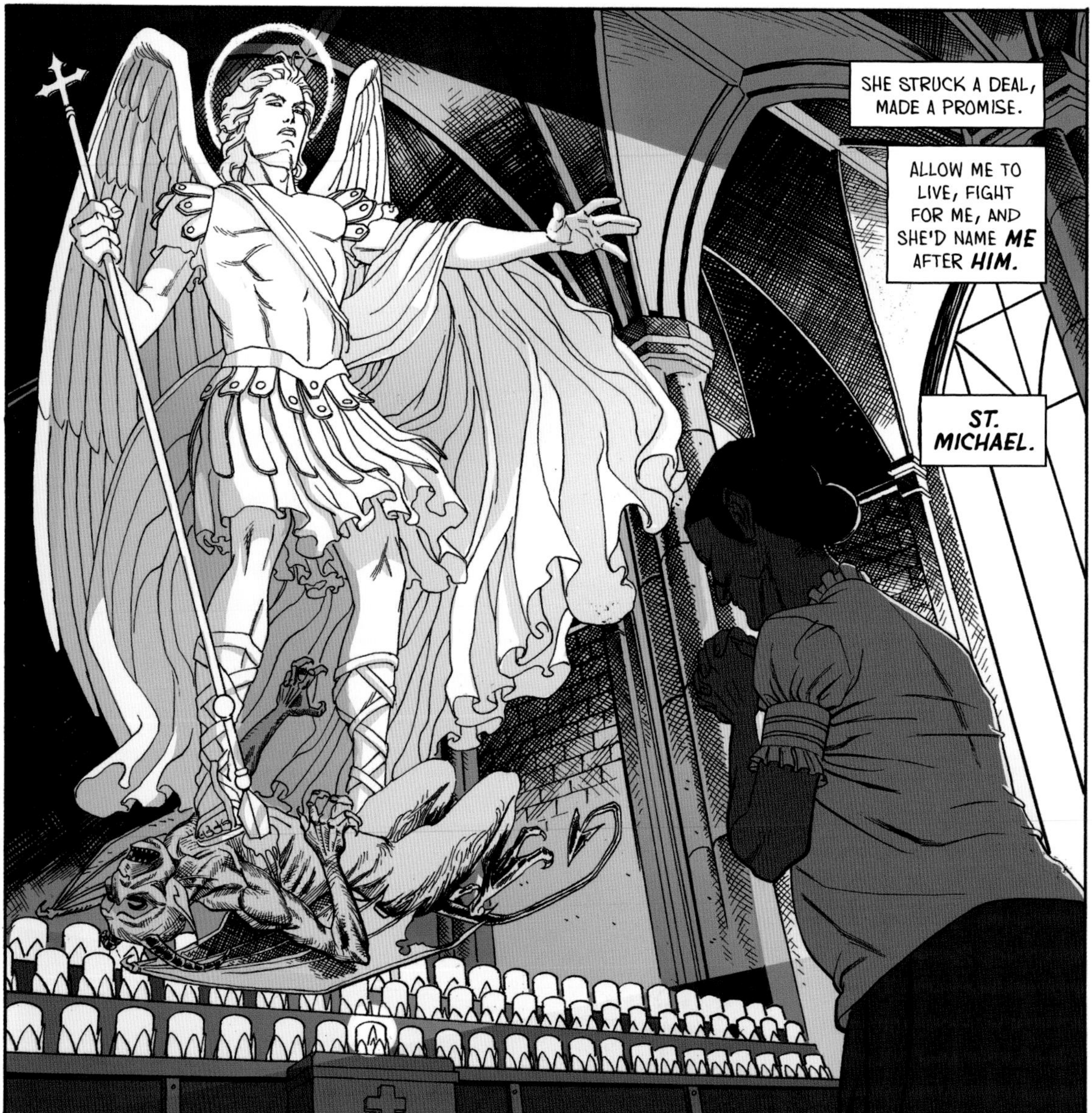
SHE STRUCK A DEAL, MADE A PROMISE.
ALLOW ME TO LIVE, FIGHT FOR ME, AND SHE'D NAME **ME** AFTER **HIM.**
**ST. MICHAEL.**

ST. MIKE, NOT ONE TO BACK AWAY FROM A SCRAP, MUST HAVE TAKEN THE DEAL BECAUSE I WAS BORN HEALTHY AND HAPPY IN A LOWER MANHATTAN HOSPITAL.

MICHAEL ANTHONY HAWTHORNE.

(THE LAST NAME SWIFTLY PILFERED FROM MY FATHER WHEN HE WASN'T LOOKING, EVEN IF I WAS A BASTARD.)

HOWEVER, WHEN IT CAME TO MY FATHER, ALL THE SPELLS AND PRAYING DIDN'T HOLD.

DAD WOULD BE OUT OF HER LIFE BEFORE I WAS OUT OF DIAPERS.

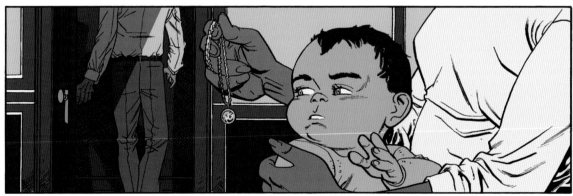

AFTER ALL, HE HAD A WIFE AND *OTHER* KIDS TO TAKE CARE OF.

BUT HE DID LEAVE A CONSOLATION PRIZE BEHIND.

THE FAILURE OF THE LOVE POTIONS DIDN'T CAUSE BLANCA TO LOSE FAITH IN SANTERIA ALTOGETHER.

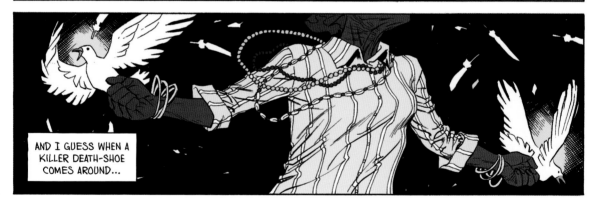

THIS **NEW** PROBLEM NEEDED A FIX THAT **ONLY** THE OLD WORLD COULD PROVIDE.

AND I GUESS WHEN A KILLER DEATH-SHOE COMES AROUND...

...YOU SURE AS **HELL** DON'T LOOK TO ST. MICHAEL AGAIN FOR PROTECTION.

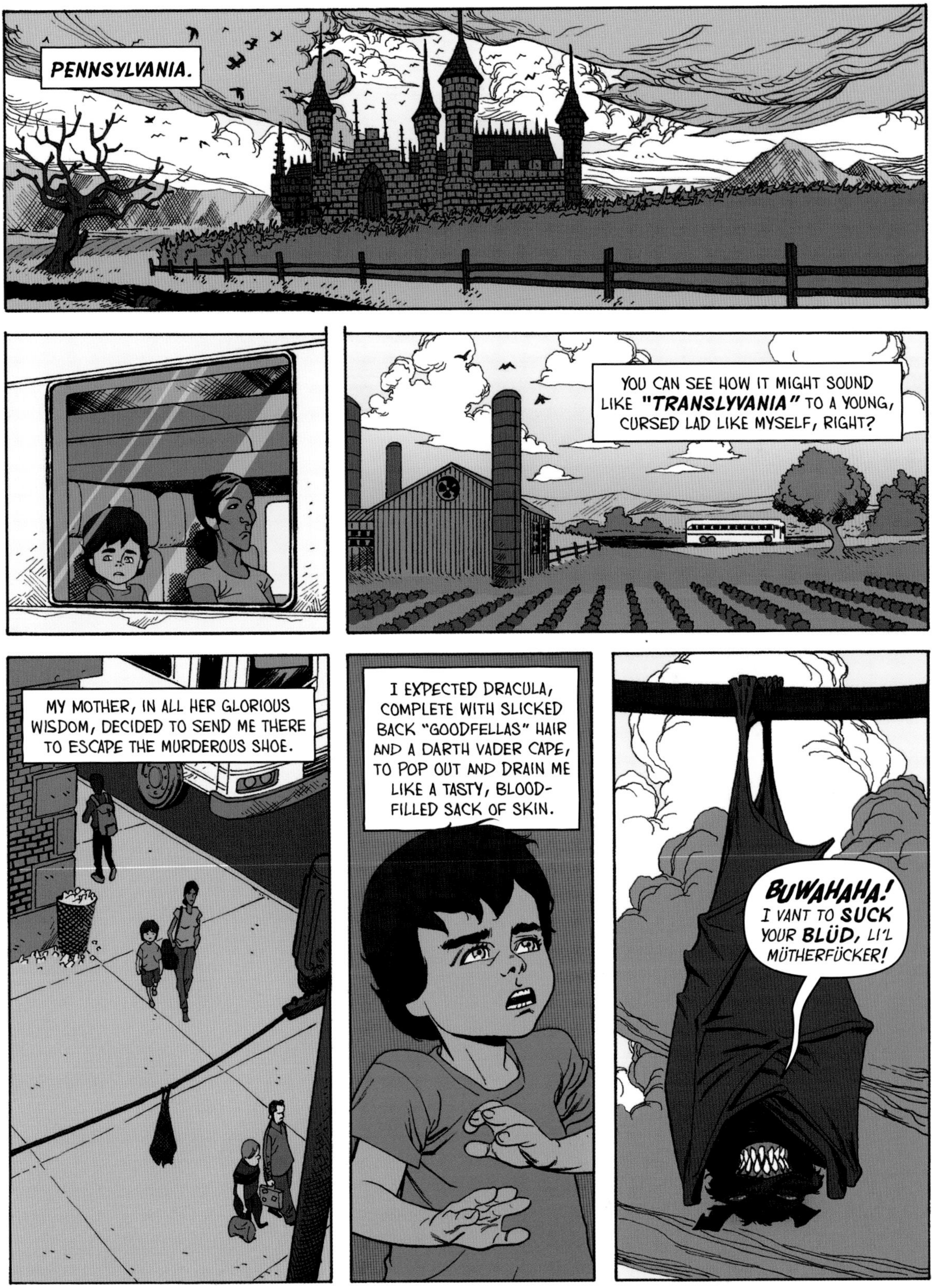
PENNSYLVANIA.
YOU CAN SEE HOW IT MIGHT SOUND LIKE "TRANSLYVANIA" TO A YOUNG, CURSED LAD LIKE MYSELF, RIGHT?
MY MOTHER, IN ALL HER GLORIOUS WISDOM, DECIDED TO SEND ME THERE TO ESCAPE THE MURDEROUS SHOE.
I EXPECTED DRACULA, COMPLETE WITH SLICKED BACK "GOODFELLAS" HAIR AND A DARTH VADER CAPE, TO POP OUT AND DRAIN ME LIKE A TASTY, BLOOD-FILLED SACK OF SKIN.
BUWAHAHA! I VANT TO SUCK YOUR BLÜD, LI'L MÜTHERFÜCKER!

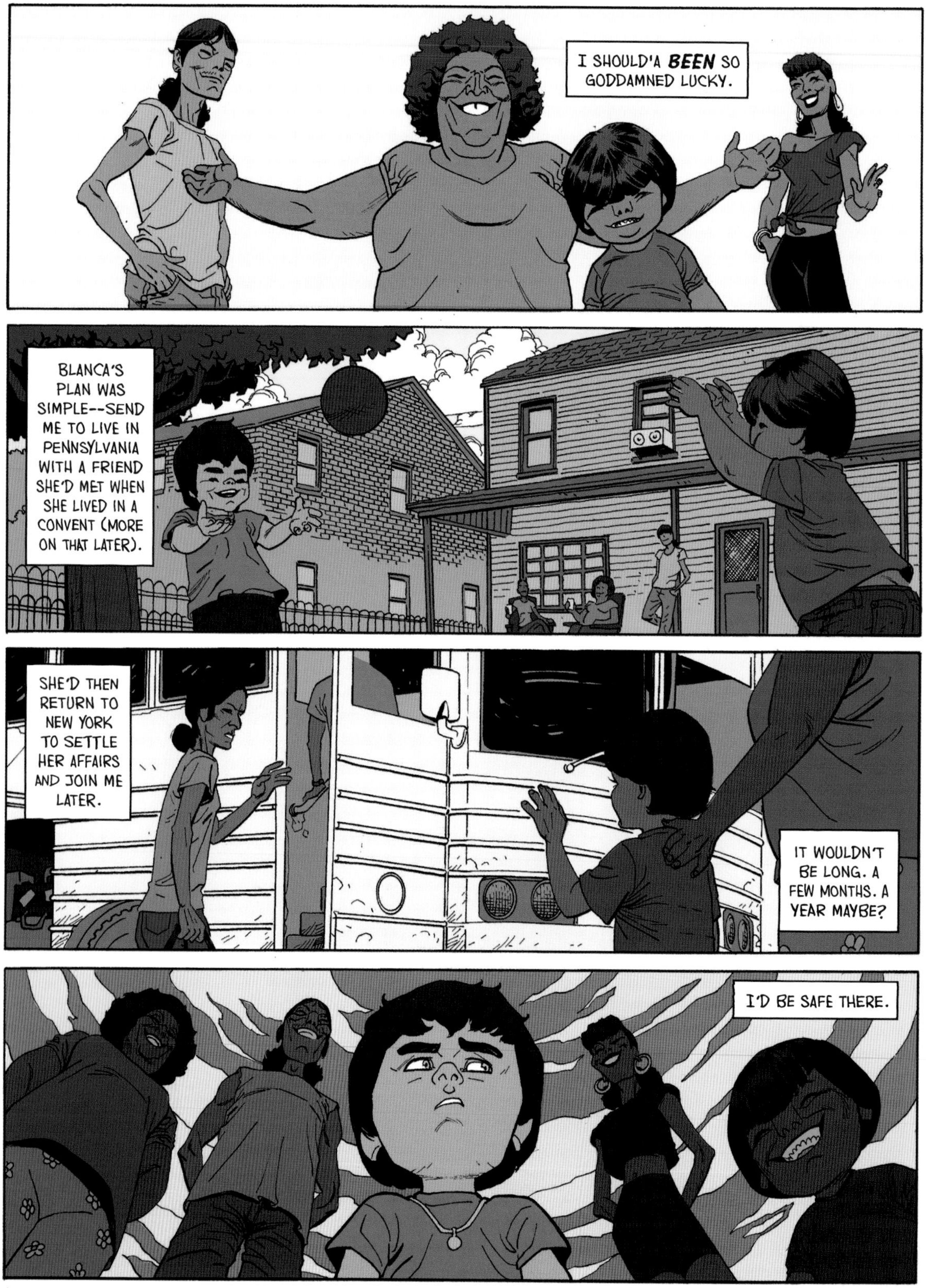
I SHOULD'A **BEEN** SO GODDAMNED LUCKY.
BLANCA'S PLAN WAS SIMPLE--SEND ME TO LIVE IN PENNSYLVANIA WITH A FRIEND SHE'D MET WHEN SHE LIVED IN A CONVENT (MORE ON THAT LATER).
SHE'D THEN RETURN TO NEW YORK TO SETTLE HER AFFAIRS AND JOIN ME LATER.
IT WOULDN'T BE LONG. A FEW MONTHS. A YEAR MAYBE?
I'D BE SAFE THERE.

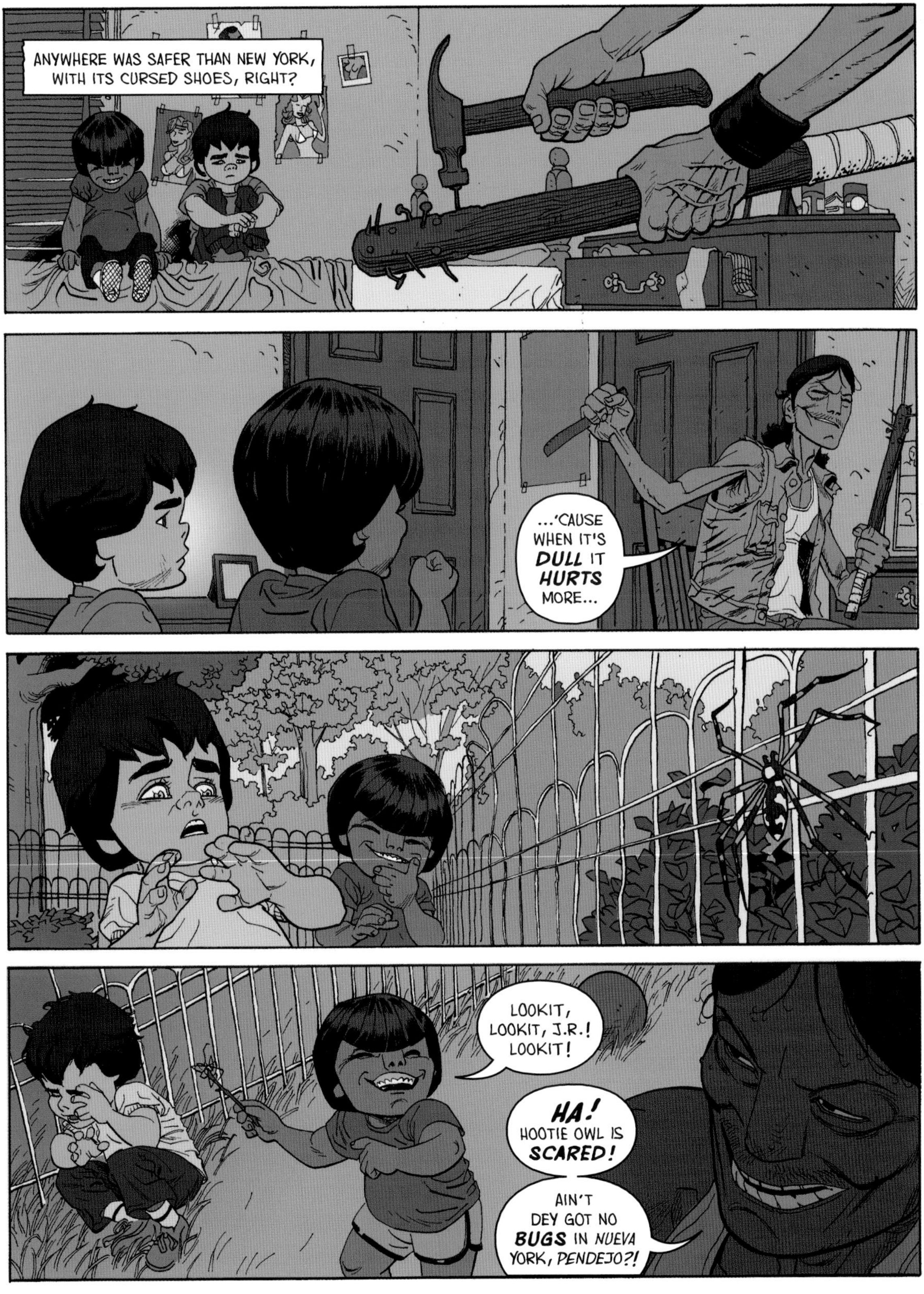
ANYWHERE WAS SAFER THAN NEW YORK, WITH ITS CURSED SHOES, RIGHT?
...'CAUSE WHEN IT'S *DULL* IT *HURTS* MORE...
LOOKIT, LOOKIT, J.R.! LOOKIT!
*HA!* HOOTIE OWL IS *SCARED!*
AIN'T DEY GOT NO *BUGS* IN *NUEVA* YORK, *PENDEJO?!*

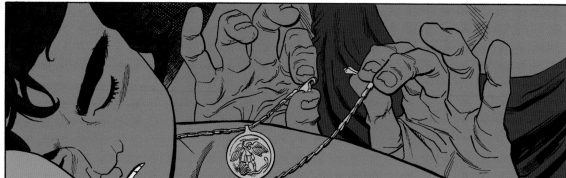

I'D HAVE GIVEN UP ON "SAFETY" TO HAVE STAYED WITH BLANCA.

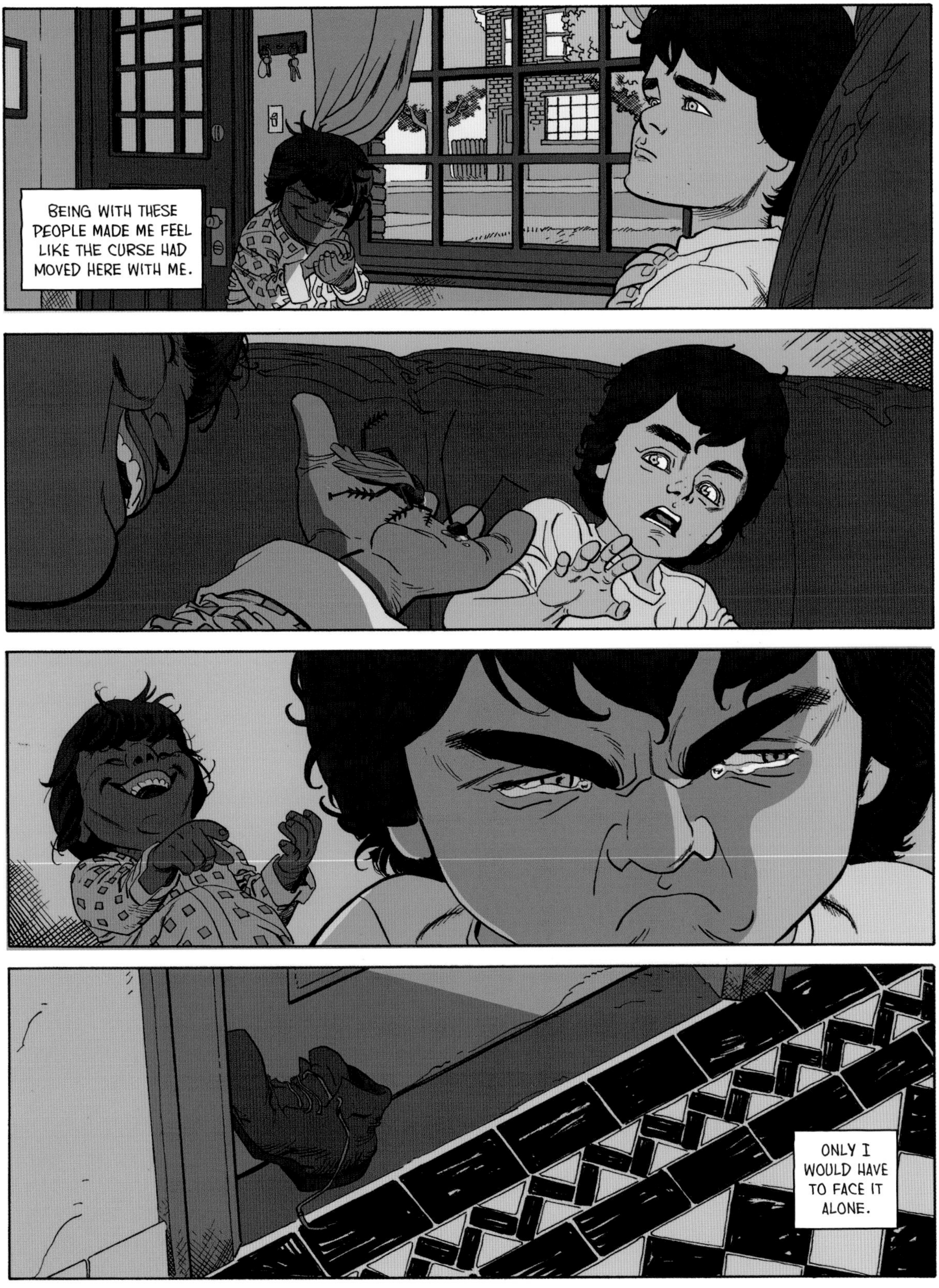
BEING WITH THESE PEOPLE MADE ME FEEL LIKE THE CURSE HAD MOVED HERE WITH ME.
ONLY I WOULD HAVE TO FACE IT ALONE.

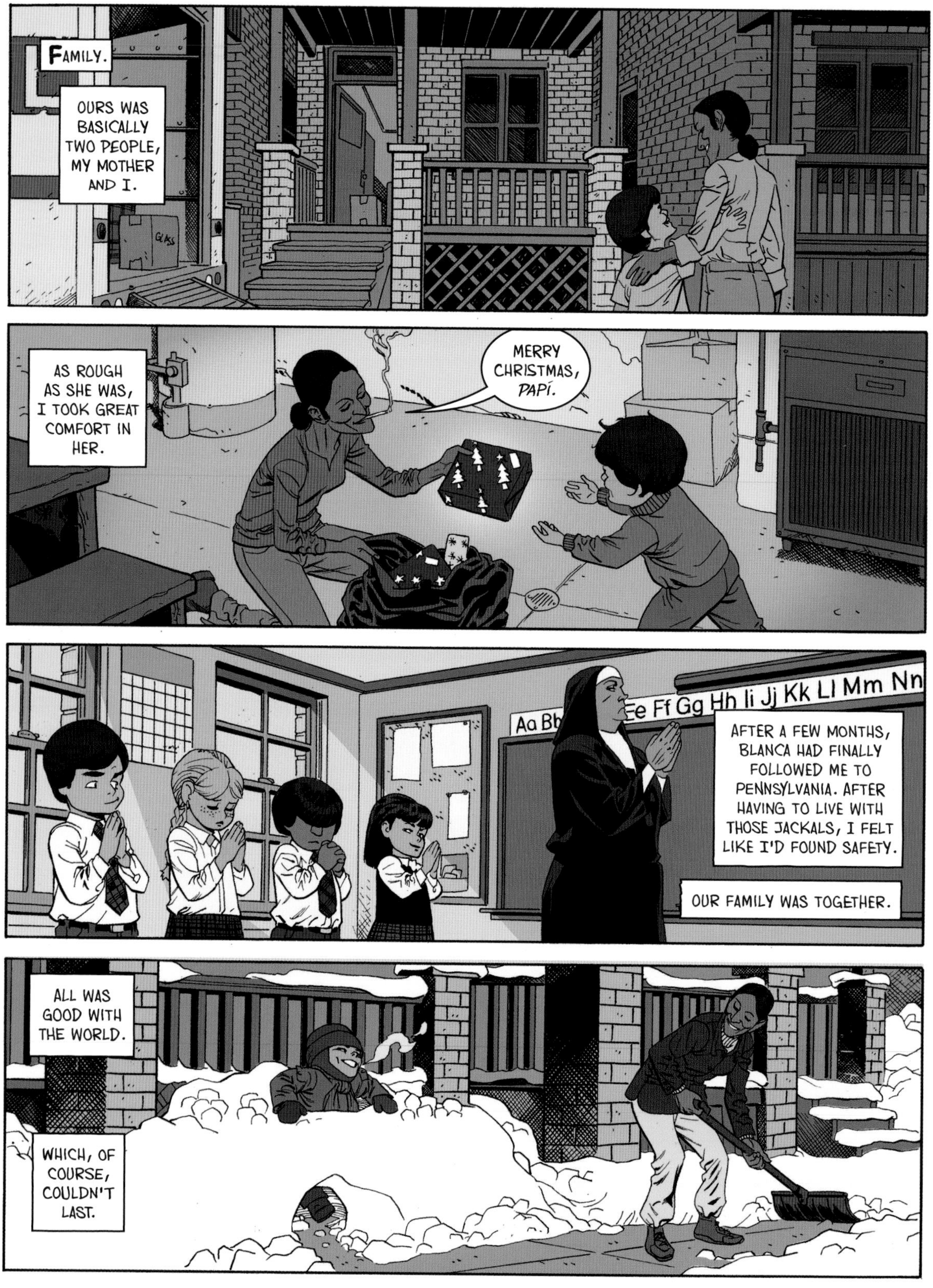
FAMILY.
OURS WAS BASICALLY TWO PEOPLE, MY MOTHER AND I.
GLASS
AS ROUGH AS SHE WAS, I TOOK GREAT COMFORT IN HER.
MERRY CHRISTMAS, *PAPÍ.*
Aa Bb Ee Ff Gg Hh Ii Jj Kk Ll Mm Nn
AFTER A FEW MONTHS, BLANCA HAD FINALLY FOLLOWED ME TO PENNSYLVANIA. AFTER HAVING TO LIVE WITH THOSE JACKALS, I FELT LIKE I'D FOUND SAFETY.
OUR FAMILY WAS TOGETHER.
ALL WAS GOOD WITH THE WORLD.
WHICH, OF COURSE, COULDN'T LAST.

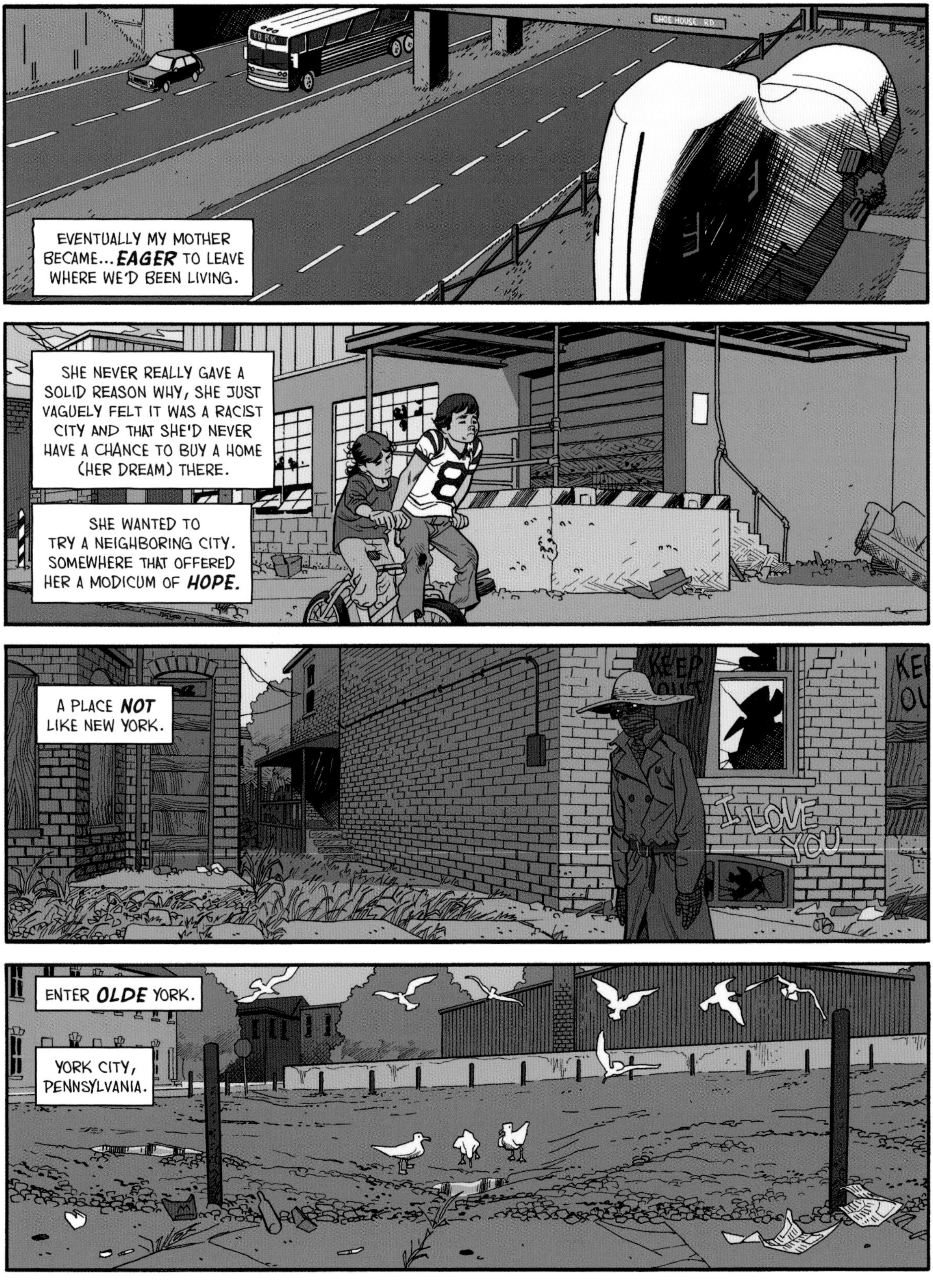

SHOE HOUSE RD.
EVENTUALLY MY MOTHER BECAME... **EAGER** TO LEAVE WHERE WE'D BEEN LIVING.
SHE NEVER REALLY GAVE A SOLID REASON WHY, SHE JUST VAGUELY FELT IT WAS A RACIST CITY AND THAT SHE'D NEVER HAVE A CHANCE TO BUY A HOME (HER DREAM) THERE.
SHE WANTED TO TRY A NEIGHBORING CITY. SOMEWHERE THAT OFFERED HER A MODICUM OF **HOPE.**
A PLACE **NOT** LIKE NEW YORK.
I LOVE YOU
ENTER **OLDE** YORK.
YORK CITY, PENNSYLVANIA.

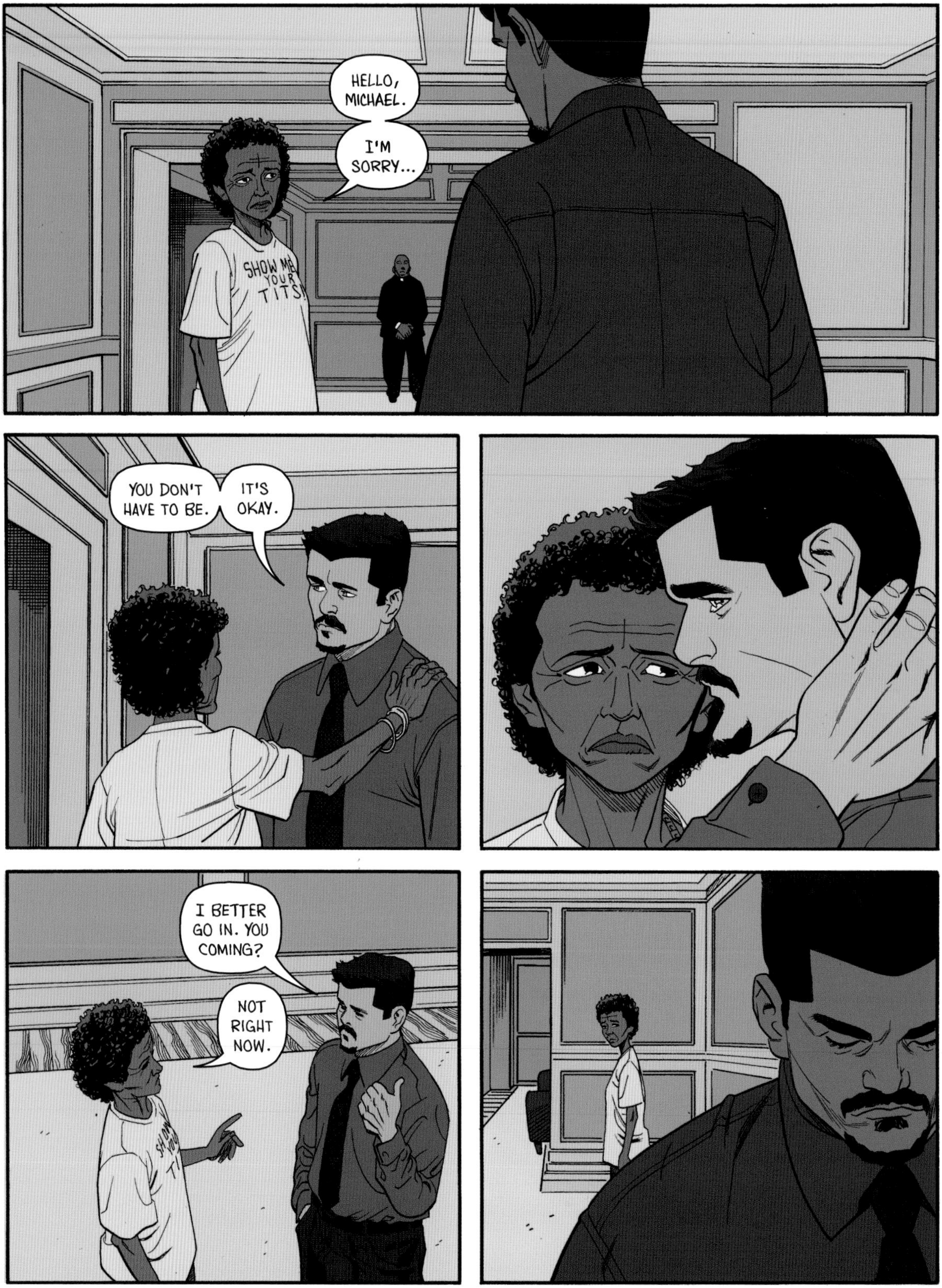
HELLO, MICHAEL.
I'M SORRY...
SHOW ME YOUR TITS!
YOU DON'T HAVE TO BE.
IT'S OKAY.
I BETTER GO IN. YOU COMING?
NOT RIGHT NOW.

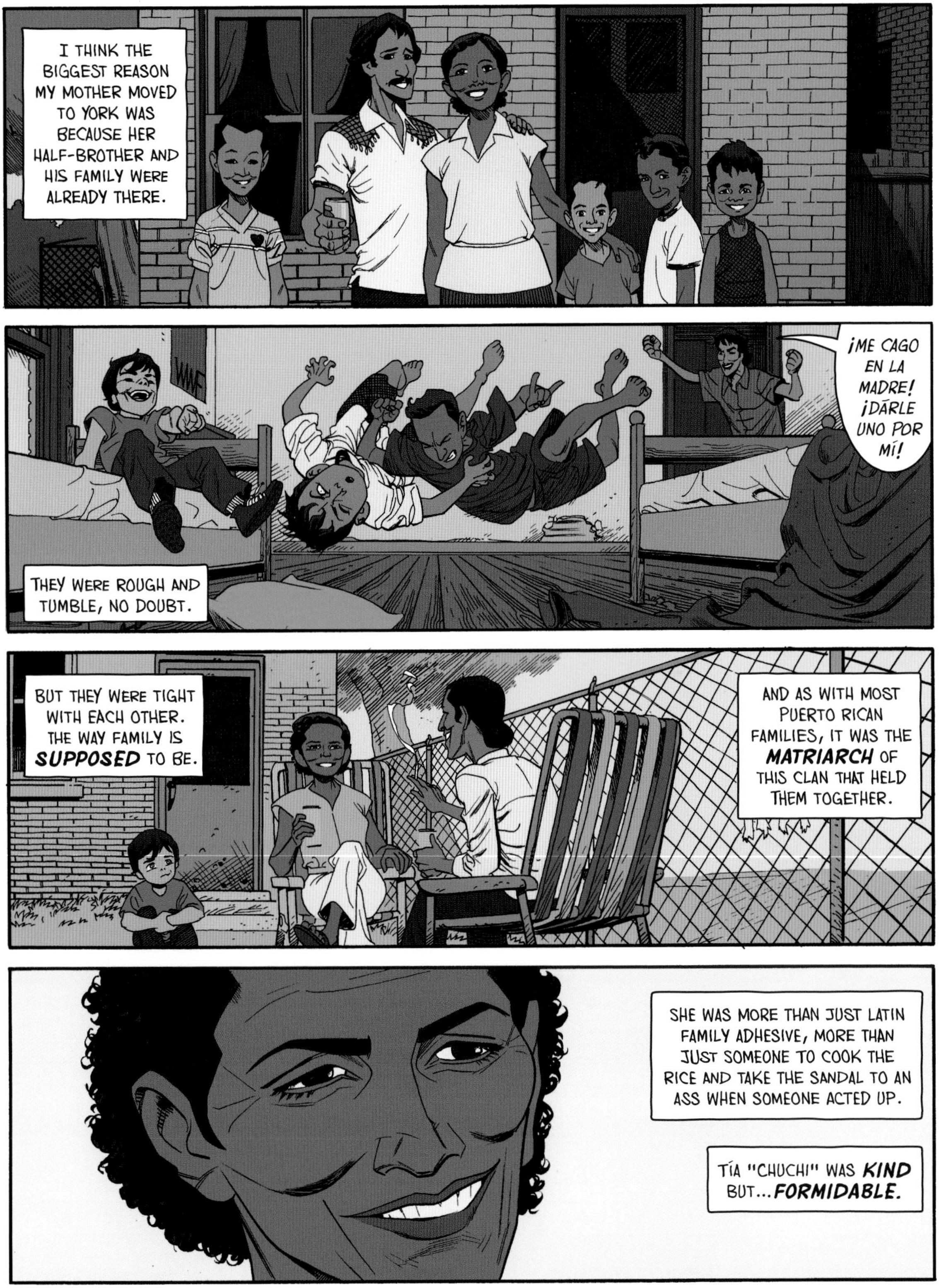
I THINK THE BIGGEST REASON MY MOTHER MOVED TO YORK WAS BECAUSE HER HALF-BROTHER AND HIS FAMILY WERE ALREADY THERE.
¡ME CAGO EN LA MADRE! ¡DÁRLE UNO POR MÍ!
THEY WERE ROUGH AND TUMBLE, NO DOUBT.
BUT THEY WERE TIGHT WITH EACH OTHER. THE WAY FAMILY IS **SUPPOSED** TO BE.
AND AS WITH MOST PUERTO RICAN FAMILIES, IT WAS THE **MATRIARCH** OF THIS CLAN THAT HELD THEM TOGETHER.
SHE WAS MORE THAN JUST LATIN FAMILY ADHESIVE, MORE THAN JUST SOMEONE TO COOK THE RICE AND TAKE THE SANDAL TO AN ASS WHEN SOMEONE ACTED UP.
TÍA "CHUCHI" WAS **KIND** BUT... **FORMIDABLE.**

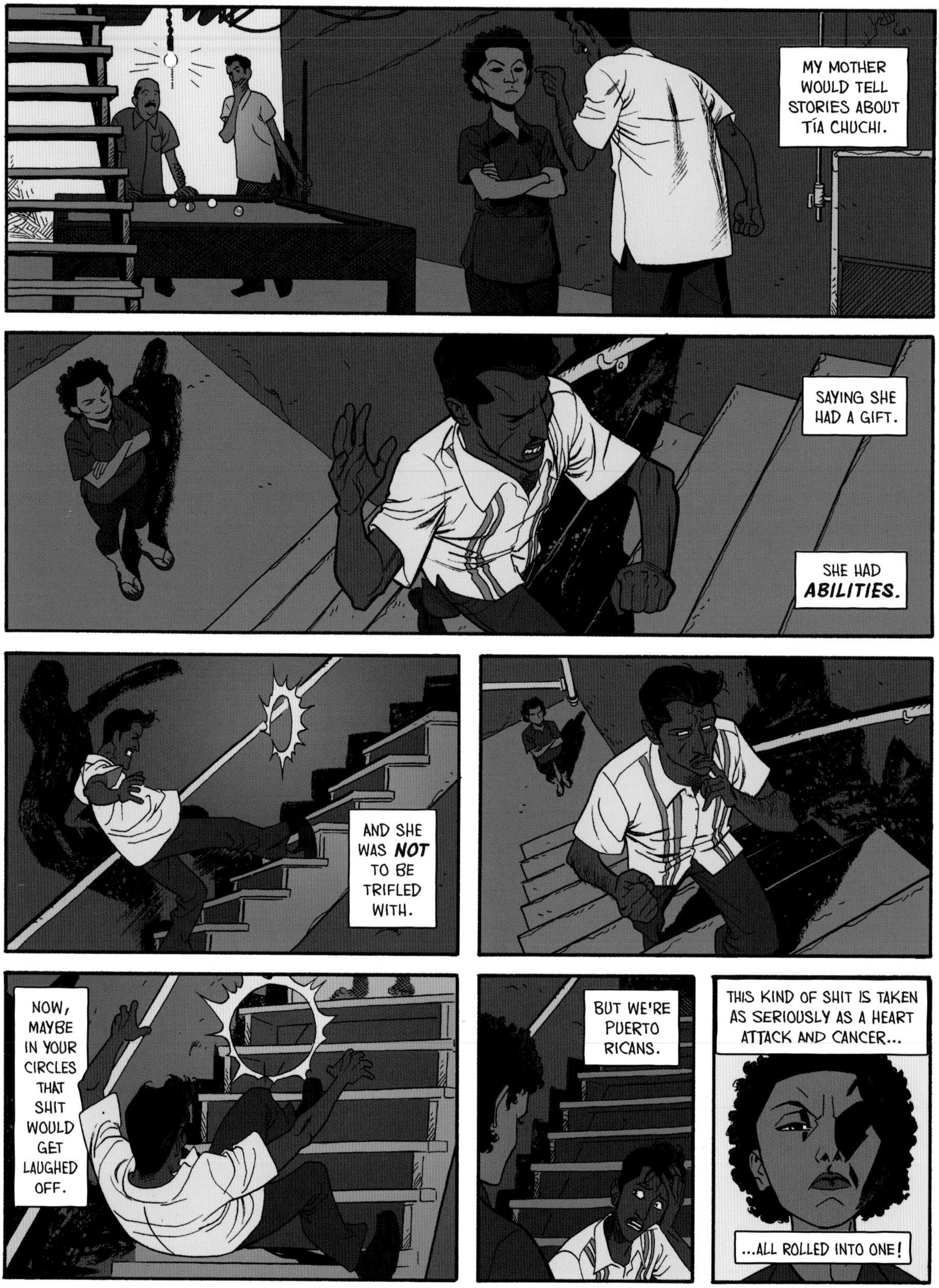
MY MOTHER WOULD TELL STORIES ABOUT TÍA CHUCHI.
SAYING SHE HAD A GIFT.
SHE HAD ABILITIES.
AND SHE WAS NOT TO BE TRIFLED WITH.
NOW, MAYBE IN YOUR CIRCLES THAT SHIT WOULD GET LAUGHED OFF.
BUT WE'RE PUERTO RICANS.
THIS KIND OF SHIT IS TAKEN AS SERIOUSLY AS A HEART ATTACK AND CANCER...
...ALL ROLLED INTO ONE!

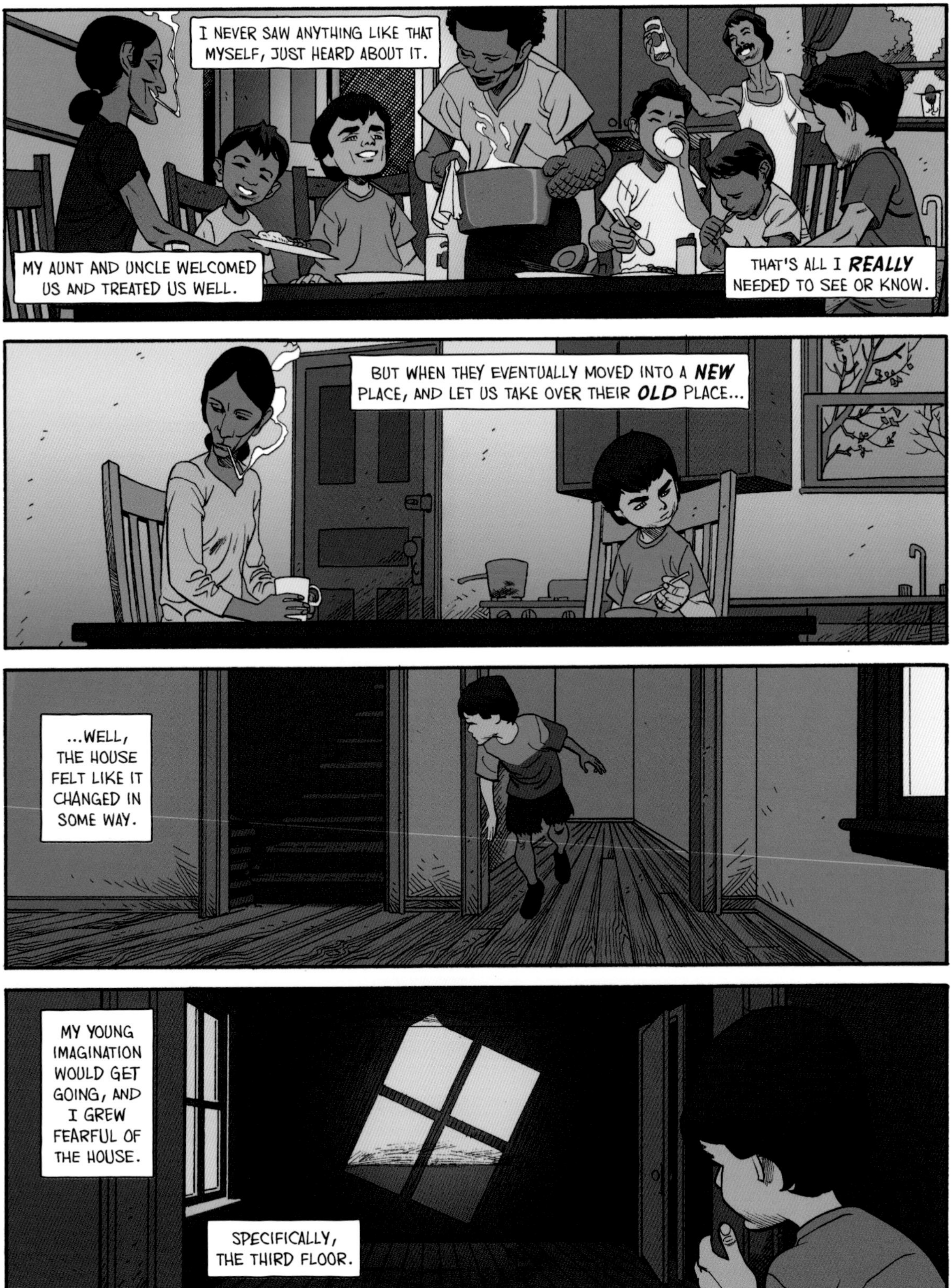
I NEVER SAW ANYTHING LIKE THAT MYSELF, JUST HEARD ABOUT IT.
MY AUNT AND UNCLE WELCOMED US AND TREATED US WELL.
THAT'S ALL I REALLY NEEDED TO SEE OR KNOW.
BUT WHEN THEY EVENTUALLY MOVED INTO A NEW PLACE, AND LET US TAKE OVER THEIR OLD PLACE...
...WELL, THE HOUSE FELT LIKE IT CHANGED IN SOME WAY.
MY YOUNG IMAGINATION WOULD GET GOING, AND I GREW FEARFUL OF THE HOUSE.
SPECIFICALLY, THE THIRD FLOOR.

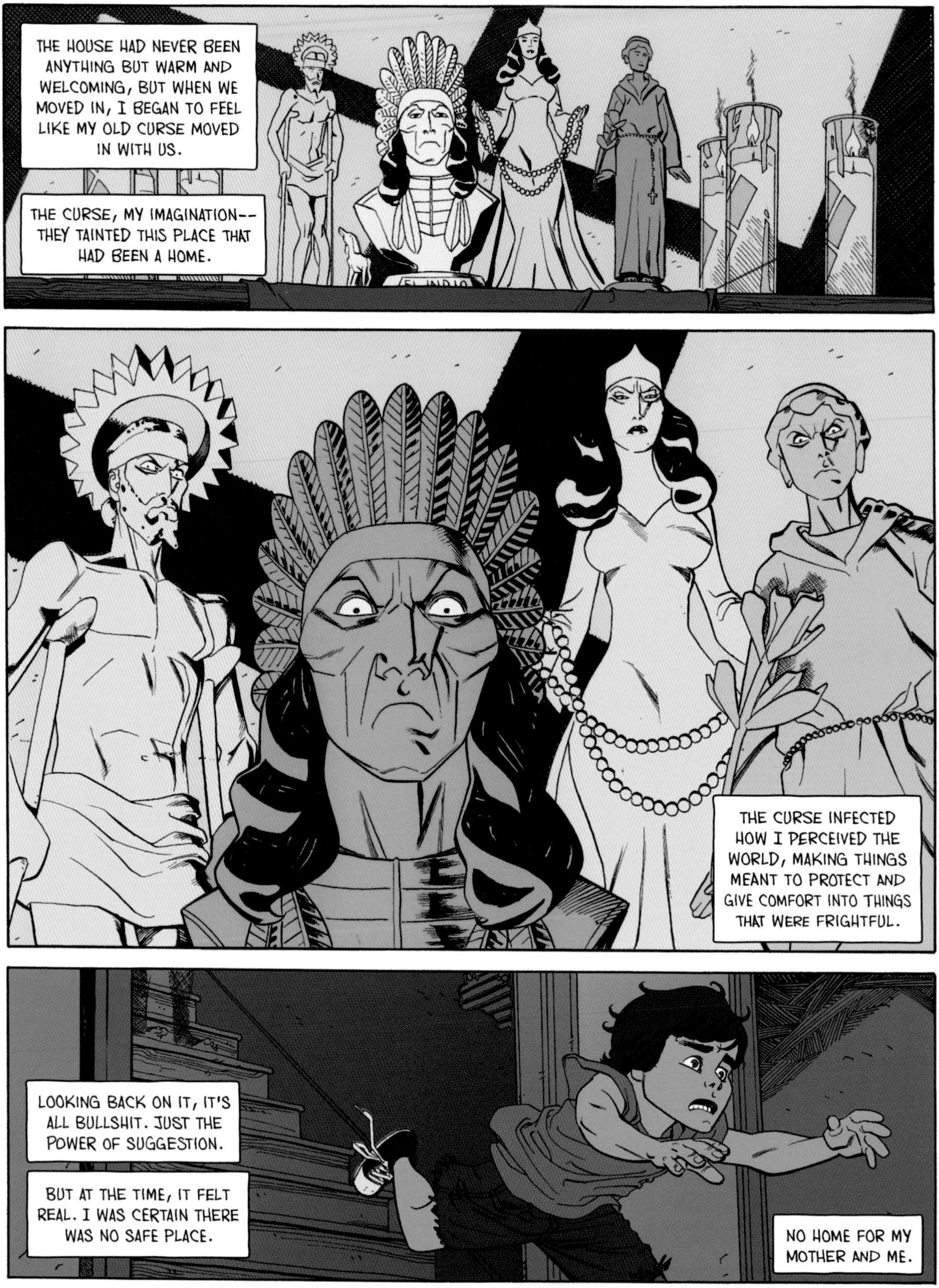
THE HOUSE HAD NEVER BEEN ANYTHING BUT WARM AND WELCOMING, BUT WHEN WE MOVED IN, I BEGAN TO FEEL LIKE MY OLD CURSE MOVED IN WITH US.
THE CURSE, MY IMAGINATION-- THEY TAINTED THIS PLACE THAT HAD BEEN A HOME.
THE CURSE INFECTED HOW I PERCEIVED THE WORLD, MAKING THINGS MEANT TO PROTECT AND GIVE COMFORT INTO THINGS THAT WERE FRIGHTFUL.
LOOKING BACK ON IT, IT'S ALL BULLSHIT. JUST THE POWER OF SUGGESTION.
BUT AT THE TIME, IT FELT REAL. I WAS CERTAIN THERE WAS NO SAFE PLACE.
NO HOME FOR MY MOTHER AND ME.

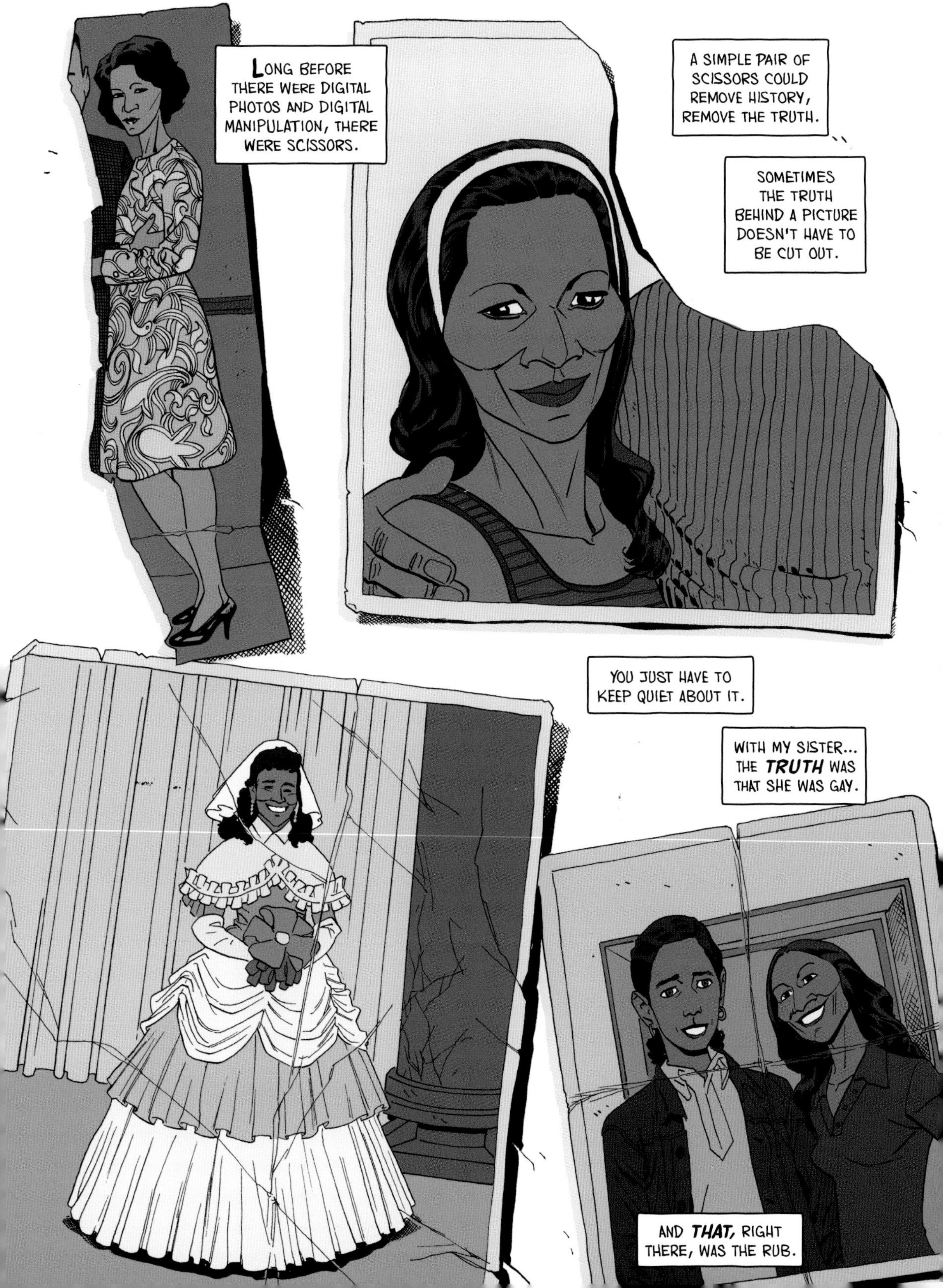
LONG BEFORE THERE WERE DIGITAL PHOTOS AND DIGITAL MANIPULATION, THERE WERE SCISSORS.
A SIMPLE PAIR OF SCISSORS COULD REMOVE HISTORY, REMOVE THE TRUTH.
SOMETIMES THE TRUTH BEHIND A PICTURE DOESN'T HAVE TO BE CUT OUT.
YOU JUST HAVE TO KEEP QUIET ABOUT IT.
WITH MY SISTER... THE *TRUTH* WAS THAT SHE WAS GAY.
AND *THAT,* RIGHT THERE, WAS THE RUB.

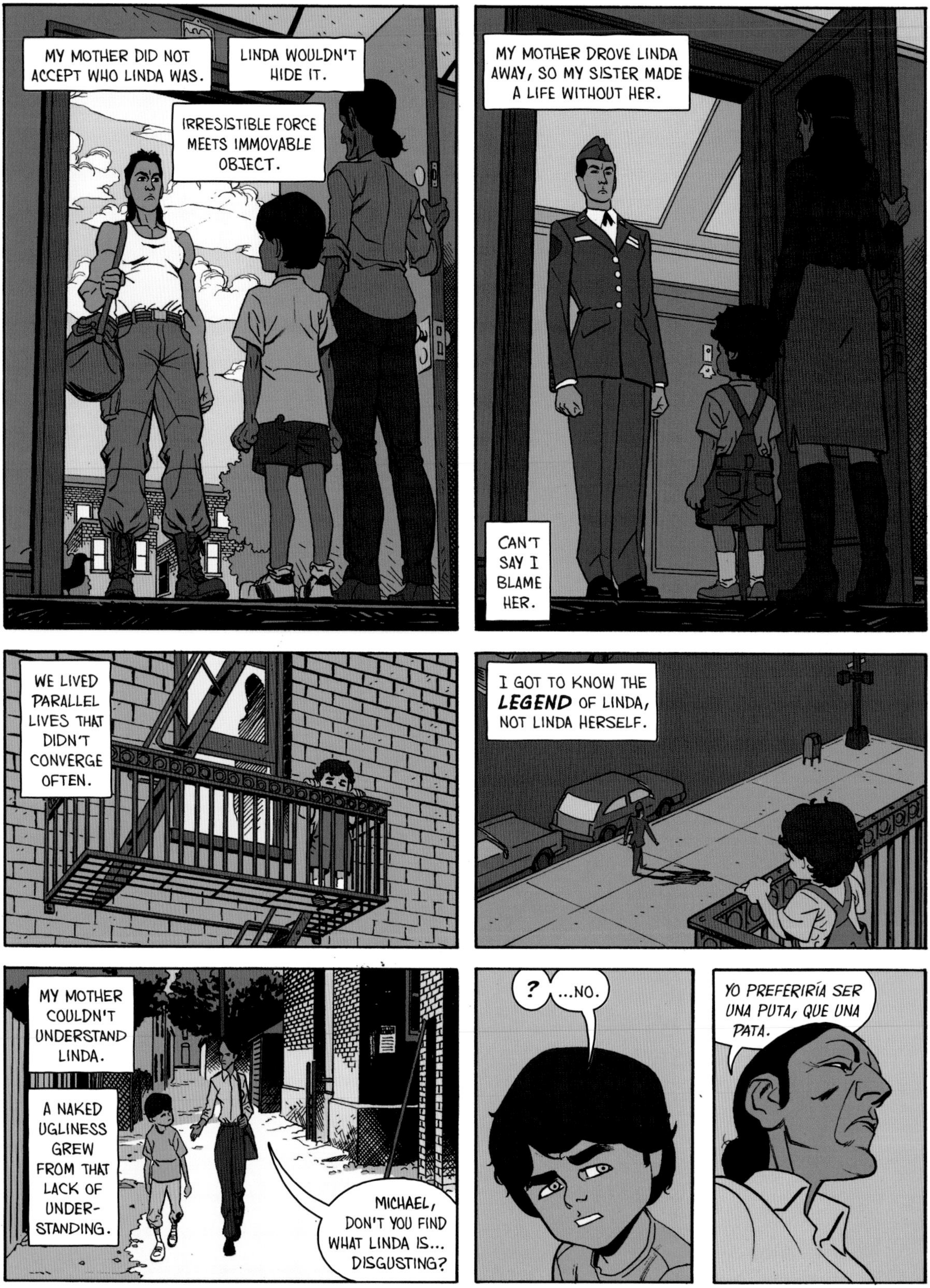
MY MOTHER DID NOT ACCEPT WHO LINDA WAS.
LINDA WOULDN'T HIDE IT.
IRRESISTIBLE FORCE MEETS IMMOVABLE OBJECT.
MY MOTHER DROVE LINDA AWAY, SO MY SISTER MADE A LIFE WITHOUT HER.
CAN'T SAY I BLAME HER.
WE LIVED PARALLEL LIVES THAT DIDN'T CONVERGE OFTEN.
I GOT TO KNOW THE LEGEND OF LINDA, NOT LINDA HERSELF.
MY MOTHER COULDN'T UNDERSTAND LINDA.
A NAKED UGLINESS GREW FROM THAT LACK OF UNDER-STANDING.
MICHAEL, DON'T YOU FIND WHAT LINDA IS... DISGUSTING?
?
...NO.
YO PREFERIRÍA SER UNA PUTA, QUE UNA PATA.

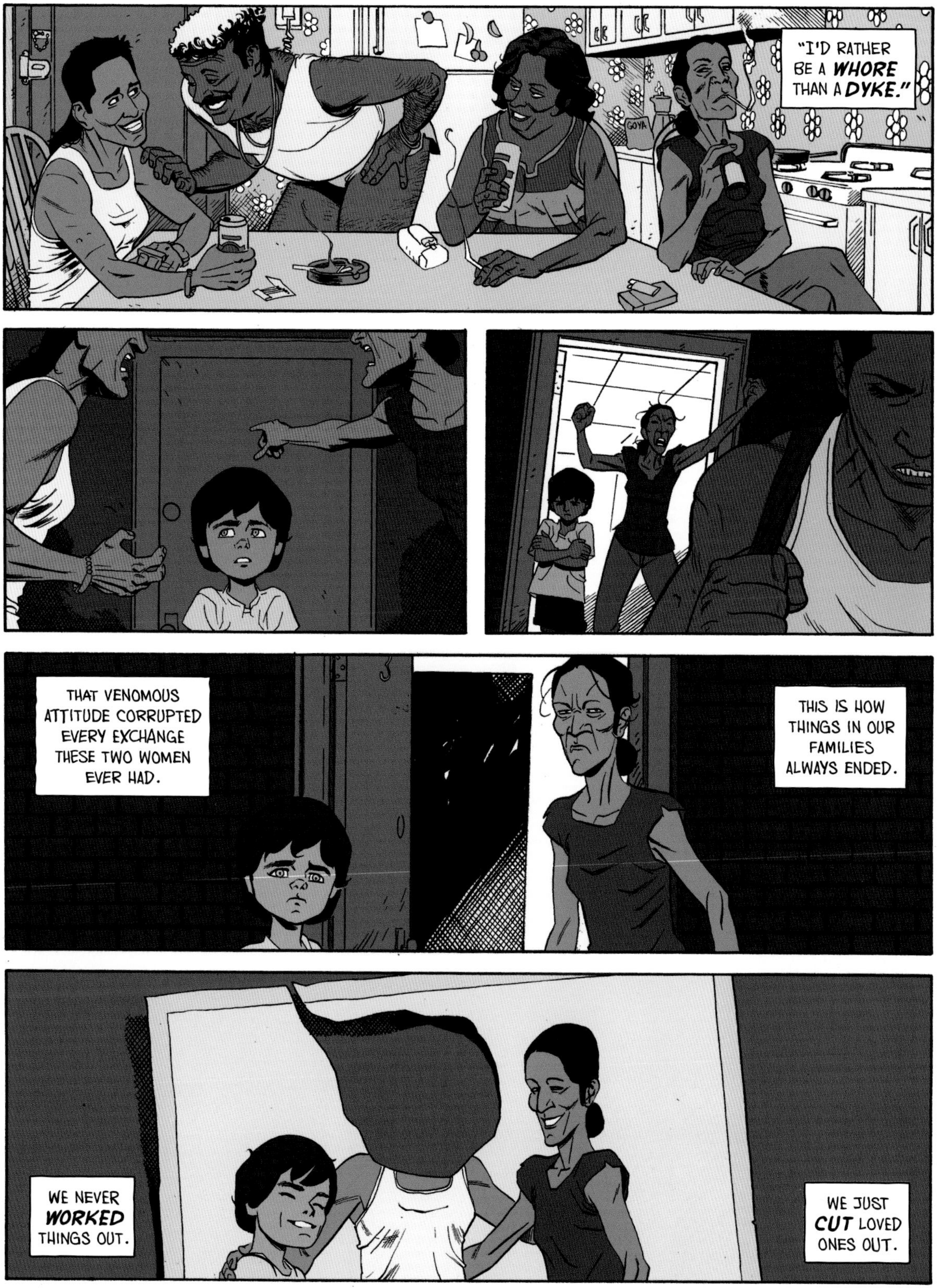
"I'D RATHER BE A **WHORE** THAN A **DYKE.**"
GOYA
THAT VENOMOUS ATTITUDE CORRUPTED EVERY EXCHANGE THESE TWO WOMEN EVER HAD.
THIS IS HOW THINGS IN OUR FAMILIES ALWAYS ENDED.
WE NEVER **WORKED** THINGS OUT.
WE JUST **CUT** LOVED ONES OUT.

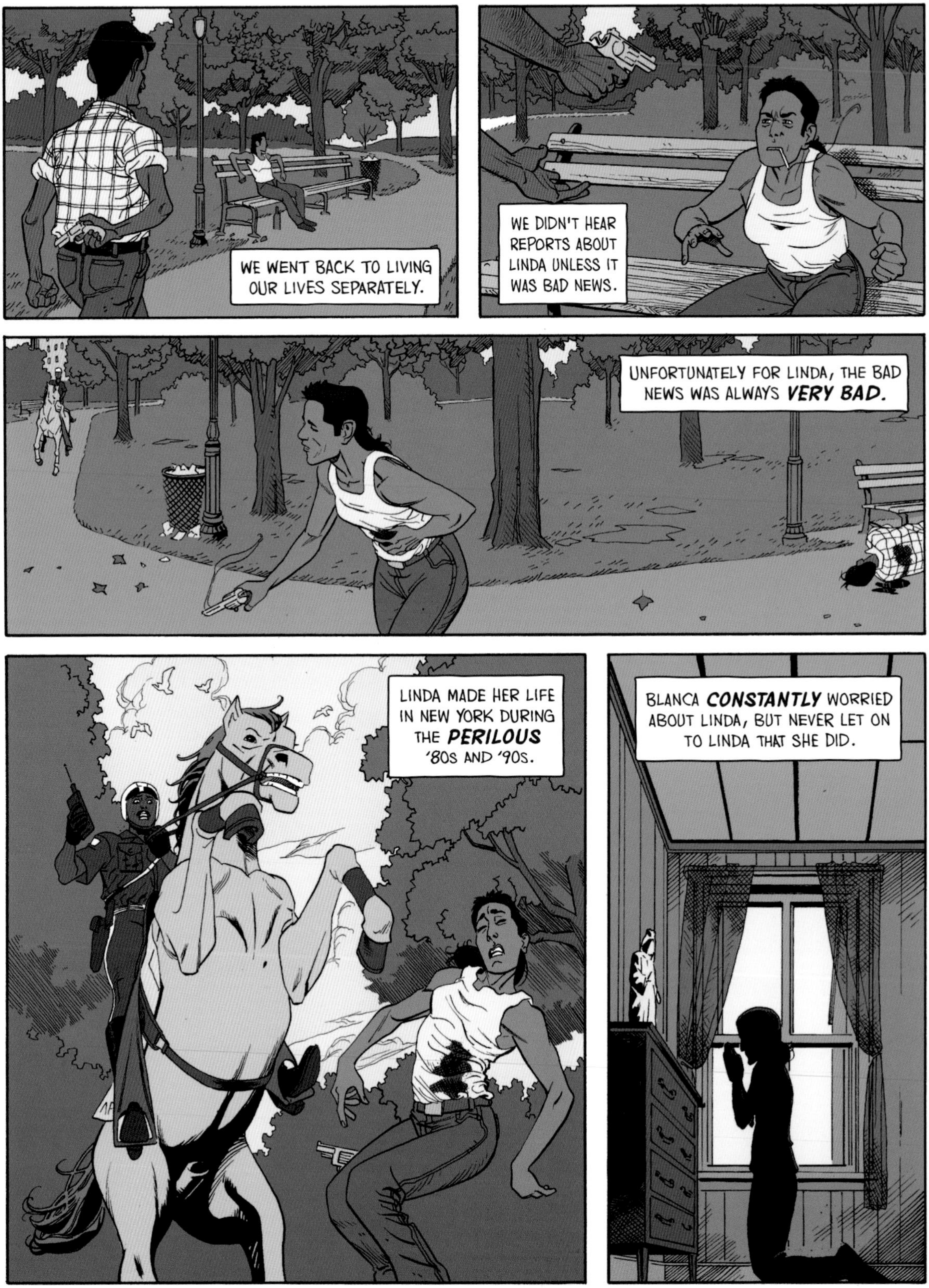
WE WENT BACK TO LIVING OUR LIVES SEPARATELY.
WE DIDN'T HEAR REPORTS ABOUT LINDA UNLESS IT WAS BAD NEWS.
UNFORTUNATELY FOR LINDA, THE BAD NEWS WAS ALWAYS VERY BAD.
LINDA MADE HER LIFE IN NEW YORK DURING THE PERILOUS '80S AND '90S.
BLANCA CONSTANTLY WORRIED ABOUT LINDA, BUT NEVER LET ON TO LINDA THAT SHE DID.

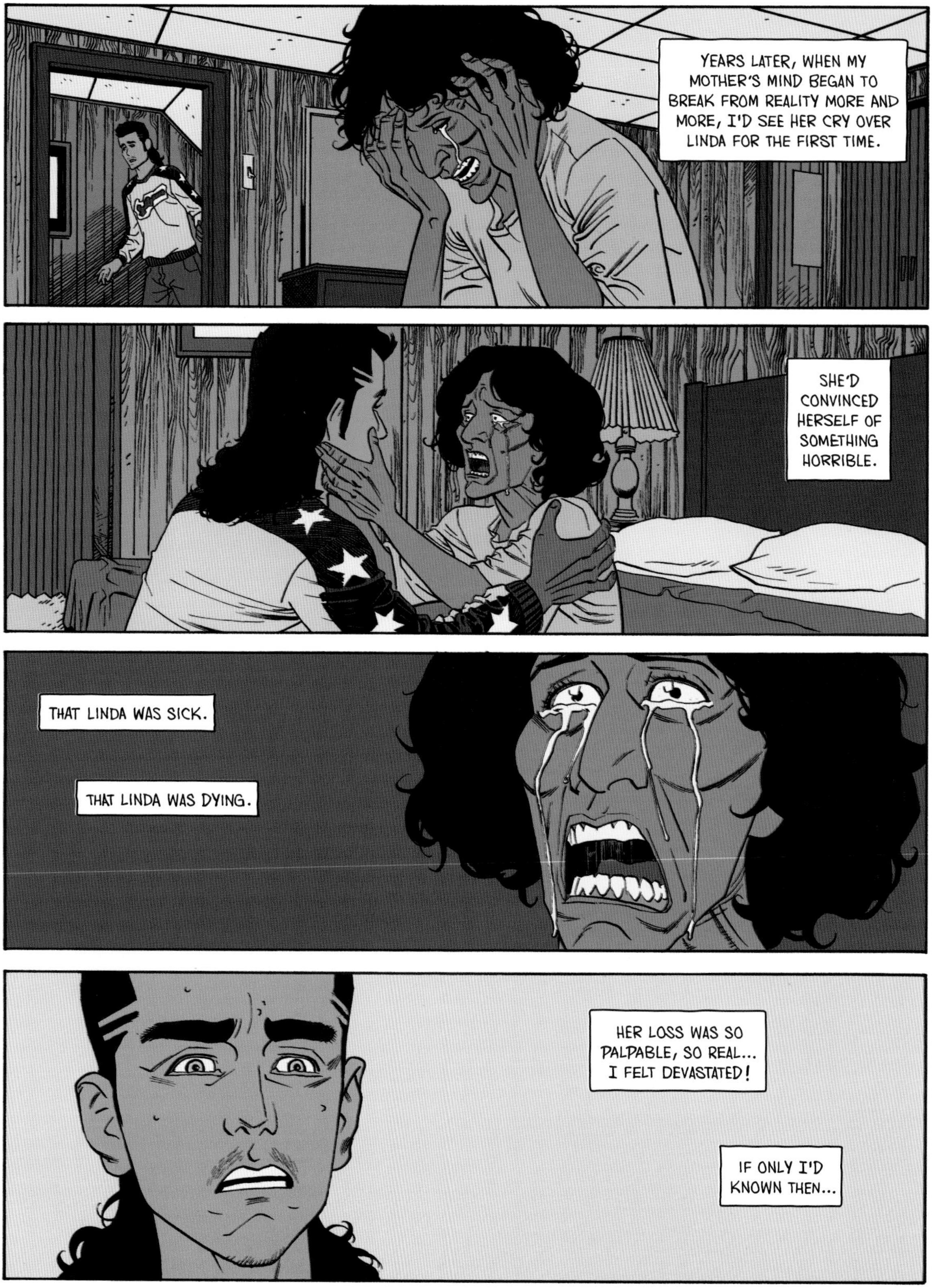
YEARS LATER, WHEN MY MOTHER'S MIND BEGAN TO BREAK FROM REALITY MORE AND MORE, I'D SEE HER CRY OVER LINDA FOR THE FIRST TIME.
SHE'D CONVINCED HERSELF OF SOMETHING HORRIBLE.
THAT LINDA WAS SICK.
THAT LINDA WAS DYING.
HER LOSS WAS SO PALPABLE, SO REAL... I FELT DEVASTATED!
IF ONLY I'D KNOWN THEN...

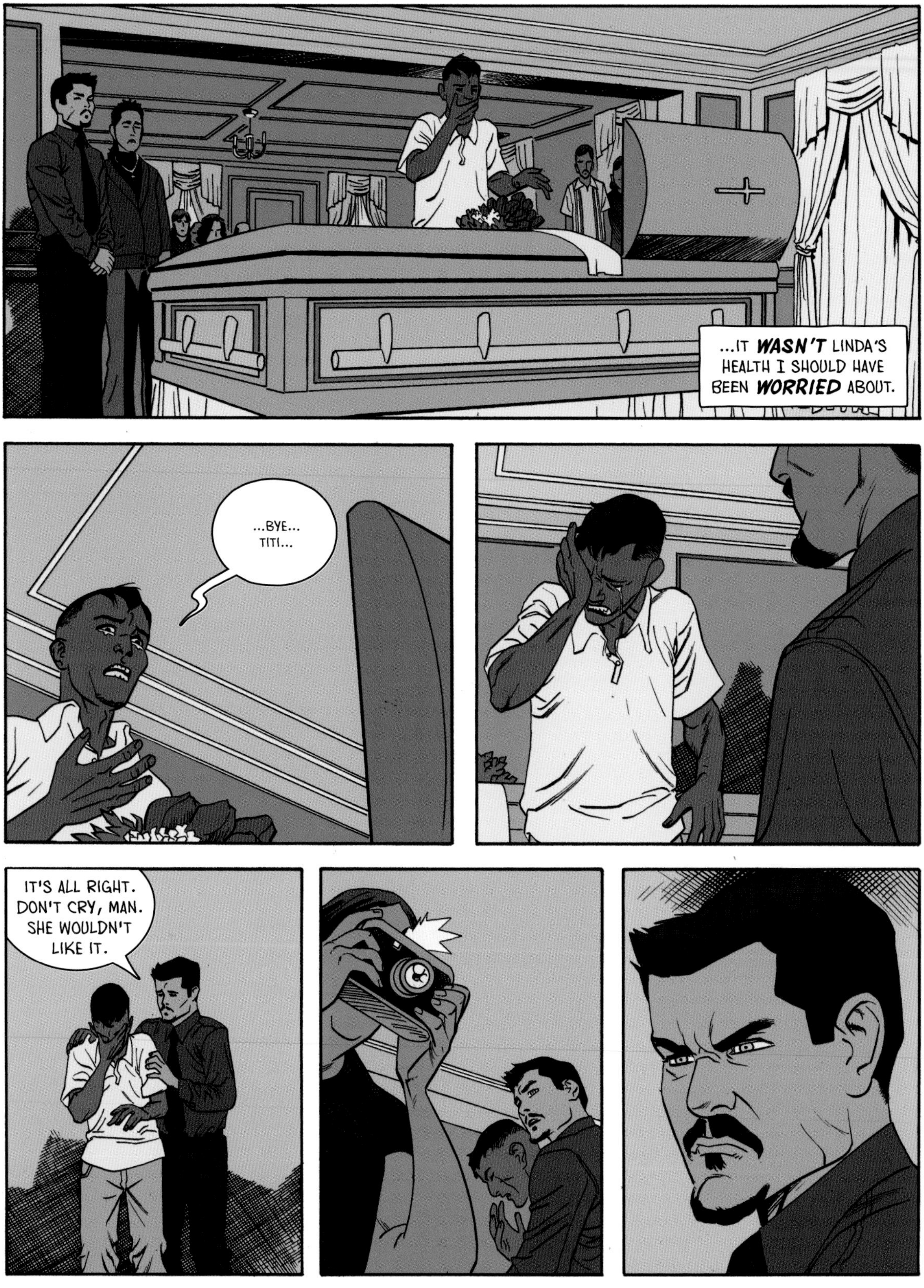
...IT WASN'T LINDA'S HEALTH I SHOULD HAVE BEEN WORRIED ABOUT.
...BYE... TITI...
IT'S ALL RIGHT. DON'T CRY, MAN. SHE WOULDN'T LIKE IT.

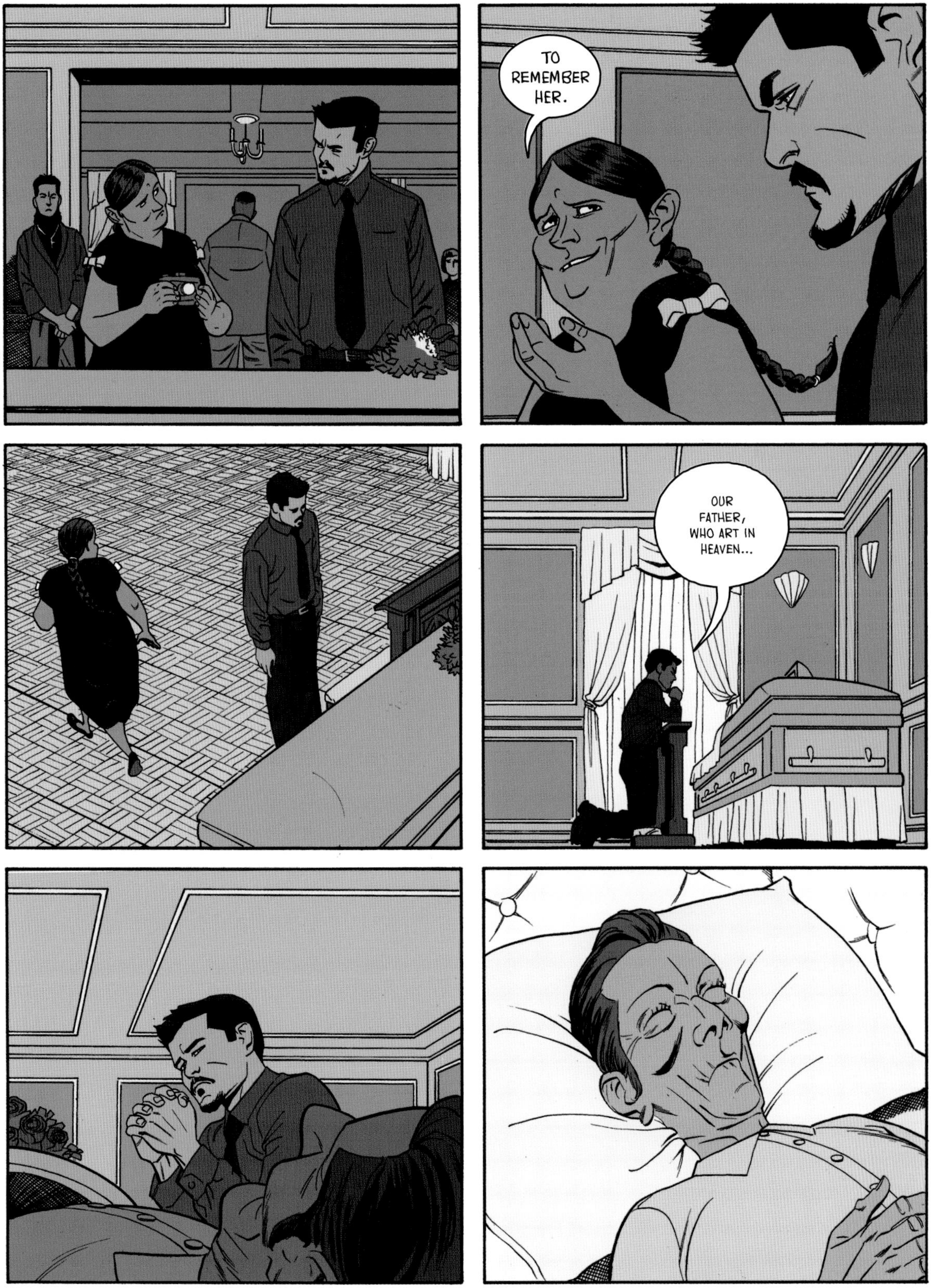
TO REMEMBER HER.
OUR FATHER, WHO ART IN HEAVEN...

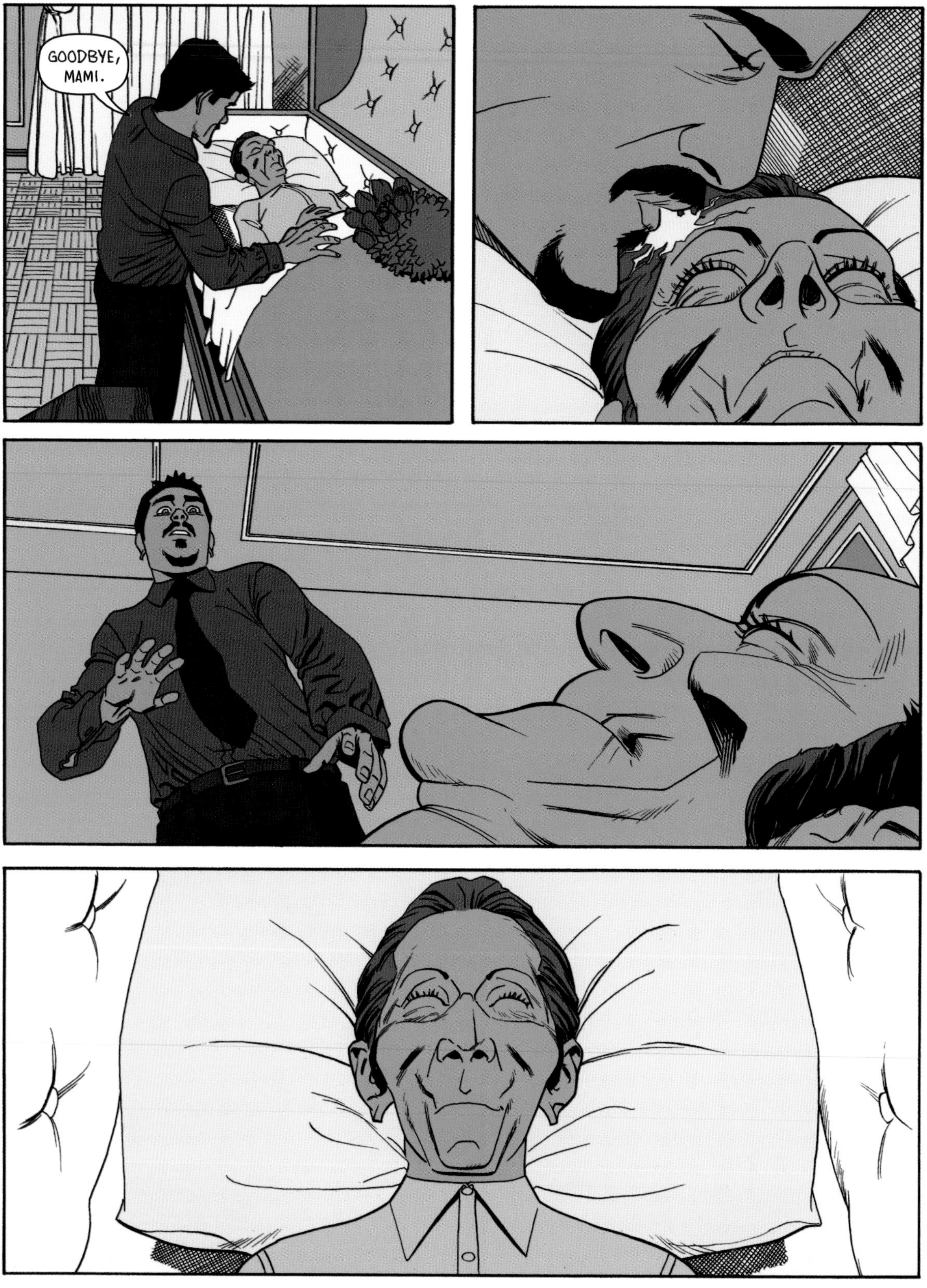
GOODBYE, MAMI.

GROWING UP, I GOT MY ASS BEAT.

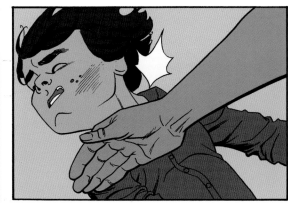

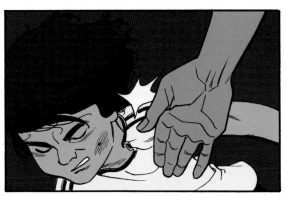

OFTEN.

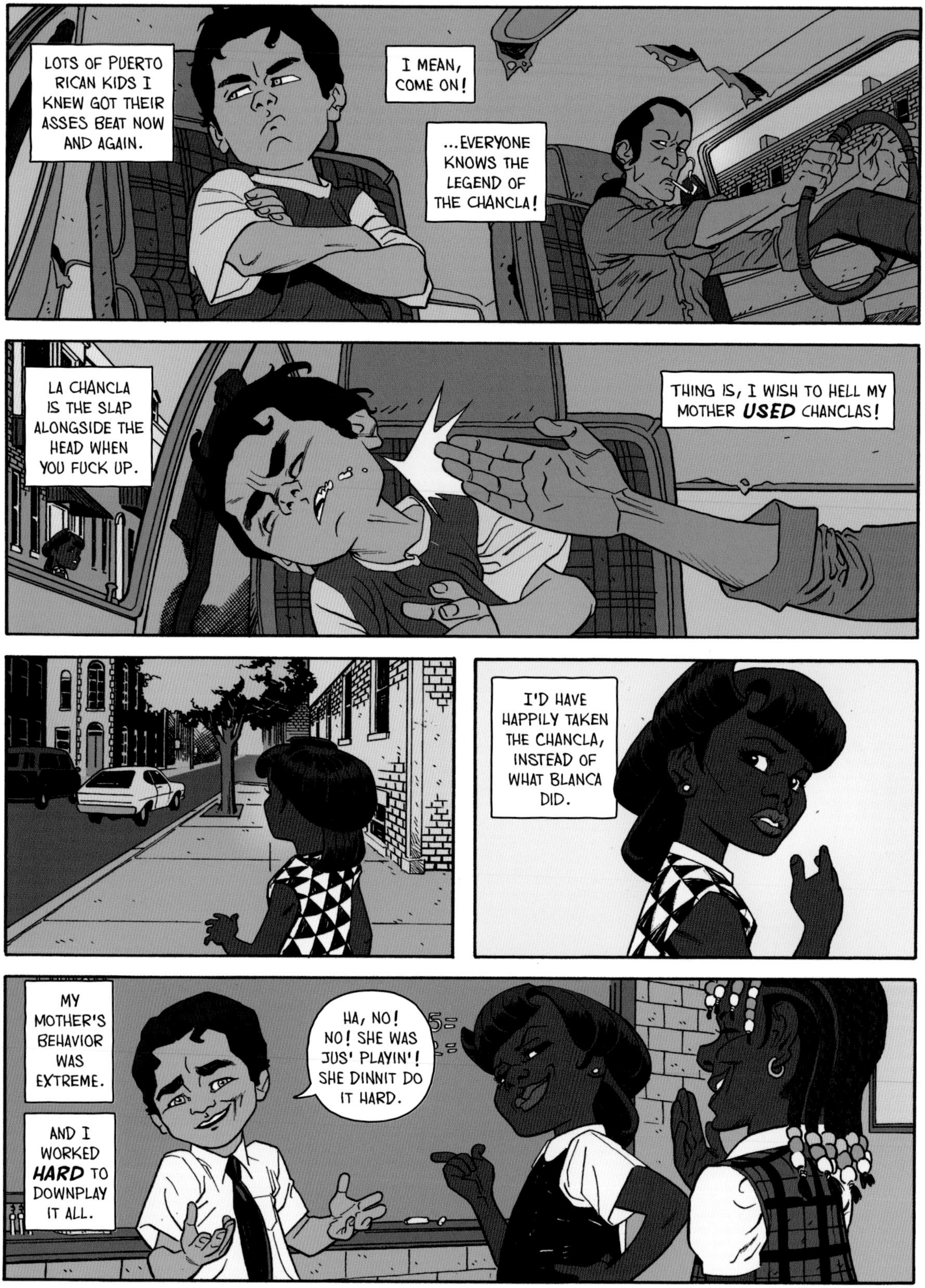

LOTS OF PUERTO RICAN KIDS I KNEW GOT THEIR ASSES BEAT NOW AND AGAIN.
I MEAN, COME ON!
...EVERYONE KNOWS THE LEGEND OF THE CHANCLA!
LA CHANCLA IS THE SLAP ALONGSIDE THE HEAD WHEN YOU FUCK UP.
THING IS, I WISH TO HELL MY MOTHER USED CHANCLAS!
I'D HAVE HAPPILY TAKEN THE CHANCLA, INSTEAD OF WHAT BLANCA DID.
MY MOTHER'S BEHAVIOR WAS EXTREME.
AND I WORKED HARD TO DOWNPLAY IT ALL.
HA, NO! NO! SHE WAS JUS' PLAYIN'! SHE DINNIT DO IT HARD.

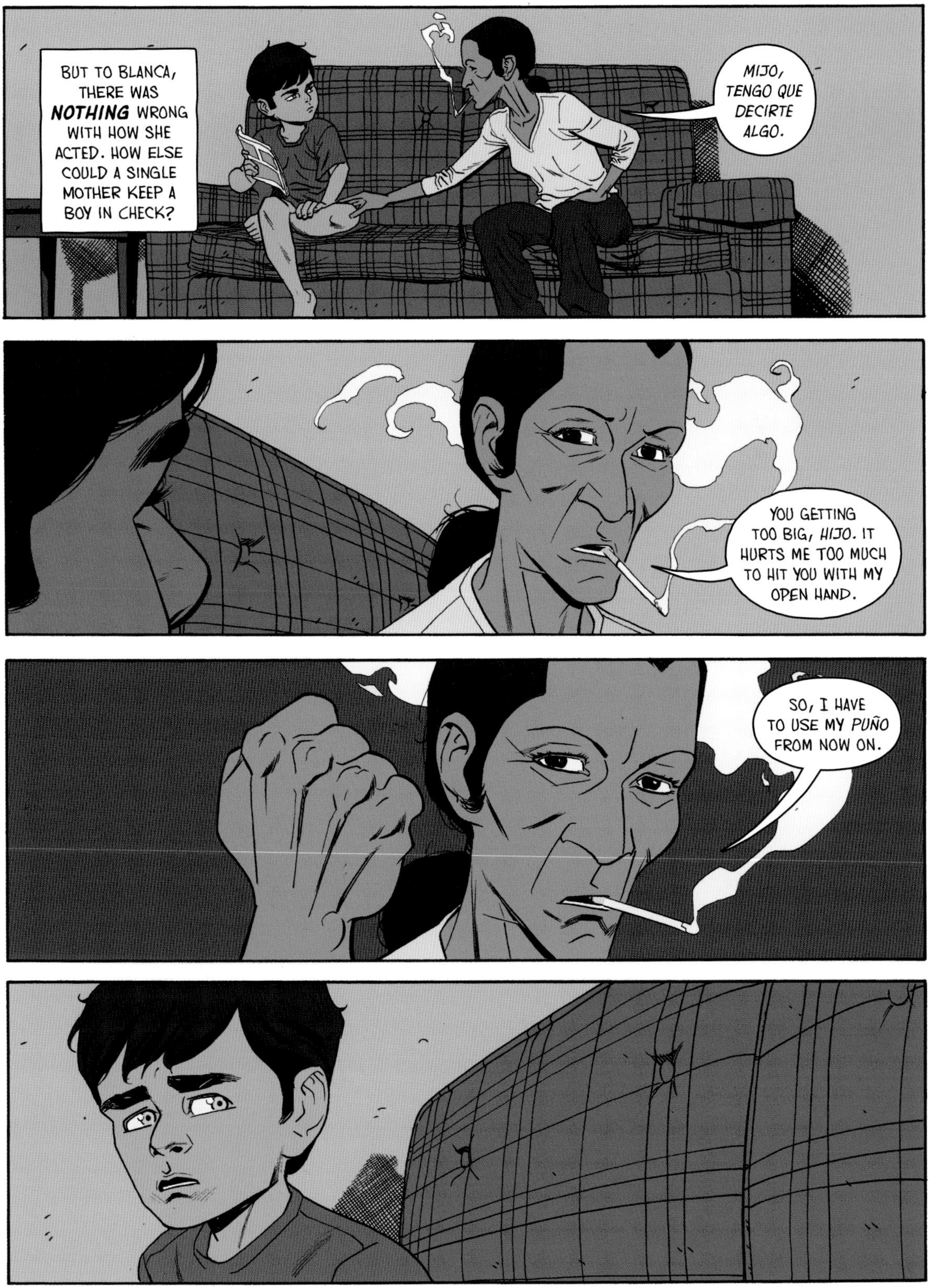
BUT TO BLANCA, THERE WAS **NOTHING** WRONG WITH HOW SHE ACTED. HOW ELSE COULD A SINGLE MOTHER KEEP A BOY IN CHECK?
*MIJO, TENGO QUE DECIRTE ALGO.*
YOU GETTING TOO BIG, *HIJO*. IT HURTS ME TOO MUCH TO HIT YOU WITH MY OPEN HAND.
SO, I HAVE TO USE MY *PUÑO* FROM NOW ON.

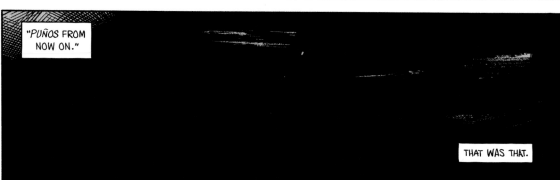

"*PUÑOS* FROM NOW ON."

THAT WAS THAT.

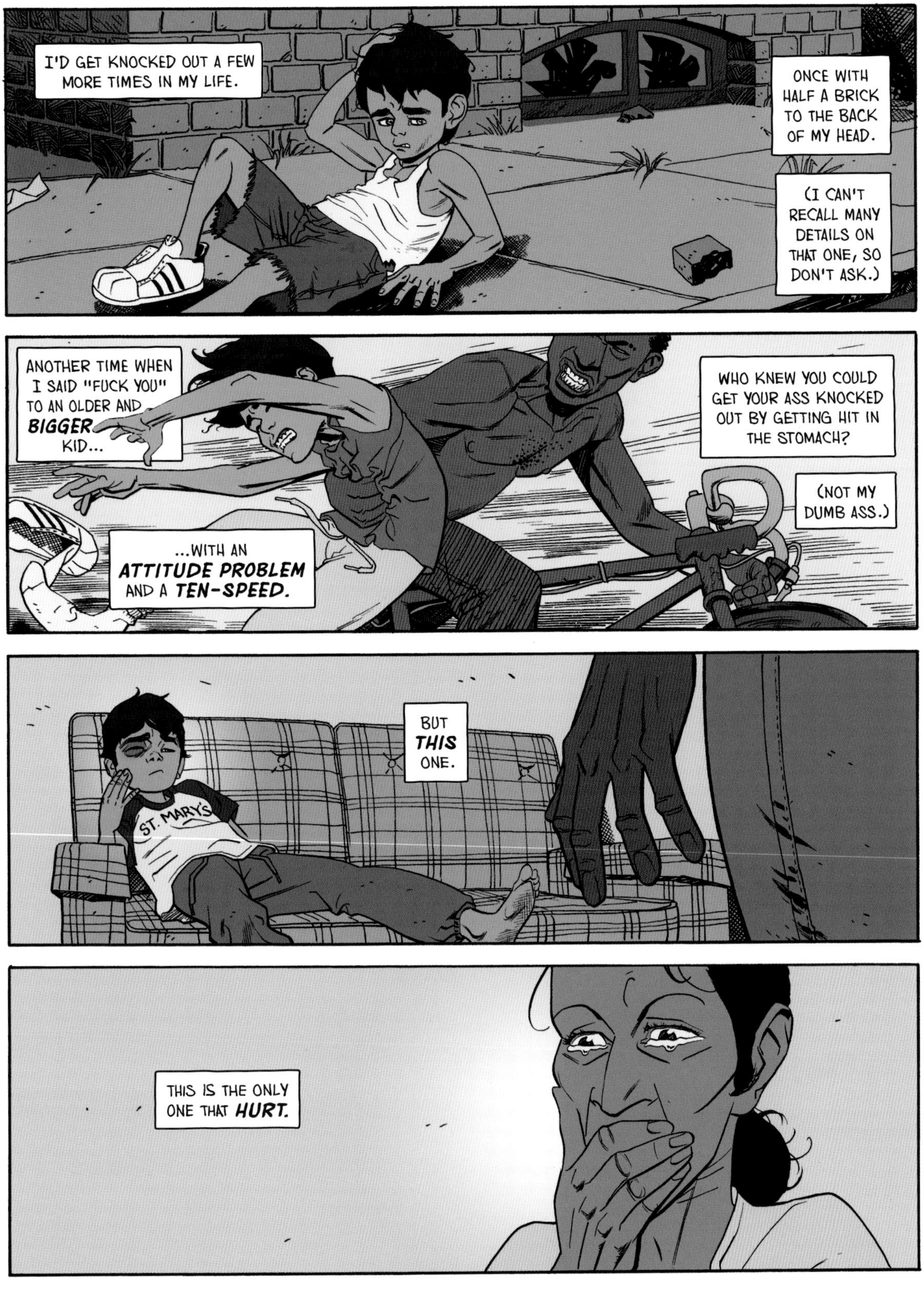
I'D GET KNOCKED OUT A FEW MORE TIMES IN MY LIFE.
ONCE WITH HALF A BRICK TO THE BACK OF MY HEAD.
(I CAN'T RECALL MANY DETAILS ON THAT ONE, SO DON'T ASK.)
ANOTHER TIME WHEN I SAID "FUCK YOU" TO AN OLDER AND BIGGER KID...
...WITH AN ATTITUDE PROBLEM AND A TEN-SPEED.
WHO KNEW YOU COULD GET YOUR ASS KNOCKED OUT BY GETTING HIT IN THE STOMACH?
(NOT MY DUMB ASS.)
ST. MARY'S
BUT THIS ONE.
THIS IS THE ONLY ONE THAT HURT.

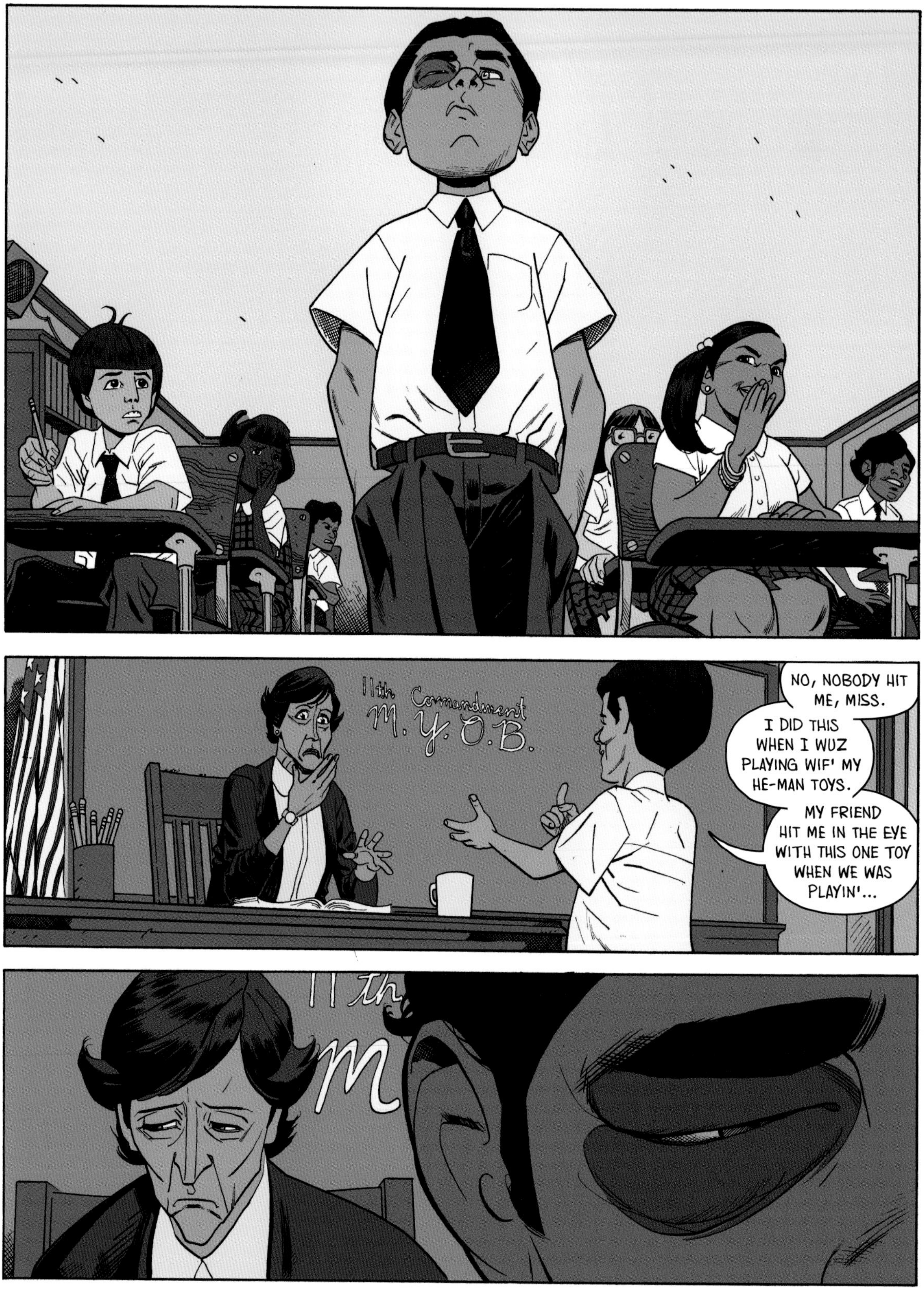
11th Commandment
M. Y. O. B.
NO, NOBODY HIT ME, MISS.
I DID THIS WHEN I WUZ PLAYING WIF' MY HE-MAN TOYS.
MY FRIEND HIT ME IN THE EYE WITH THIS ONE TOY WHEN WE WAS PLAYIN'...
11th
M

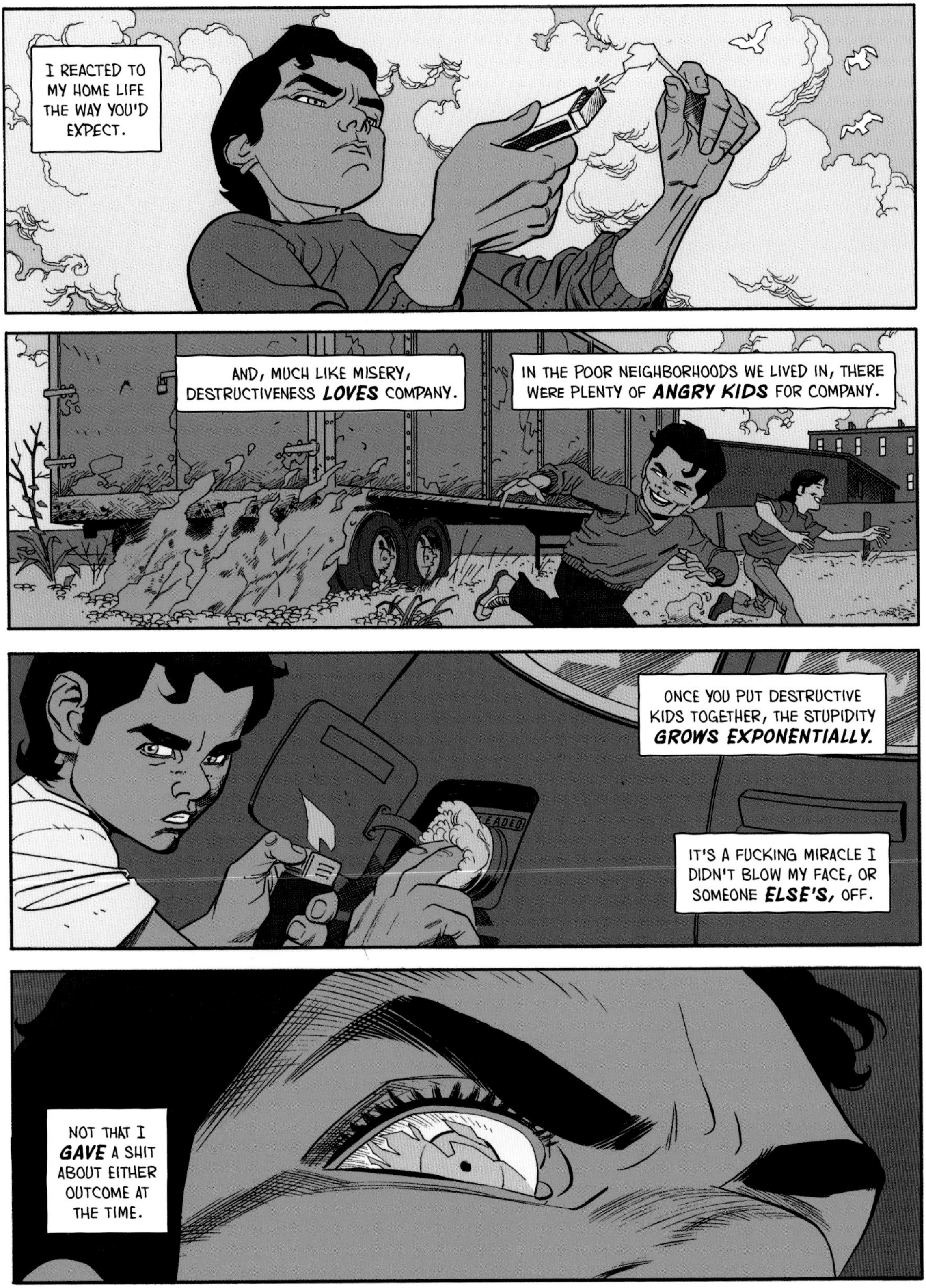
I REACTED TO MY HOME LIFE THE WAY YOU'D EXPECT.
AND, MUCH LIKE MISERY, DESTRUCTIVENESS LOVES COMPANY.
IN THE POOR NEIGHBORHOODS WE LIVED IN, THERE WERE PLENTY OF ANGRY KIDS FOR COMPANY.
ONCE YOU PUT DESTRUCTIVE KIDS TOGETHER, THE STUPIDITY GROWS EXPONENTIALLY.
IT'S A FUCKING MIRACLE I DIDN'T BLOW MY FACE, OR SOMEONE ELSE'S, OFF.
NOT THAT I GAVE A SHIT ABOUT EITHER OUTCOME AT THE TIME.

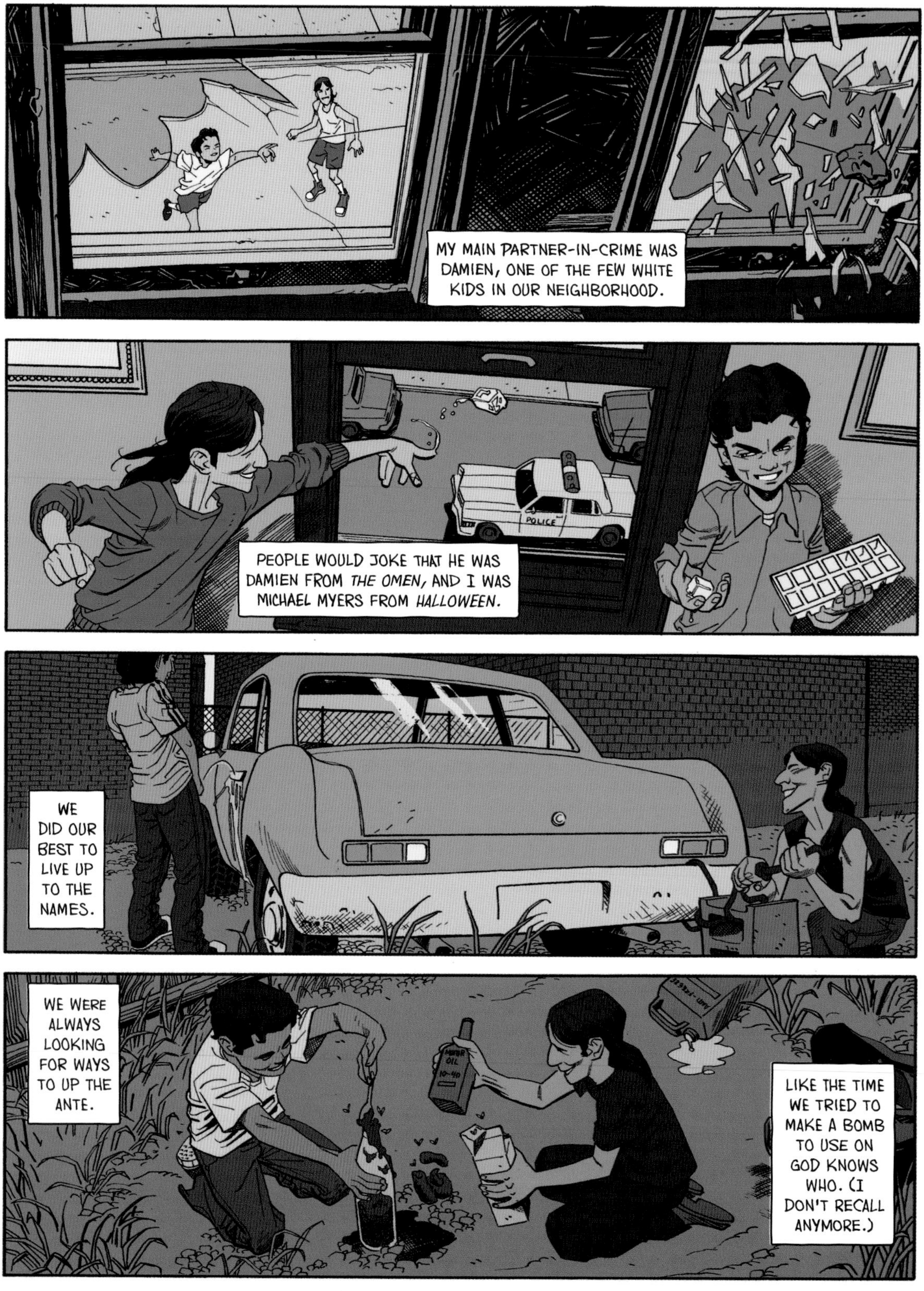
MY MAIN PARTNER-IN-CRIME WAS DAMIEN, ONE OF THE FEW WHITE KIDS IN OUR NEIGHBORHOOD.
POLICE
PEOPLE WOULD JOKE THAT HE WAS DAMIEN FROM *THE OMEN*, AND I WAS MICHAEL MYERS FROM *HALLOWEEN*.
WE DID OUR BEST TO LIVE UP TO THE NAMES.
WE WERE ALWAYS LOOKING FOR WAYS TO UP THE ANTE.
MOTOR OIL 10-40
LIKE THE TIME WE TRIED TO MAKE A BOMB TO USE ON GOD KNOWS WHO. (I DON'T RECALL ANYMORE.)

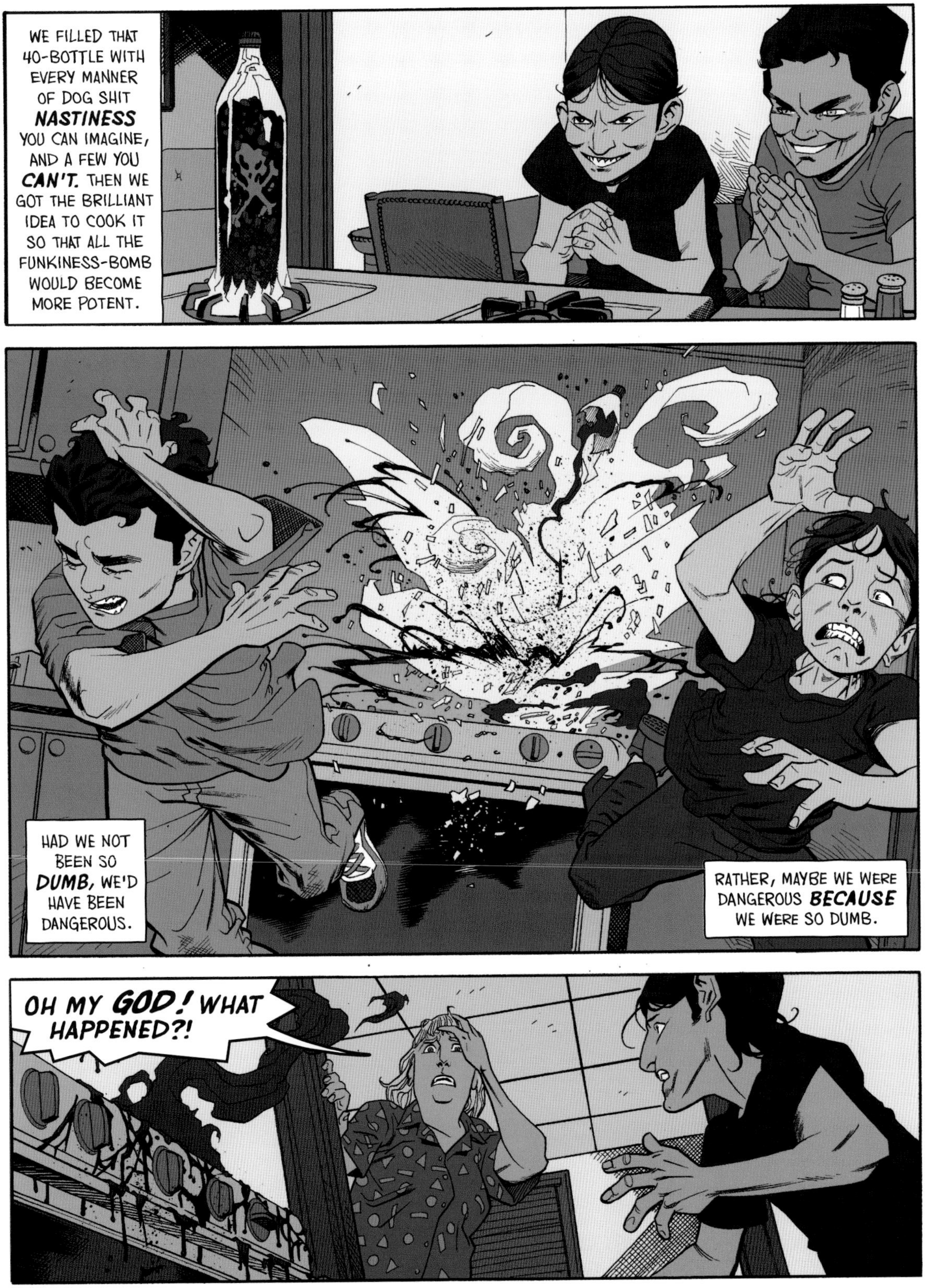

WE FILLED THAT 40-BOTTLE WITH EVERY MANNER OF DOG SHIT **NASTINESS** YOU CAN IMAGINE, AND A FEW YOU **CAN'T.** THEN WE GOT THE BRILLIANT IDEA TO COOK IT SO THAT ALL THE FUNKINESS-BOMB WOULD BECOME MORE POTENT.
HAD WE NOT BEEN SO **DUMB,** WE'D HAVE BEEN DANGEROUS.
RATHER, MAYBE WE WERE DANGEROUS **BECAUSE** WE WERE SO DUMB.
OH MY **GOD!** WHAT HAPPENED?!

I EXPECTED TO BE **KILLED** WHEN THE BOTTLE BLEW UP.

NOT BY THE BOTTLE.

BY DAMIEN'S **MOTHER.**

IF I PULLED A STUNT LIKE THAT IN **MY** HOUSE...

...BLANCA WOULD HAVE PUT A BEATING ON MY LITTLE ASS THE LIKES OF WHICH HAVE RARELY BEEN PUT UPON **MAN** OR **BEAST.**

INSTEAD, SHE FRANTICALLY BEGAN CLEANING UP **OUR** MESS!

I COULDN'T UNDER-STAND WHAT WAS HAPPENING.

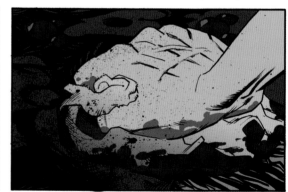

DAMIEN'S MOTHER, HOWEVER, WAS REACTING LIKE **SHE** WAS THE ONE ABOUT TO CATCH A BAD ONE.

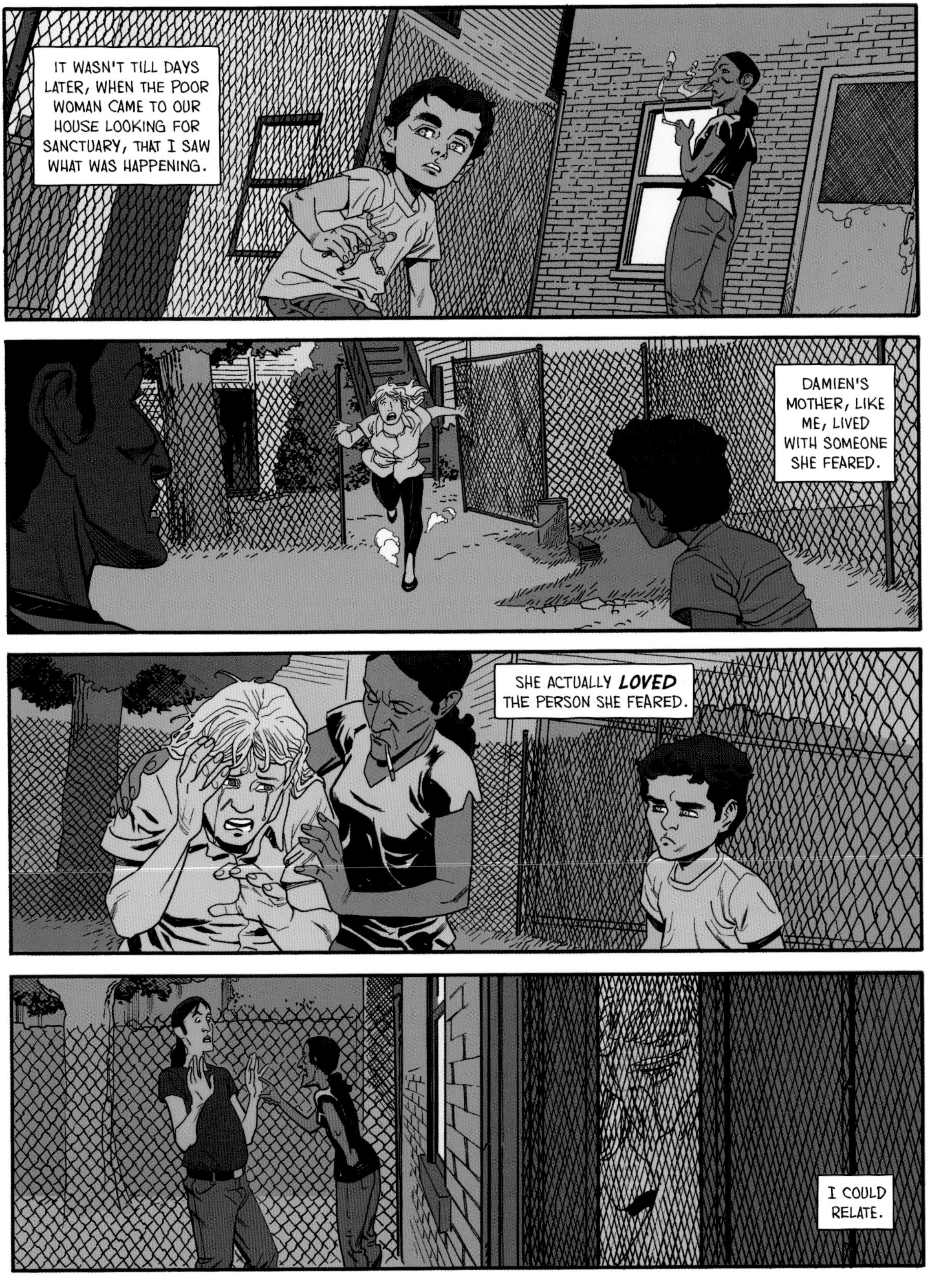
IT WASN'T TILL DAYS LATER, WHEN THE POOR WOMAN CAME TO OUR HOUSE LOOKING FOR SANCTUARY, THAT I SAW WHAT WAS HAPPENING.
DAMIEN'S MOTHER, LIKE ME, LIVED WITH SOMEONE SHE FEARED.
SHE ACTUALLY LOVED THE PERSON SHE FEARED.
I COULD RELATE.

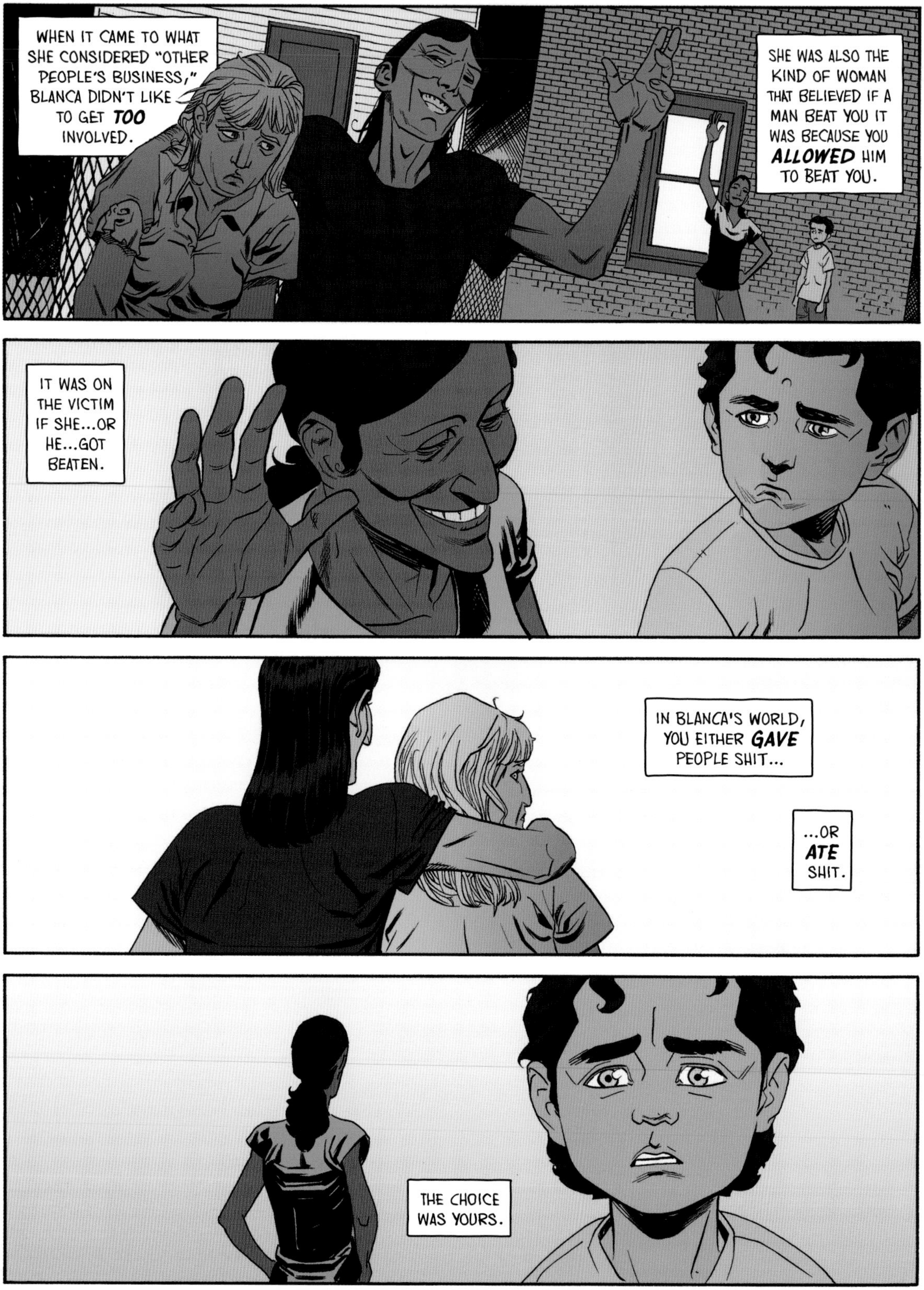
WHEN IT CAME TO WHAT SHE CONSIDERED "OTHER PEOPLE'S BUSINESS," BLANCA DIDN'T LIKE TO GET TOO INVOLVED.
SHE WAS ALSO THE KIND OF WOMAN THAT BELIEVED IF A MAN BEAT YOU IT WAS BECAUSE YOU ALLOWED HIM TO BEAT YOU.
IT WAS ON THE VICTIM IF SHE...OR HE...GOT BEATEN.
IN BLANCA'S WORLD, YOU EITHER GAVE PEOPLE SHIT...
...OR ATE SHIT.
THE CHOICE WAS YOURS.

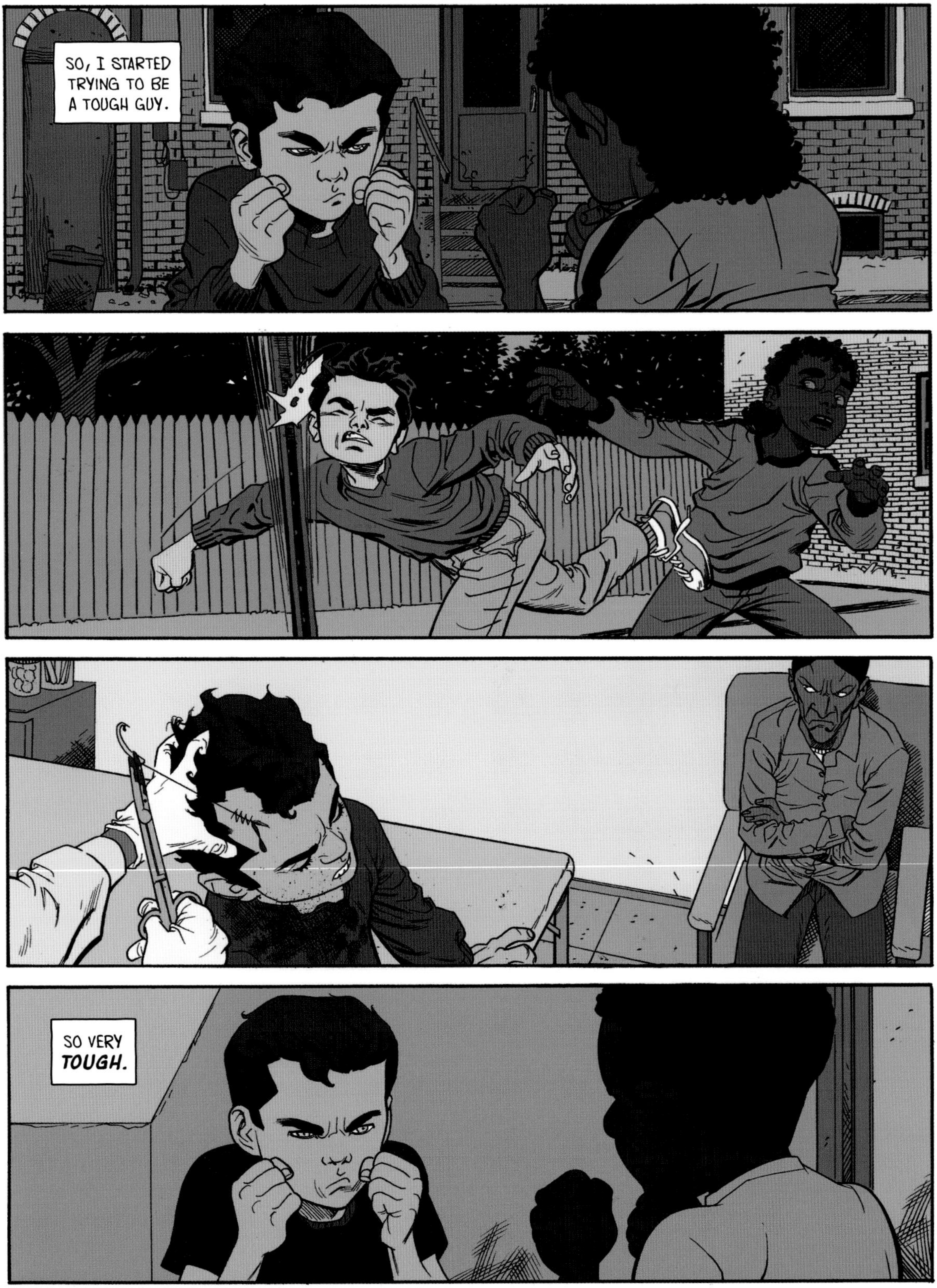
SO, I STARTED TRYING TO BE A TOUGH GUY.
SO VERY TOUGH.

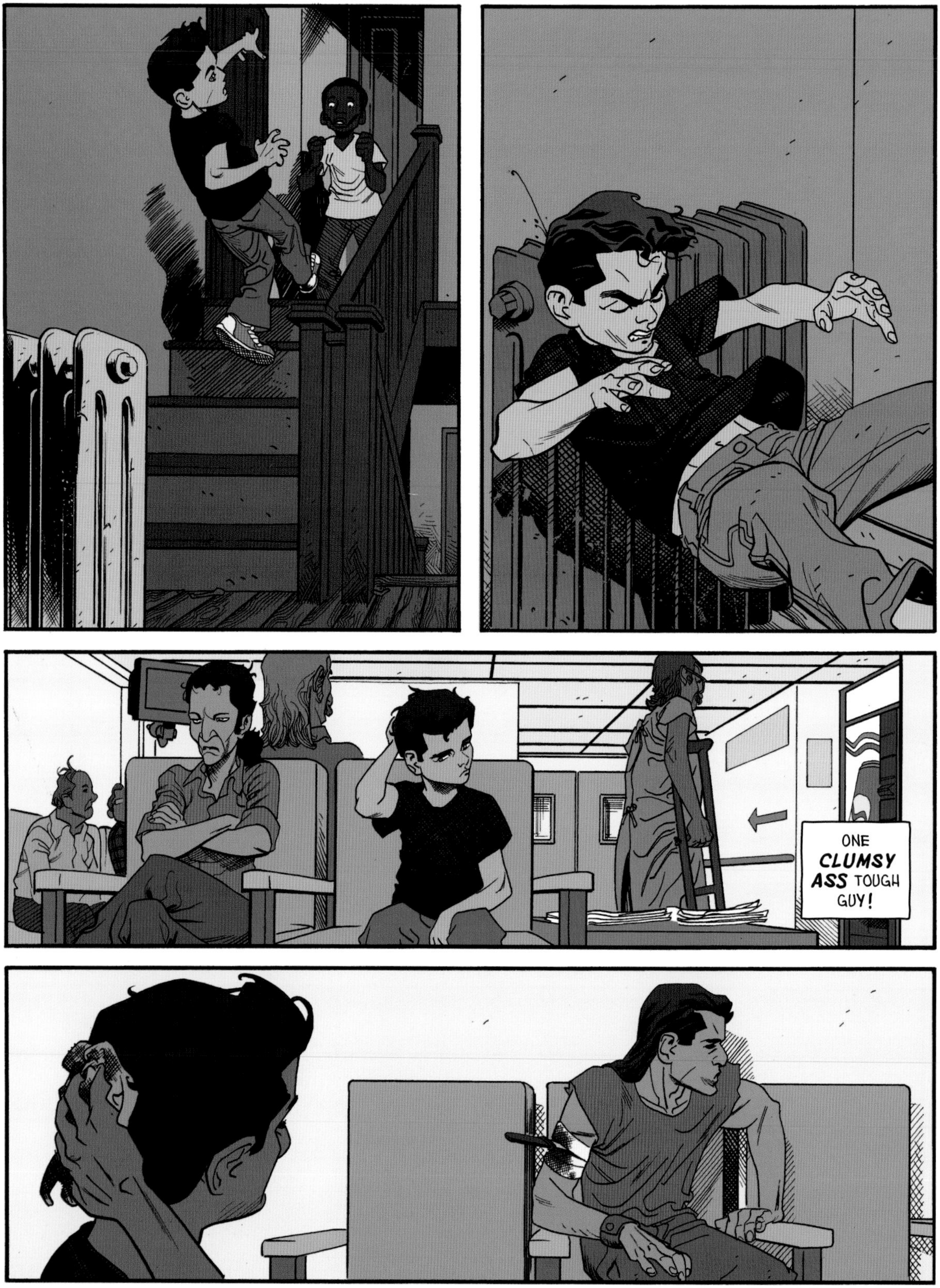
ONE CLUMSY ASS TOUGH GUY!

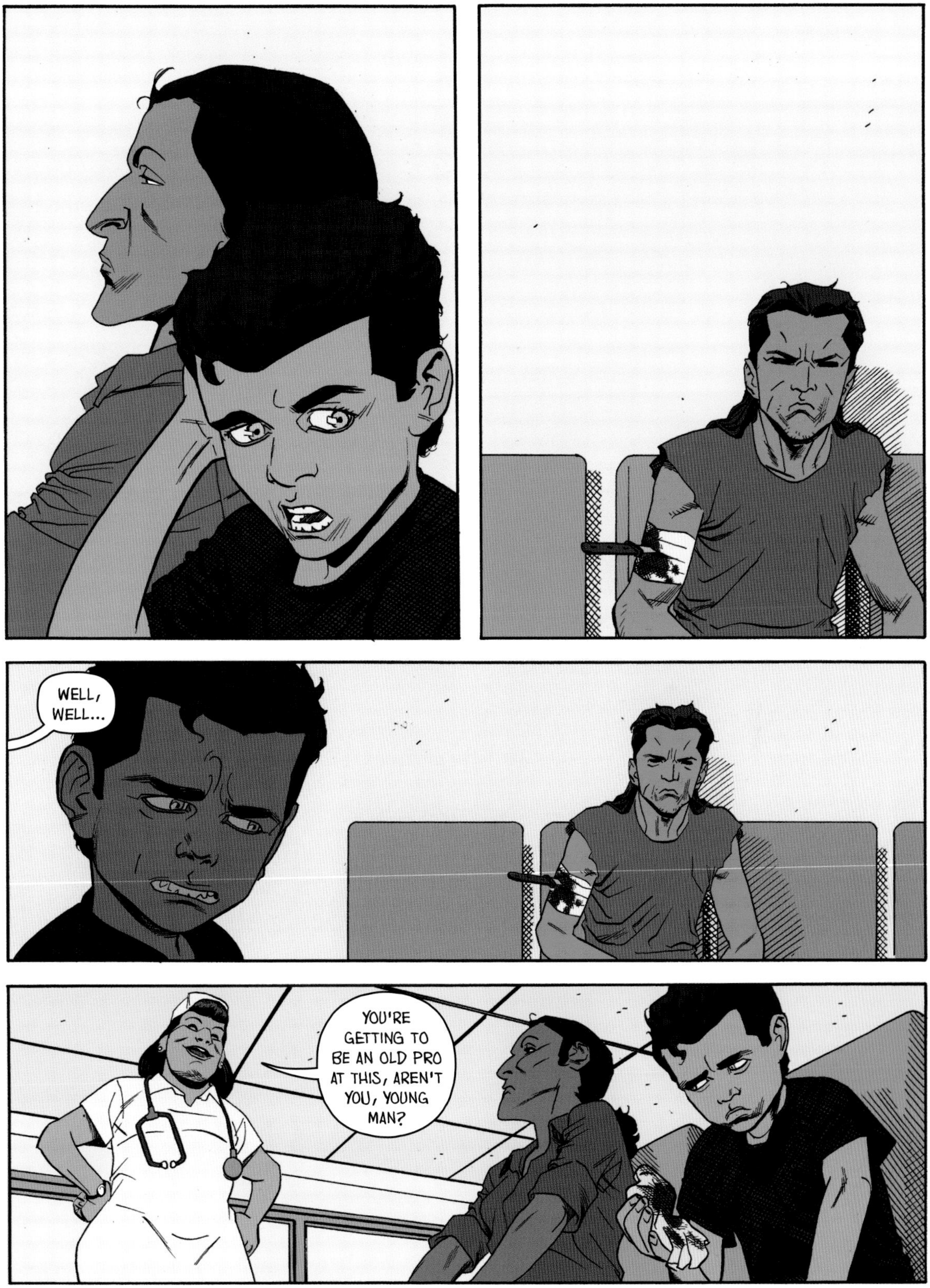
WELL, WELL...
YOU'RE GETTING TO BE AN OLD PRO AT THIS, AREN'T YOU, YOUNG MAN?

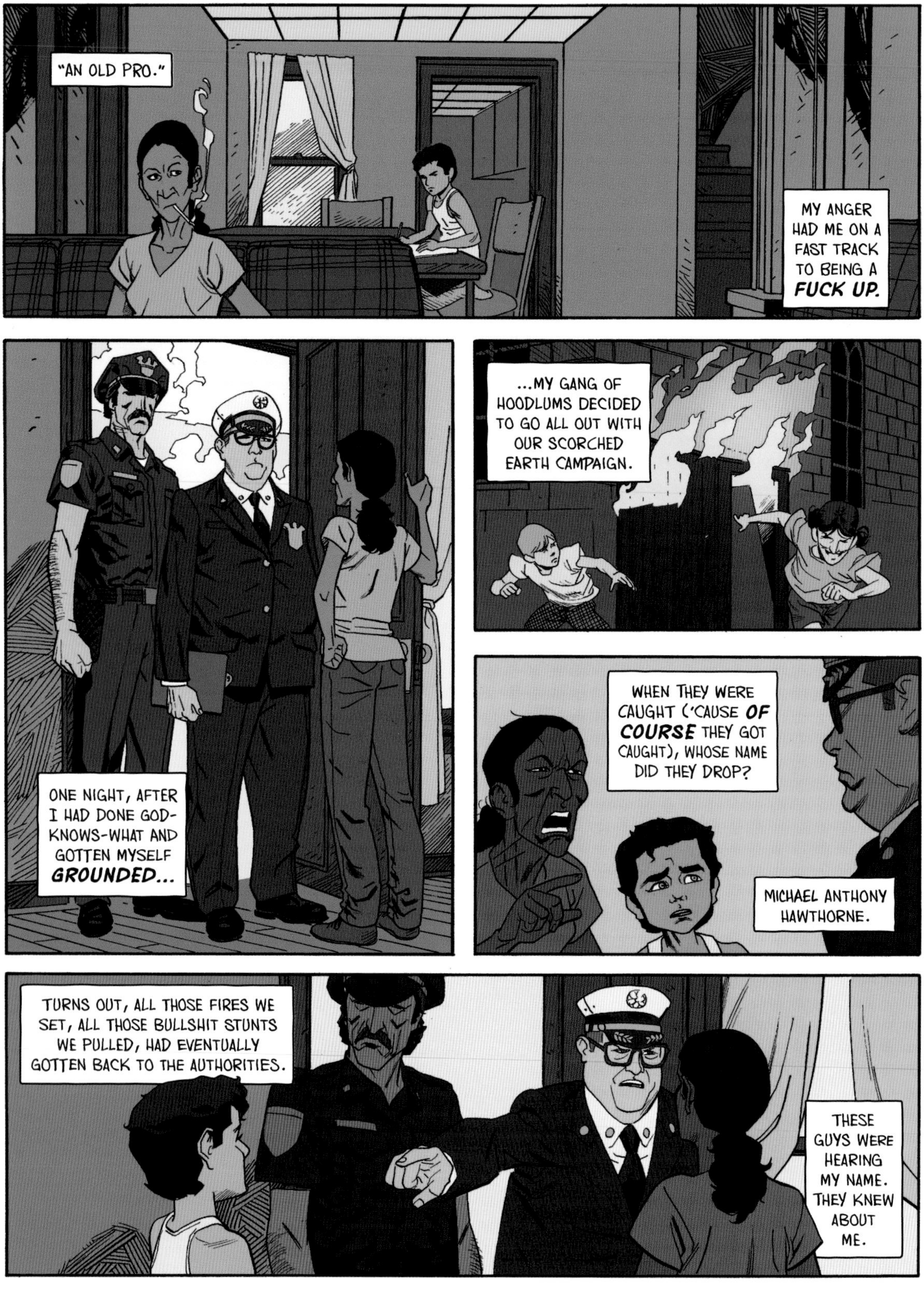
"AN OLD PRO."
MY ANGER HAD ME ON A FAST TRACK TO BEING A FUCK UP.
ONE NIGHT, AFTER I HAD DONE GOD-KNOWS-WHAT AND GOTTEN MYSELF GROUNDED...
...MY GANG OF HOODLUMS DECIDED TO GO ALL OUT WITH OUR SCORCHED EARTH CAMPAIGN.
WHEN THEY WERE CAUGHT ('CAUSE OF COURSE THEY GOT CAUGHT), WHOSE NAME DID THEY DROP?
MICHAEL ANTHONY HAWTHORNE.
TURNS OUT, ALL THOSE FIRES WE SET, ALL THOSE BULLSHIT STUNTS WE PULLED, HAD EVENTUALLY GOTTEN BACK TO THE AUTHORITIES.
THESE GUYS WERE HEARING MY NAME. THEY KNEW ABOUT ME.

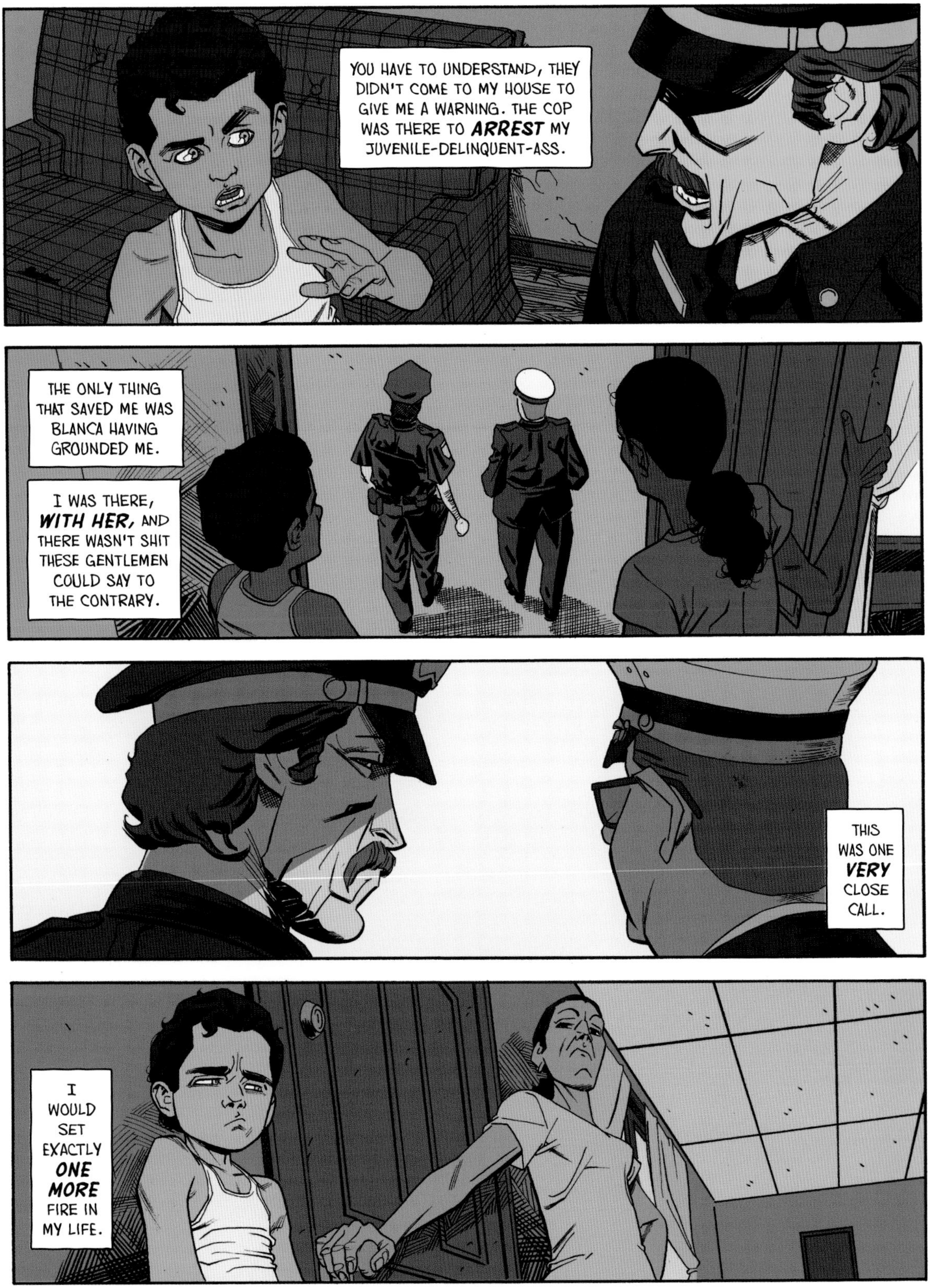
YOU HAVE TO UNDERSTAND, THEY DIDN'T COME TO MY HOUSE TO GIVE ME A WARNING. THE COP WAS THERE TO **ARREST** MY JUVENILE-DELINQUENT-ASS.
THE ONLY THING THAT SAVED ME WAS BLANCA HAVING GROUNDED ME.
I WAS THERE, **WITH HER,** AND THERE WASN'T SHIT THESE GENTLEMEN COULD SAY TO THE CONTRARY.
THIS WAS ONE **VERY** CLOSE CALL.
I WOULD SET EXACTLY **ONE MORE** FIRE IN MY LIFE.

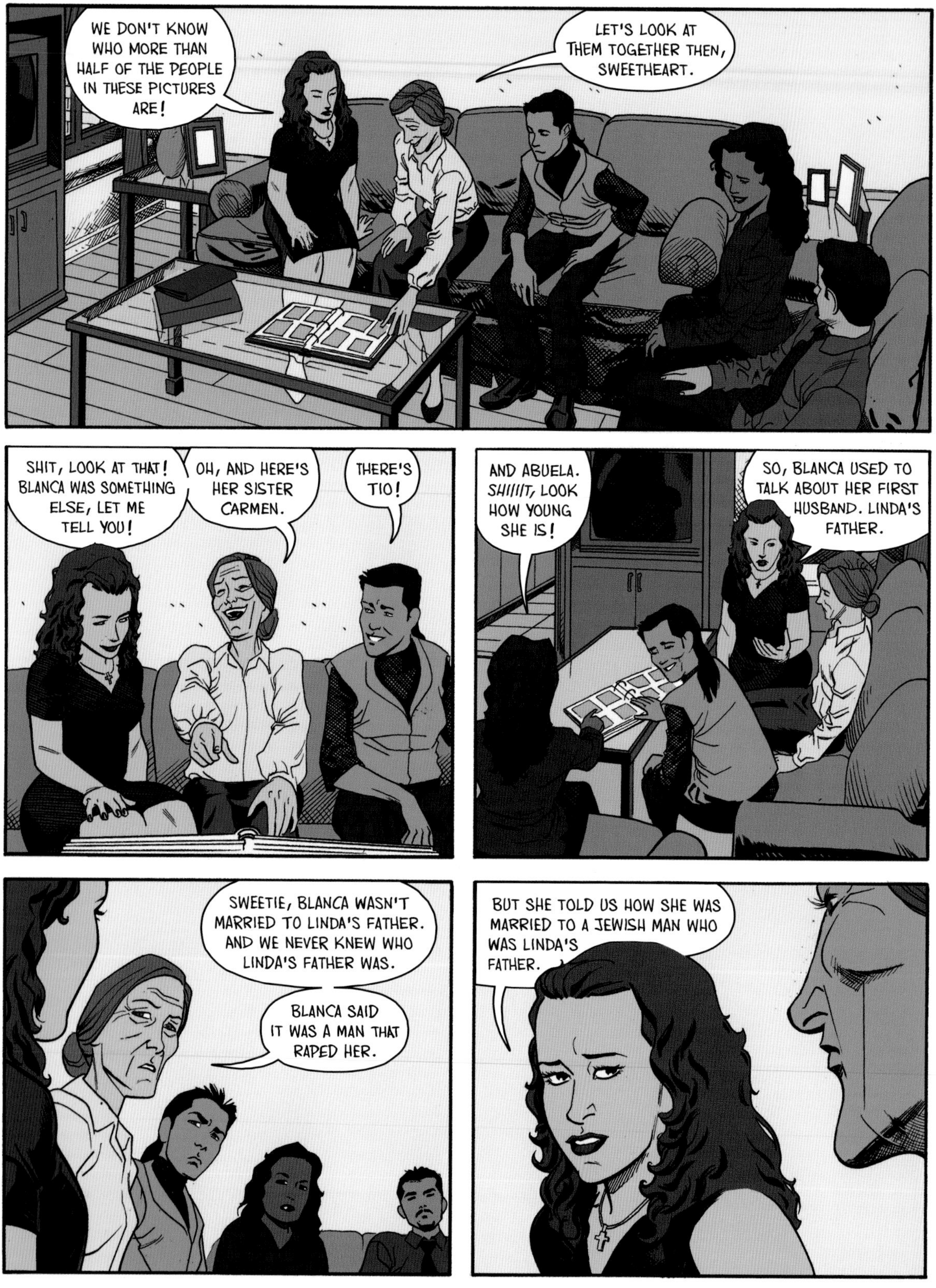
WE DON'T KNOW WHO MORE THAN HALF OF THE PEOPLE IN THESE PICTURES ARE!
LET'S LOOK AT THEM TOGETHER THEN, SWEETHEART.
SHIT, LOOK AT THAT! BLANCA WAS SOMETHING ELSE, LET ME TELL YOU!
OH, AND HERE'S HER SISTER CARMEN.
THERE'S TIO!
AND ABUELA. SHIIIIT, LOOK HOW YOUNG SHE IS!
SO, BLANCA USED TO TALK ABOUT HER FIRST HUSBAND. LINDA'S FATHER.
SWEETIE, BLANCA WASN'T MARRIED TO LINDA'S FATHER. AND WE NEVER KNEW WHO LINDA'S FATHER WAS.
BLANCA SAID IT WAS A MAN THAT RAPED HER.
BUT SHE TOLD US HOW SHE WAS MARRIED TO A JEWISH MAN WHO WAS LINDA'S FATHER.

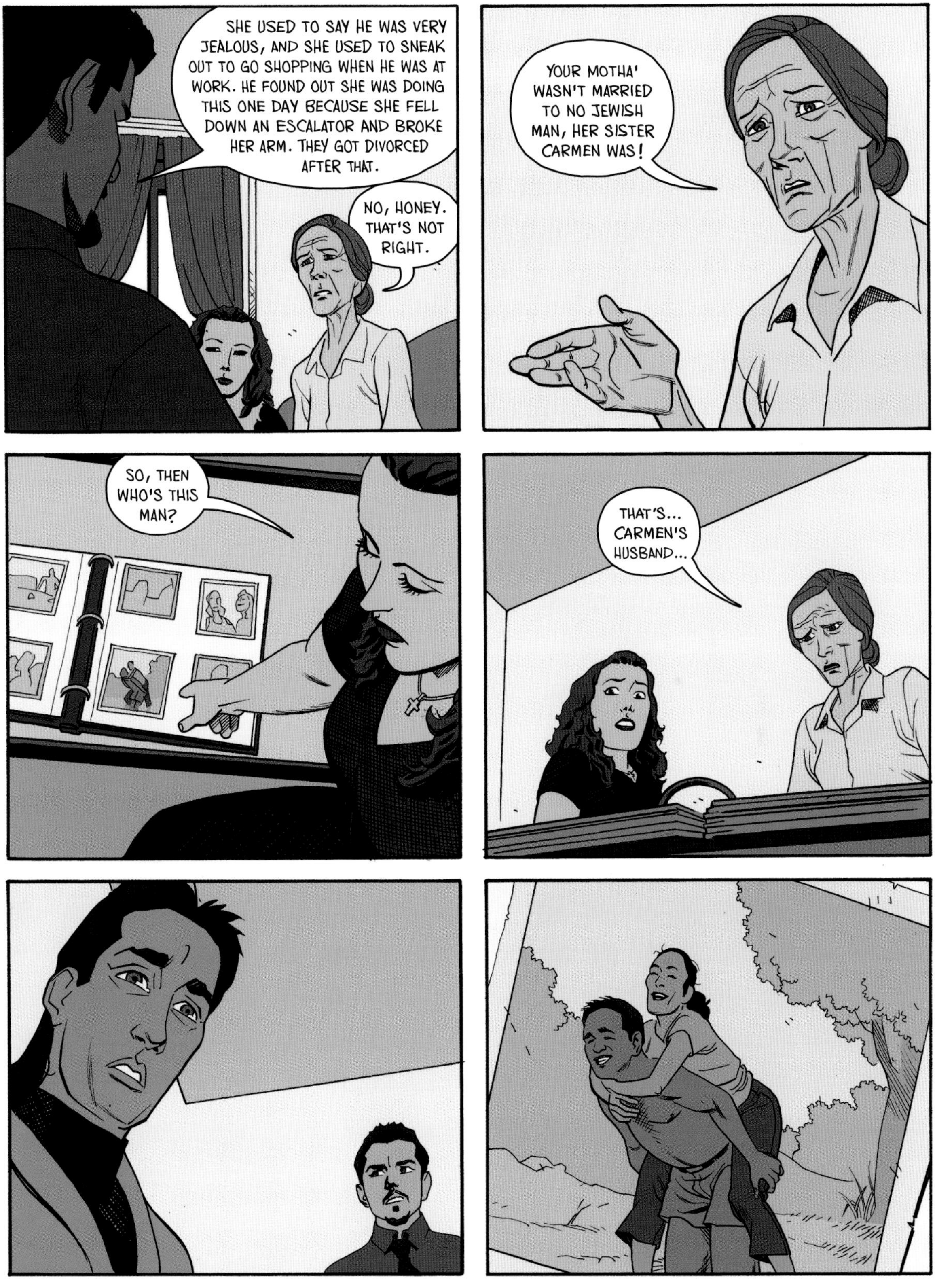
SHE USED TO SAY HE WAS VERY JEALOUS, AND SHE USED TO SNEAK OUT TO GO SHOPPING WHEN HE WAS AT WORK. HE FOUND OUT SHE WAS DOING THIS ONE DAY BECAUSE SHE FELL DOWN AN ESCALATOR AND BROKE HER ARM. THEY GOT DIVORCED AFTER THAT.
NO, HONEY. THAT'S NOT RIGHT.
YOUR MOTHA' WASN'T MARRIED TO NO JEWISH MAN, HER SISTER CARMEN WAS!
SO, THEN WHO'S THIS MAN?
THAT'S... CARMEN'S HUSBAND...

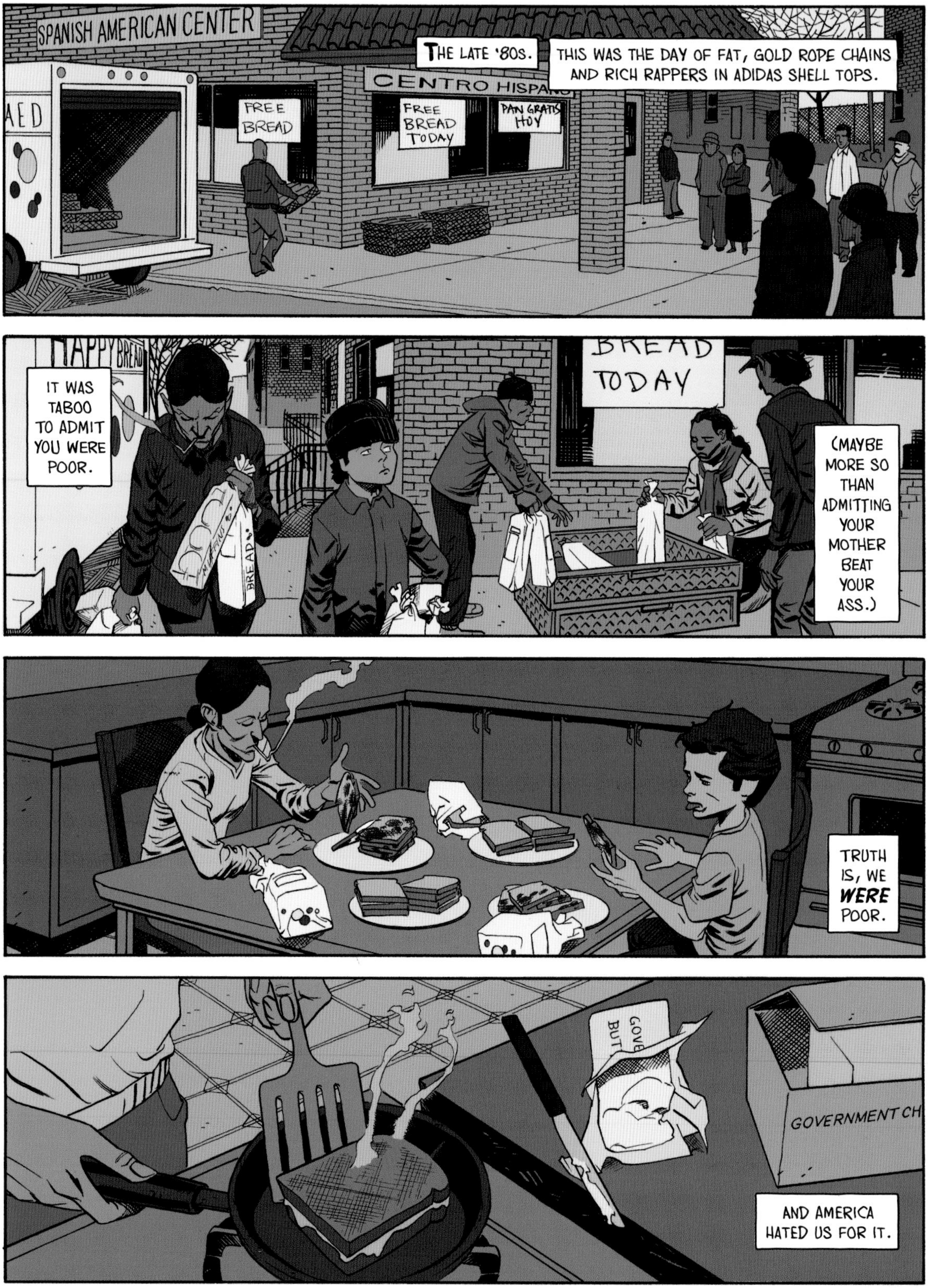
SPANISH AMERICAN CENTER
THE LATE '80S.
THIS WAS THE DAY OF FAT, GOLD ROPE CHAINS AND RICH RAPPERS IN ADIDAS SHELL TOPS.
CENTRO HISPANO
FREE BREAD
FREE BREAD TODAY
PAN GRATIS HOY
IT WAS TABOO TO ADMIT YOU WERE POOR.
BREAD TODAY
(MAYBE MORE SO THAN ADMITTING YOUR MOTHER BEAT YOUR ASS.)
TRUTH IS, WE *WERE* POOR.
GOVERNMENT CH
AND AMERICA HATED US FOR IT.

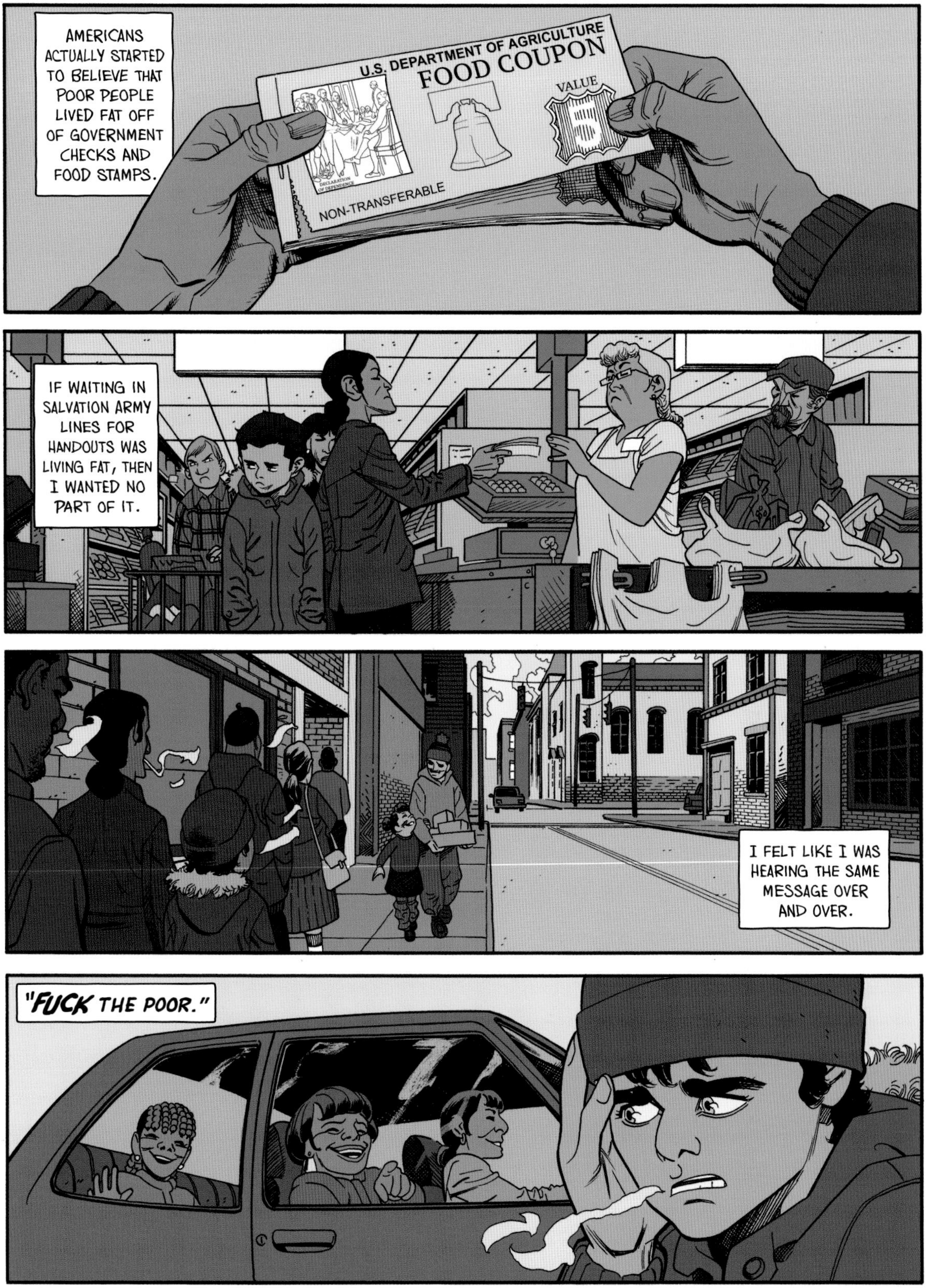
AMERICANS ACTUALLY STARTED TO BELIEVE THAT POOR PEOPLE LIVED FAT OFF OF GOVERNMENT CHECKS AND FOOD STAMPS.
U.S. DEPARTMENT OF AGRICULTURE
FOOD COUPON
VALUE
5
DECLARATION OF DEPENDENCE
NON-TRANSFERABLE
IF WAITING IN SALVATION ARMY LINES FOR HANDOUTS WAS LIVING FAT, THEN I WANTED NO PART OF IT.
I FELT LIKE I WAS HEARING THE SAME MESSAGE OVER AND OVER.
"FUCK THE POOR."

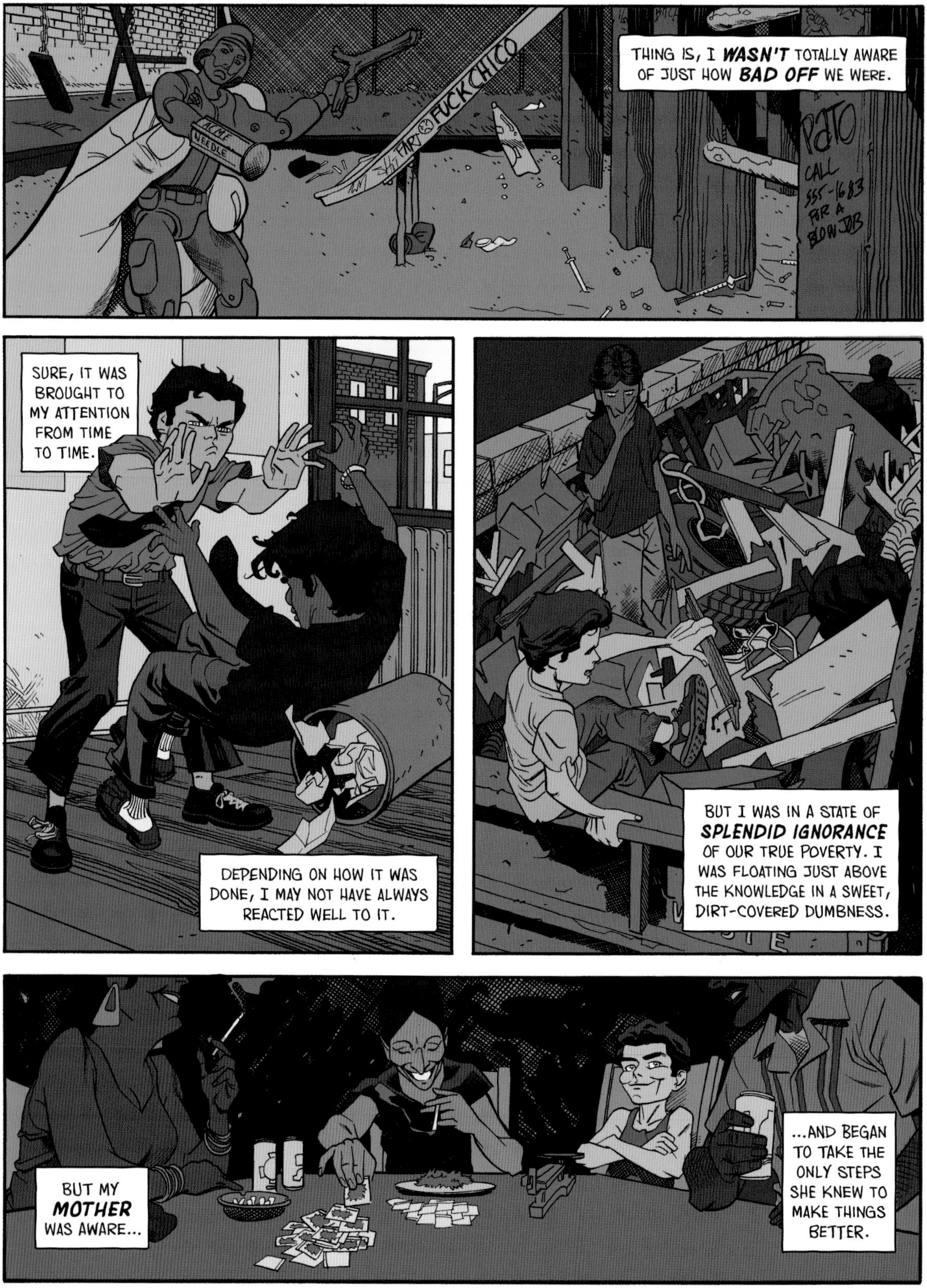

ACME NEEDLE
FUCK CHICO
FART
PATO
CALL 555-1683 FOR A BLOW JOB
THING IS, I WASN'T TOTALLY AWARE OF JUST HOW BAD OFF WE WERE.
SURE, IT WAS BROUGHT TO MY ATTENTION FROM TIME TO TIME.
DEPENDING ON HOW IT WAS DONE, I MAY NOT HAVE ALWAYS REACTED WELL TO IT.
BUT I WAS IN A STATE OF SPLENDID IGNORANCE OF OUR TRUE POVERTY. I WAS FLOATING JUST ABOVE THE KNOWLEDGE IN A SWEET, DIRT-COVERED DUMBNESS.
BUT MY MOTHER WAS AWARE...
...AND BEGAN TO TAKE THE ONLY STEPS SHE KNEW TO MAKE THINGS BETTER.

IT ACTUALLY WASN'T TILL YEARS LATER, WHEN I WAS AN ADULT, THAT I BEGAN TO **REALLY** GET WHAT HAD BEEN HAPPENING.

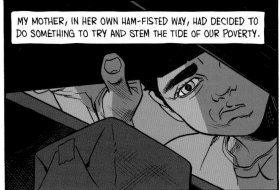

MY MOTHER, IN HER OWN HAM-FISTED WAY, HAD DECIDED TO DO SOMETHING TO TRY AND STEM THE TIDE OF OUR POVERTY.

NO, NO... THIS IS JUST SUGAR.

I'LL GET RID OF IT FOR YOU.

NO WORRY.

LET ME PUT IT TO YOU STRAIGHT, I DON'T JUDGE HER FOR IT.

SHE WAS IN A CONSTANT STATE OF DESPERATION.

SHE WAS JUST PLUGGING HOLES IN A COLLAPSING DAM.

AND SHE HAD TO TRADE IN HER PRIDE TO KEEP DISASTER AT ARM'S DISTANCE.

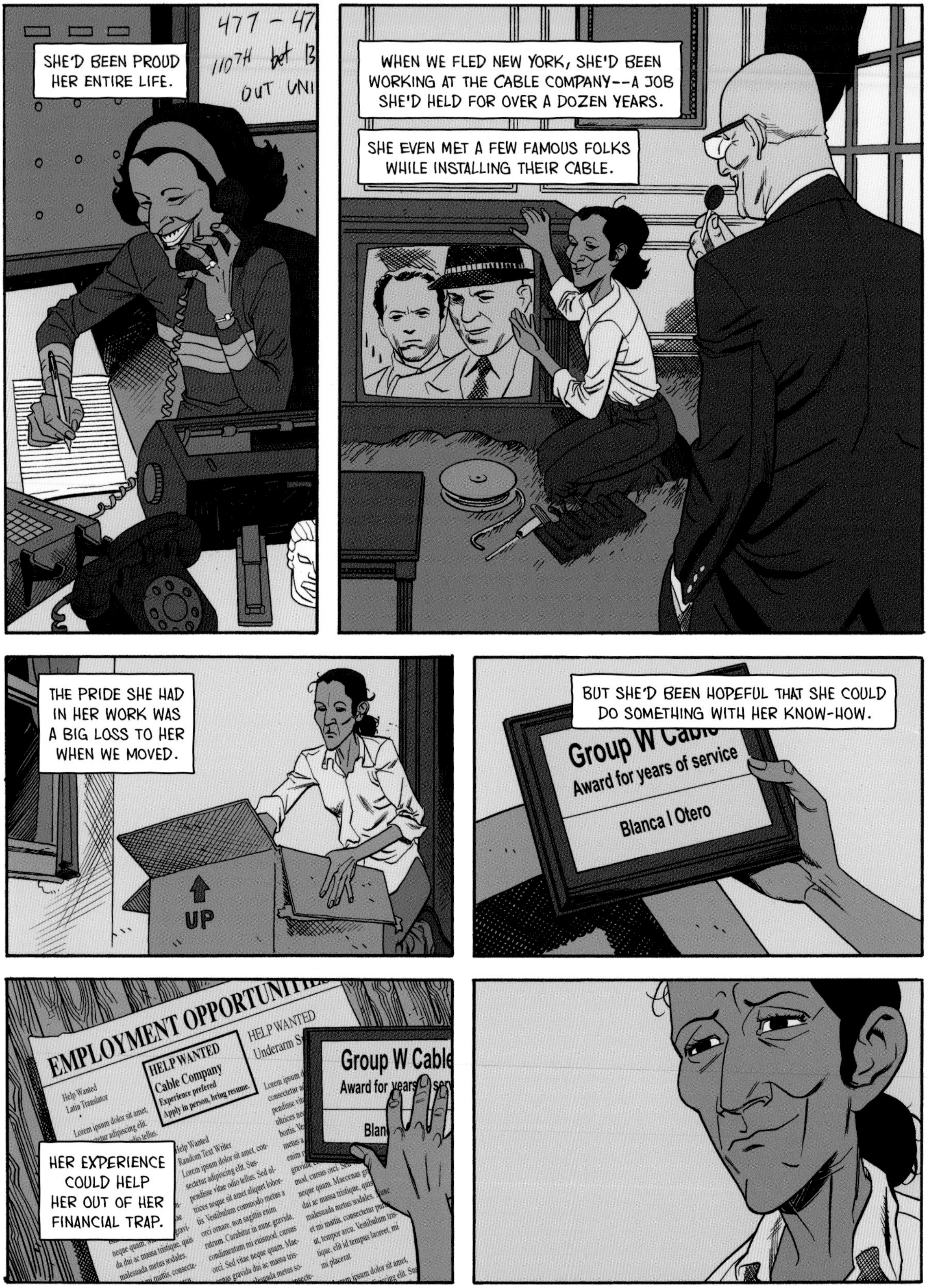
SHE'D BEEN PROUD HER ENTIRE LIFE.
WHEN WE FLED NEW YORK, SHE'D BEEN WORKING AT THE CABLE COMPANY--A JOB SHE'D HELD FOR OVER A DOZEN YEARS.
SHE EVEN MET A FEW FAMOUS FOLKS WHILE INSTALLING THEIR CABLE.
THE PRIDE SHE HAD IN HER WORK WAS A BIG LOSS TO HER WHEN WE MOVED.
UP
BUT SHE'D BEEN HOPEFUL THAT SHE COULD DO SOMETHING WITH HER KNOW-HOW.
Award for years of service
Blanca I Otero
EMPLOYMENT OPPORTUNITIES
HELP WANTED
Cable Company
Experience prefered
Apply in person, bring resume.
HELP WANTED
Help Wanted
Latin Translator
Help Wanted
Random Text Writer
Group W Cable
HER EXPERIENCE COULD HELP HER OUT OF HER FINANCIAL TRAP.

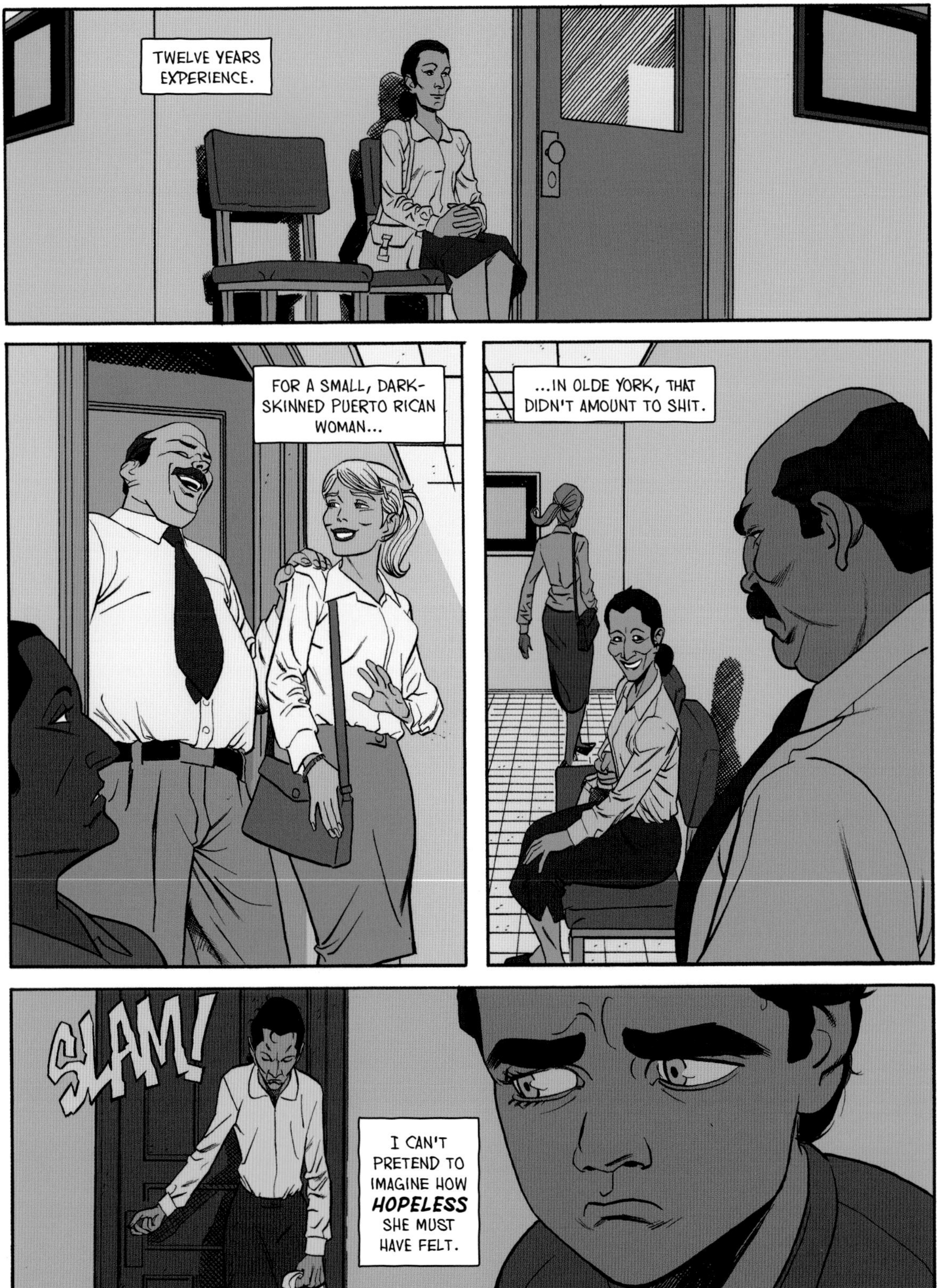
TWELVE YEARS EXPERIENCE.
FOR A SMALL, DARK-SKINNED PUERTO RICAN WOMAN...
...IN OLDE YORK, THAT DIDN'T AMOUNT TO SHIT.
SLAM!
I CAN'T PRETEND TO IMAGINE HOW **HOPELESS** SHE MUST HAVE FELT.

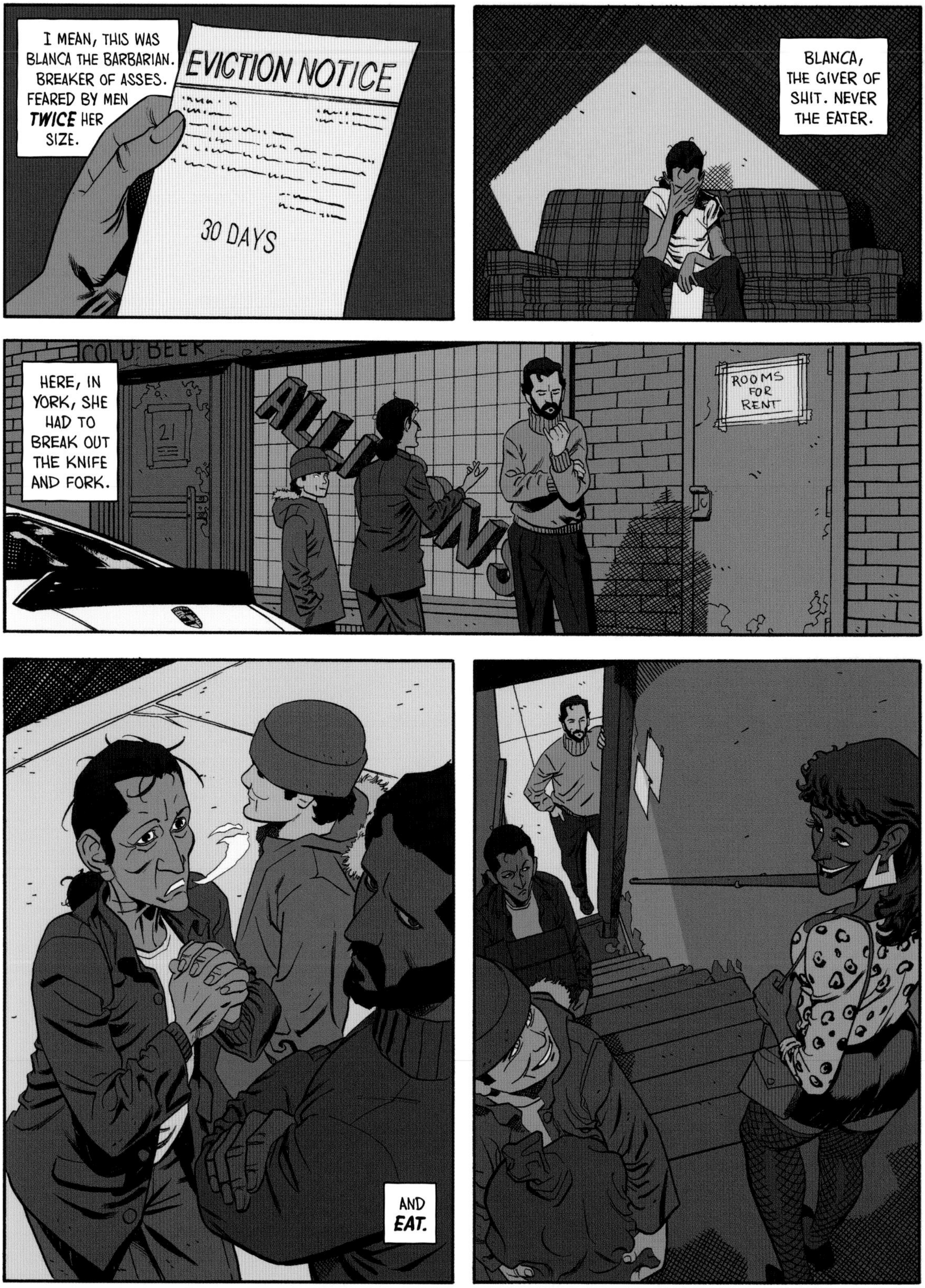
I MEAN, THIS WAS BLANCA THE BARBARIAN. BREAKER OF ASSES. FEARED BY MEN **TWICE** HER SIZE.
EVICTION NOTICE
30 DAYS
BLANCA, THE GIVER OF SHIT. NEVER THE EATER.
COLD BEER
HERE, IN YORK, SHE HAD TO BREAK OUT THE KNIFE AND FORK.
21
ROOMS FOR RENT
AND **EAT.**

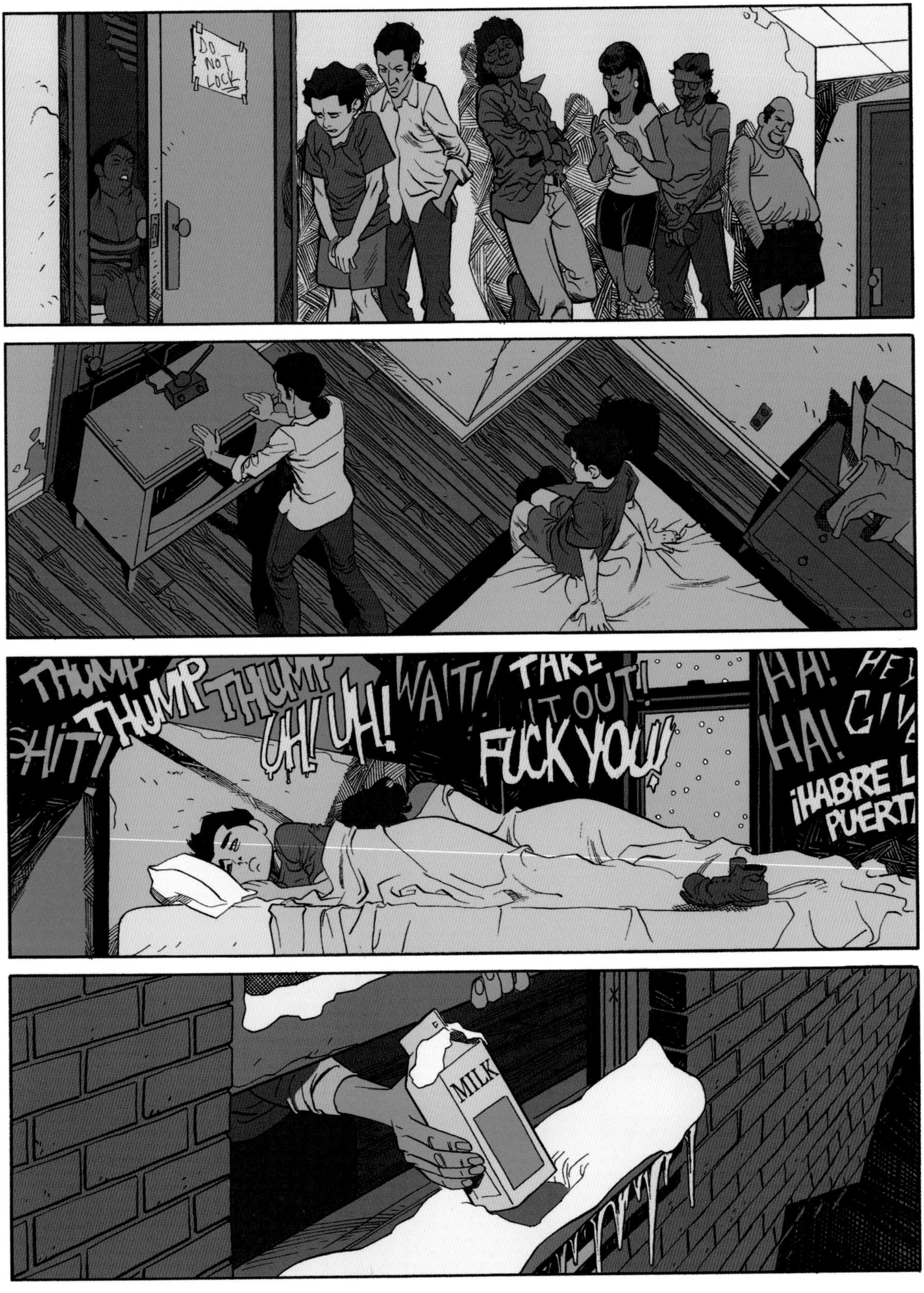
DO NOT LOCK
THUMP THUMP THUMP
SHIT!
UH! UH!
WAIT!
TAKE IT OUT!
FUCK YOU!
HA! HA!
MILK

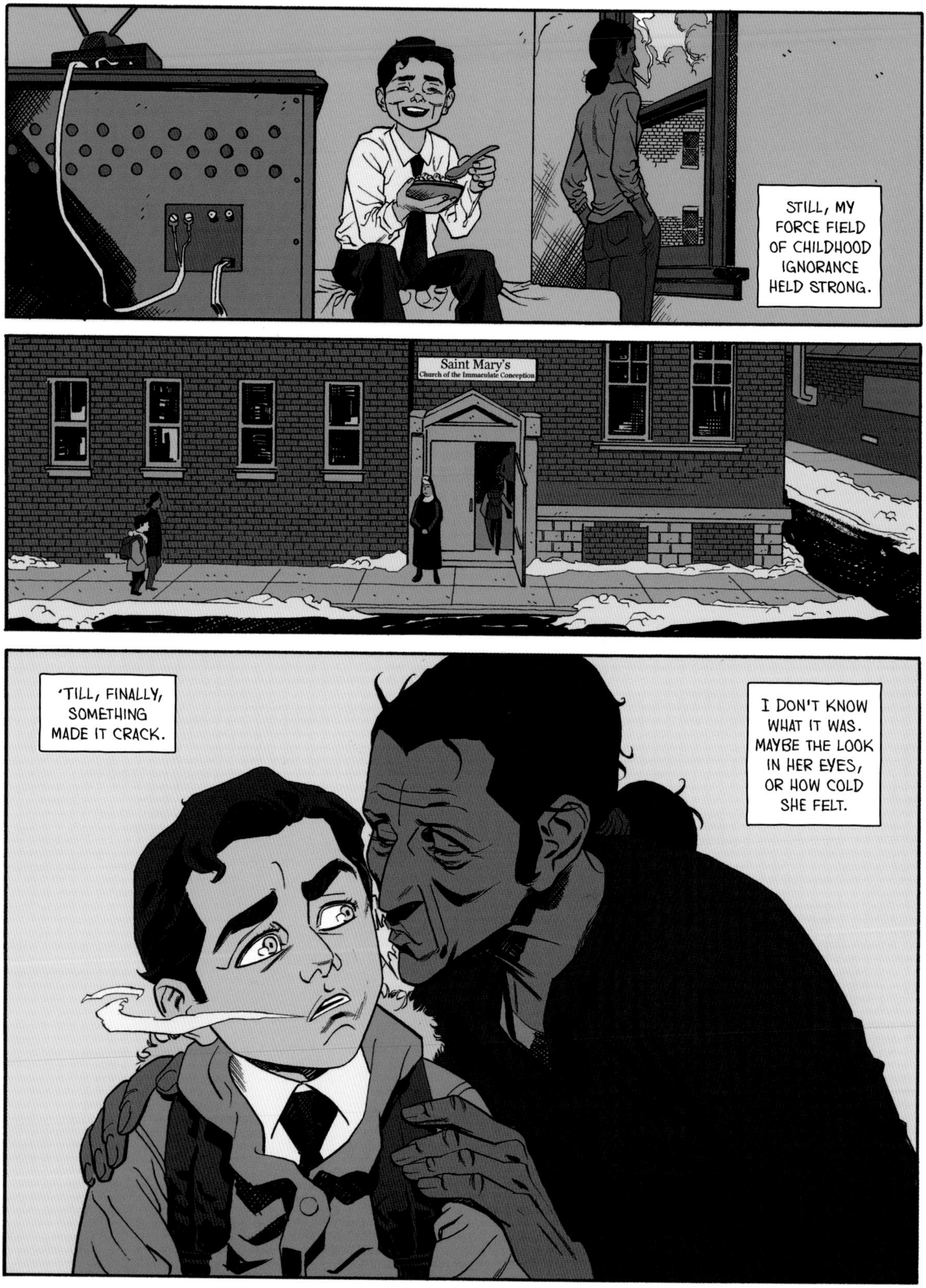
STILL, MY FORCE FIELD OF CHILDHOOD IGNORANCE HELD STRONG.
Saint Mary's
Church of the Immaculate Conception
'TILL, FINALLY, SOMETHING MADE IT CRACK.
I DON'T KNOW WHAT IT WAS. MAYBE THE LOOK IN HER EYES, OR HOW COLD SHE FELT.

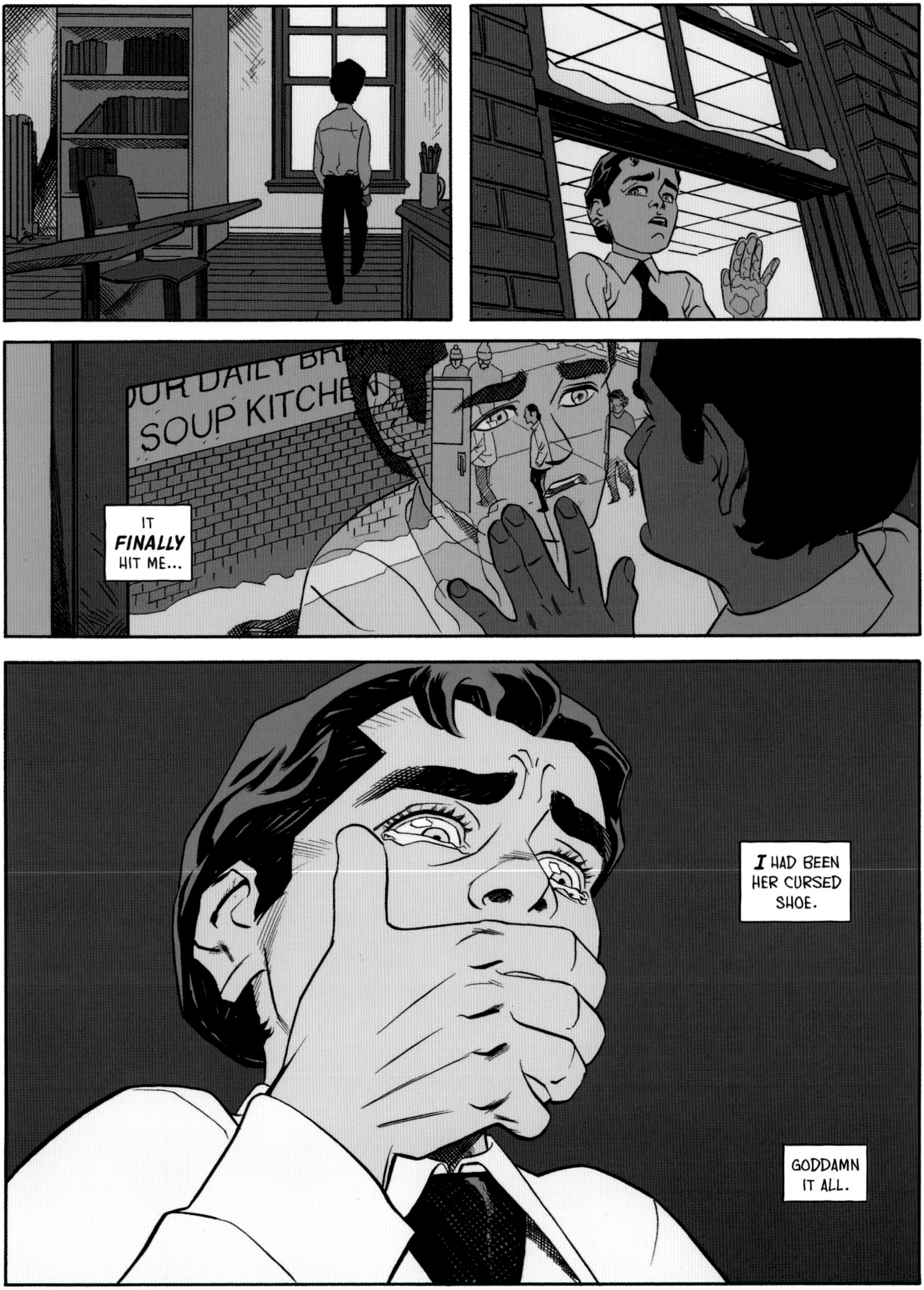

OUR DAILY BR
SOUP KITCHEN
IT FINALLY HIT ME...
I HAD BEEN HER CURSED SHOE.
GODDAMN IT ALL.

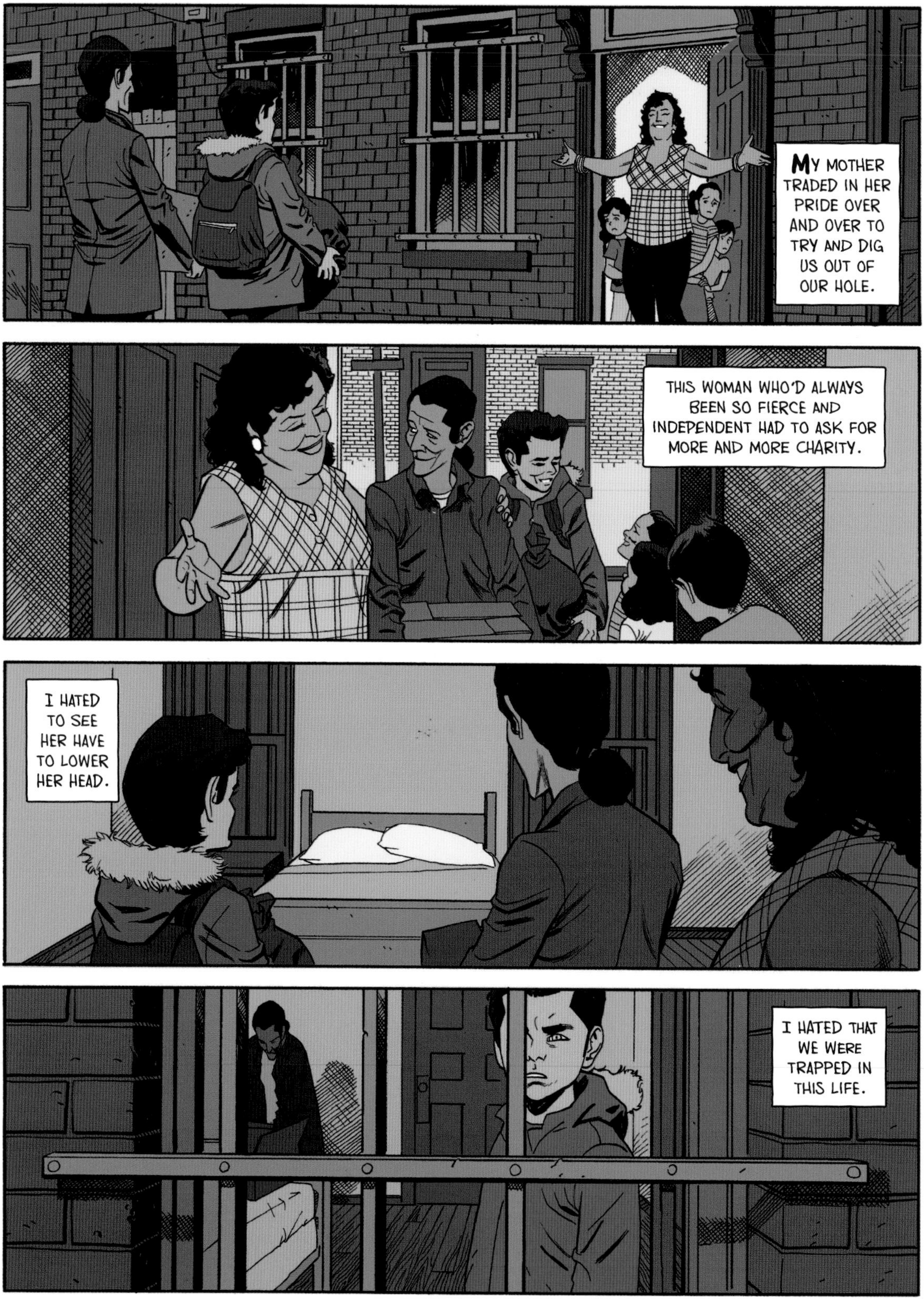
MY MOTHER TRADED IN HER PRIDE OVER AND OVER TO TRY AND DIG US OUT OF OUR HOLE.
THIS WOMAN WHO'D ALWAYS BEEN SO FIERCE AND INDEPENDENT HAD TO ASK FOR MORE AND MORE CHARITY.
I HATED TO SEE HER HAVE TO LOWER HER HEAD.
I HATED THAT WE WERE TRAPPED IN THIS LIFE.

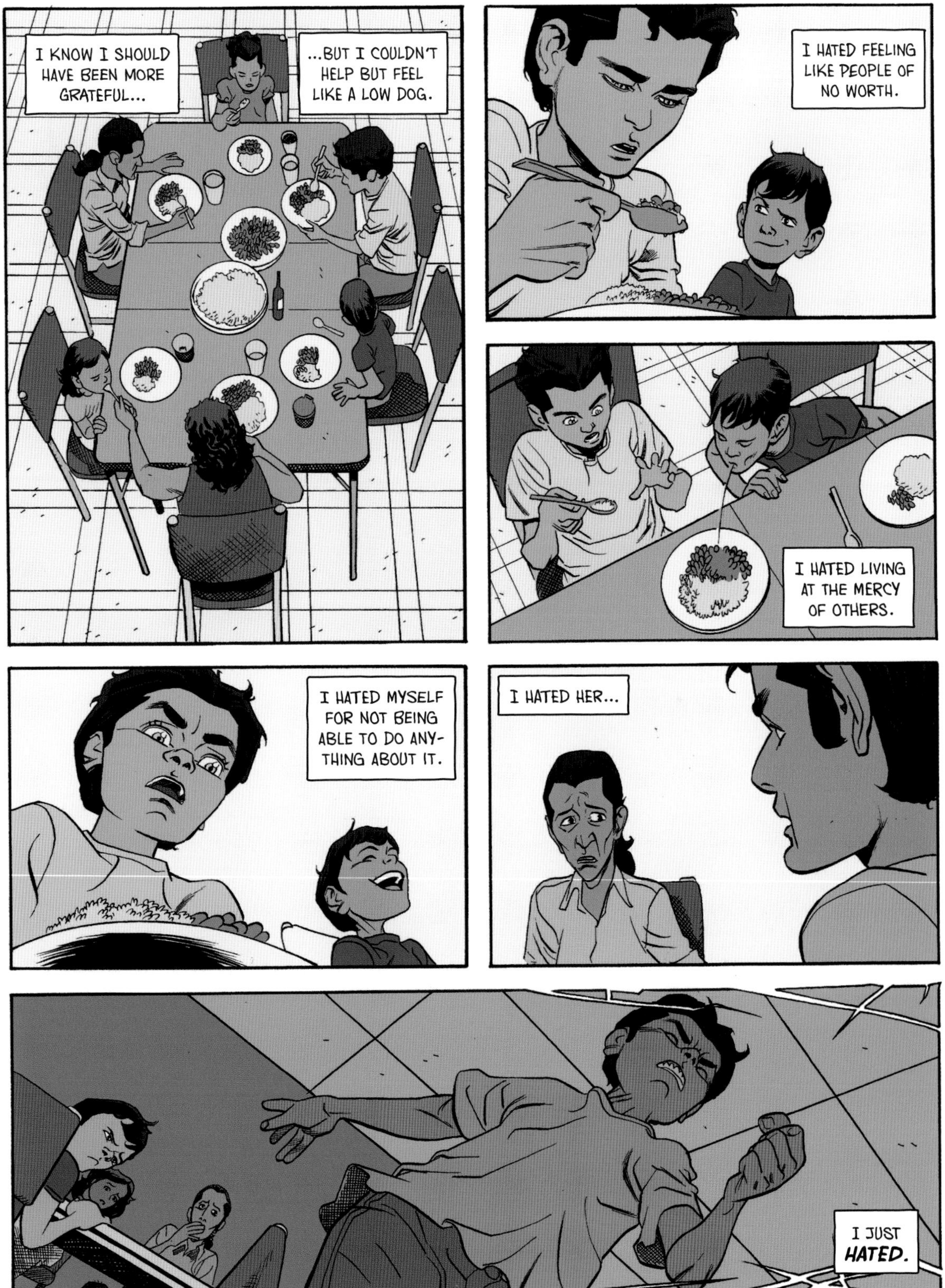
I KNOW I SHOULD HAVE BEEN MORE GRATEFUL...
...BUT I COULDN'T HELP BUT FEEL LIKE A LOW DOG.
I HATED FEELING LIKE PEOPLE OF NO WORTH.
I HATED LIVING AT THE MERCY OF OTHERS.
I HATED MYSELF FOR NOT BEING ABLE TO DO ANY-THING ABOUT IT.
I HATED HER...
I JUST *HATED.*

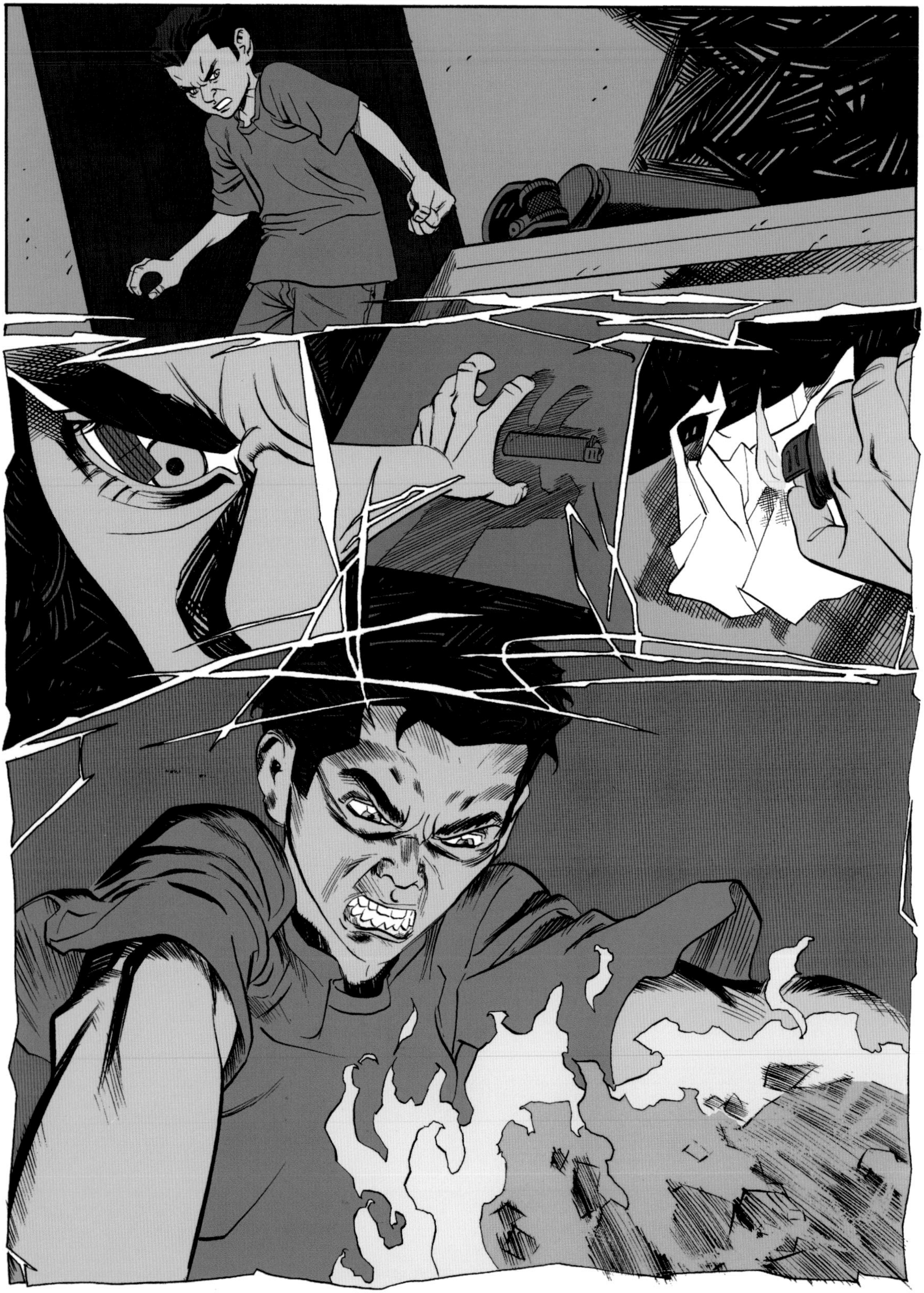

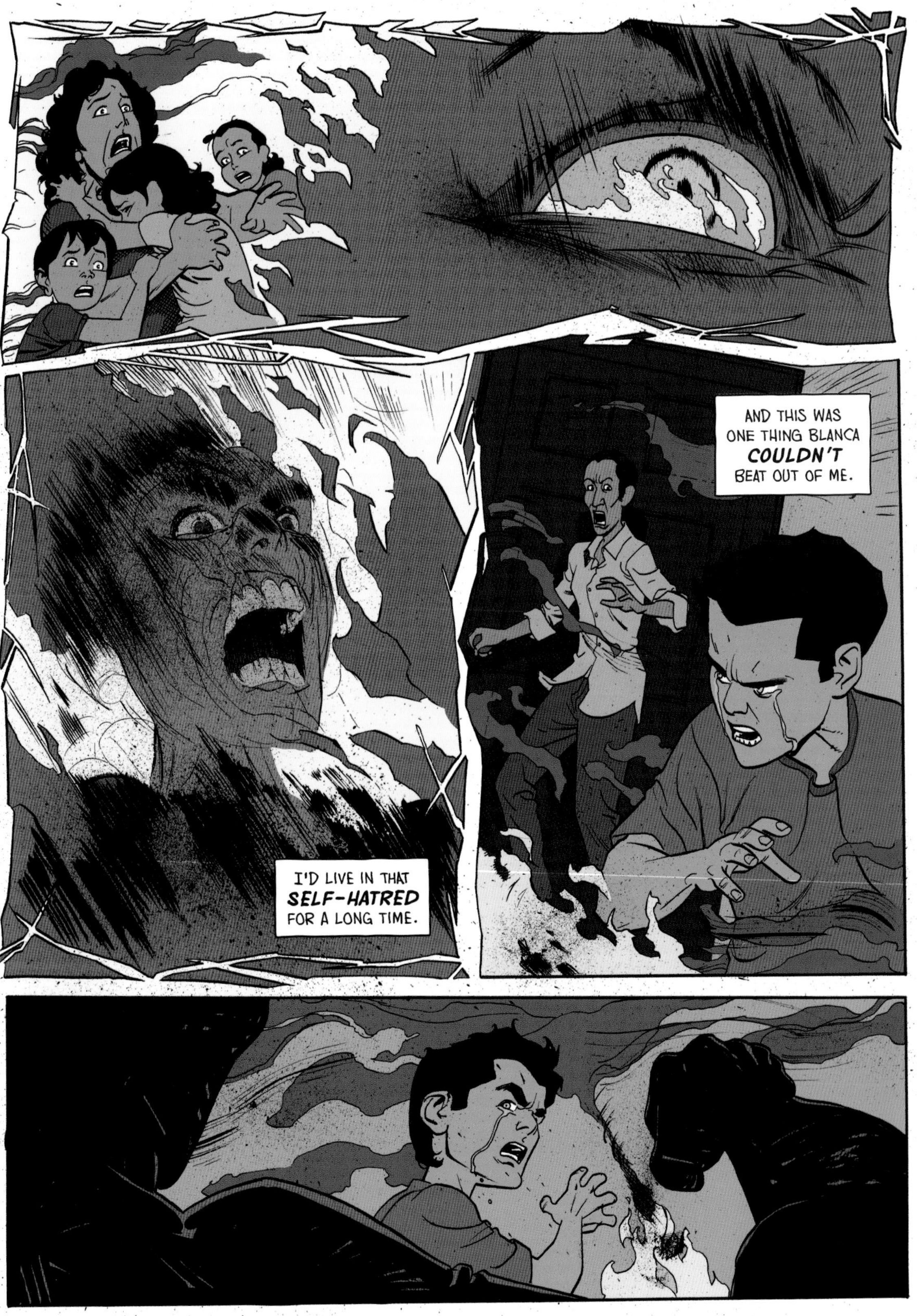
I'D LIVE IN THAT SELF-HATRED FOR A LONG TIME.
AND THIS WAS ONE THING BLANCA COULDN'T BEAT OUT OF ME.

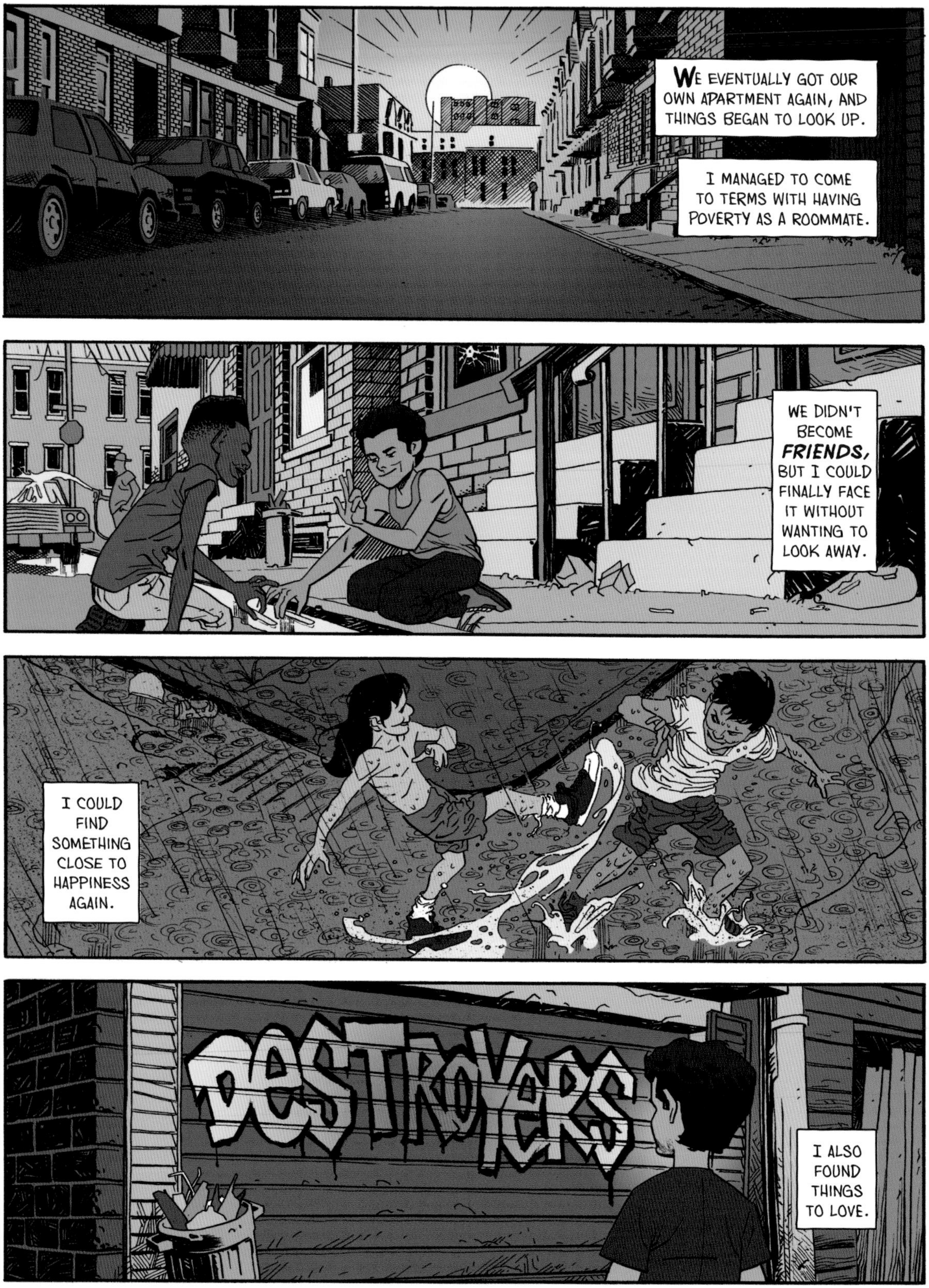
WE EVENTUALLY GOT OUR OWN APARTMENT AGAIN, AND THINGS BEGAN TO LOOK UP.
I MANAGED TO COME TO TERMS WITH HAVING POVERTY AS A ROOMMATE.
WE DIDN'T BECOME ***FRIENDS,*** BUT I COULD FINALLY FACE IT WITHOUT WANTING TO LOOK AWAY.
I COULD FIND SOMETHING CLOSE TO HAPPINESS AGAIN.
DESTROYERS
I ALSO FOUND THINGS TO LOVE.

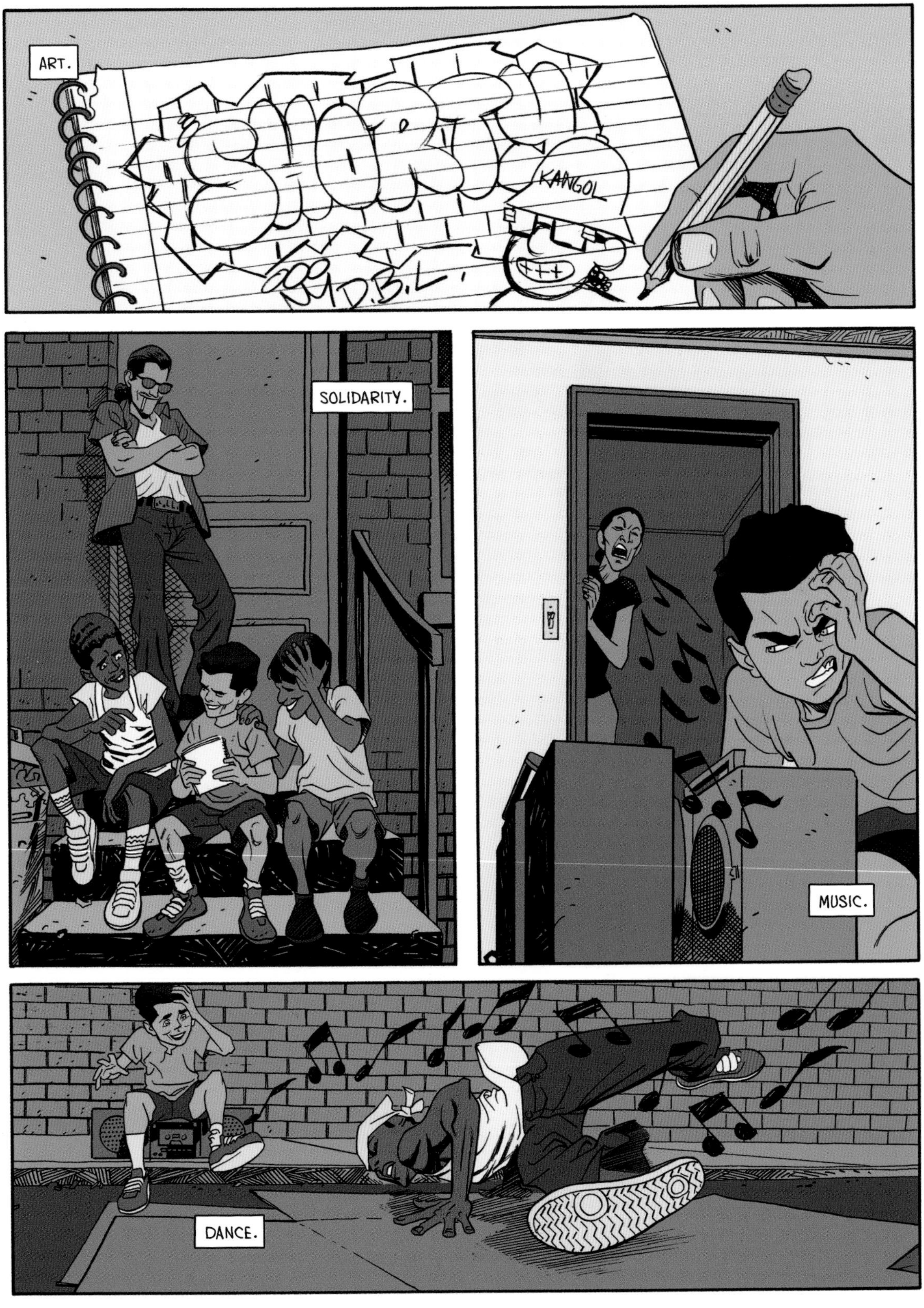
ART.
KANGOL
D.B.L
SOLIDARITY.
MUSIC.
DANCE.

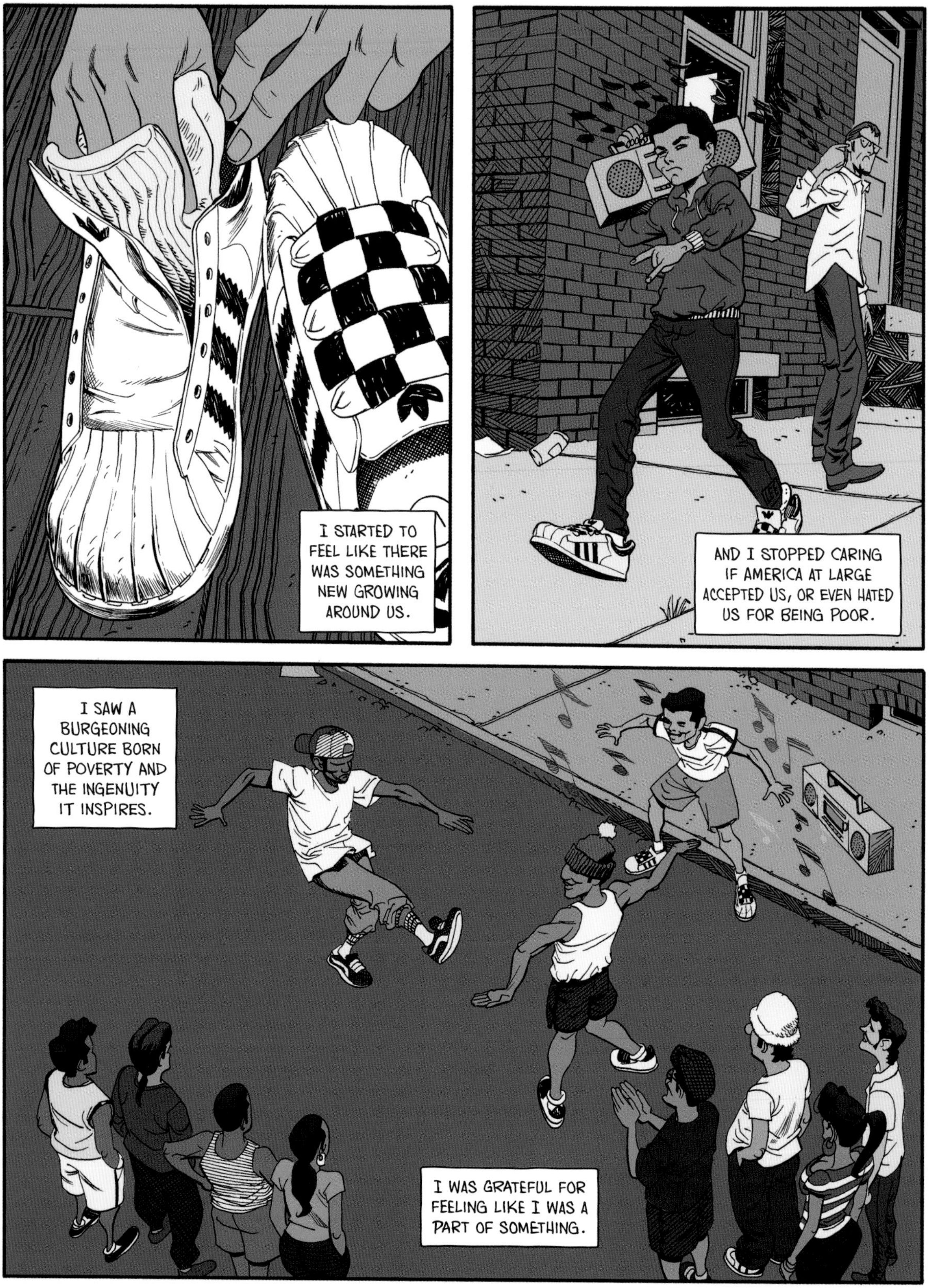
I STARTED TO FEEL LIKE THERE WAS SOMETHING NEW GROWING AROUND US.
AND I STOPPED CARING IF AMERICA AT LARGE ACCEPTED US, OR EVEN HATED US FOR BEING POOR.
I SAW A BURGEONING CULTURE BORN OF POVERTY AND THE INGENUITY IT INSPIRES.
I WAS GRATEFUL FOR FEELING LIKE I WAS A PART OF SOMETHING.

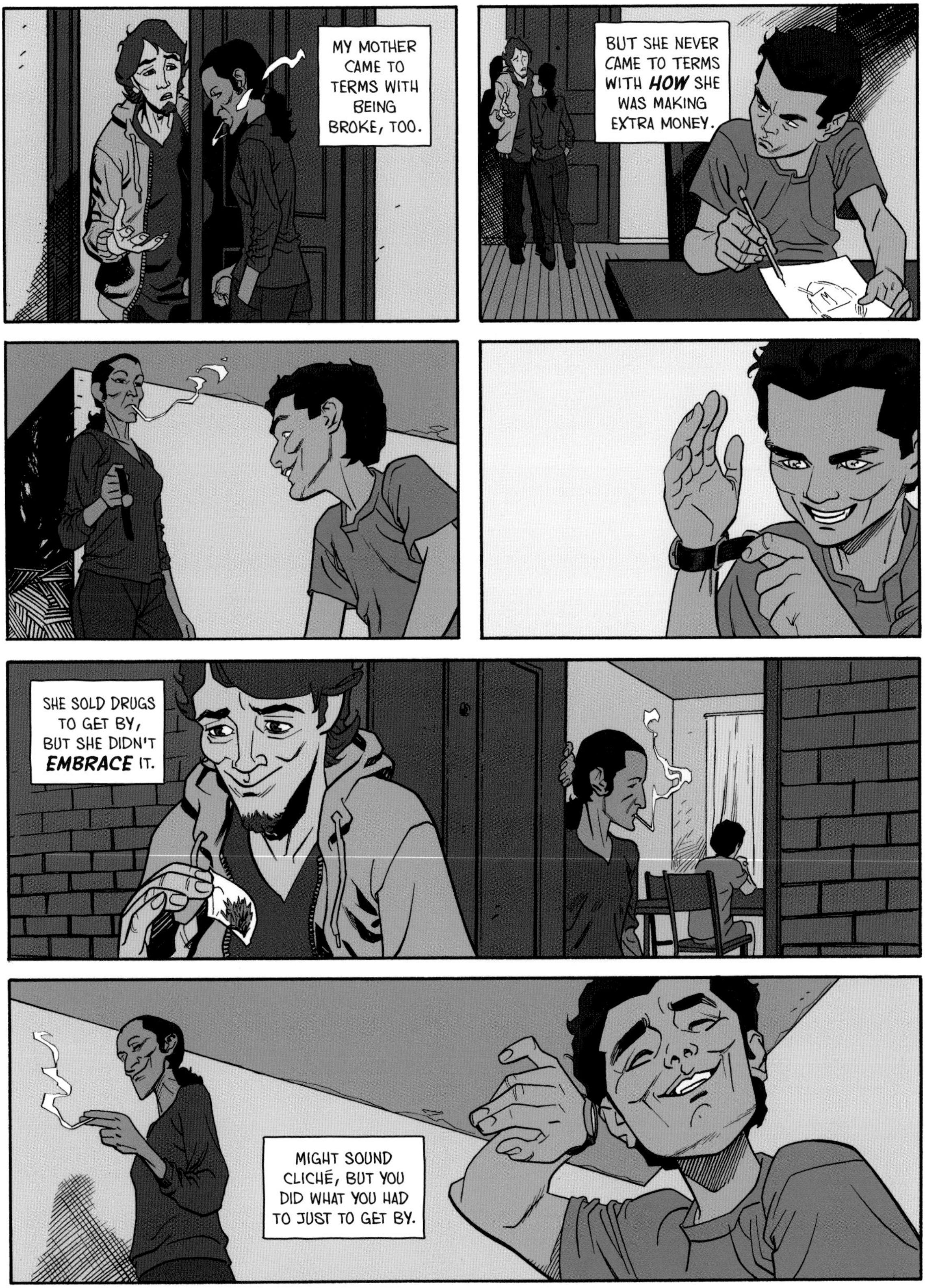
MY MOTHER CAME TO TERMS WITH BEING BROKE, TOO.
BUT SHE NEVER CAME TO TERMS WITH **HOW** SHE WAS MAKING EXTRA MONEY.
SHE SOLD DRUGS TO GET BY, BUT SHE DIDN'T **EMBRACE** IT.
MIGHT SOUND CLICHÉ, BUT YOU DID WHAT YOU HAD TO JUST TO GET BY.

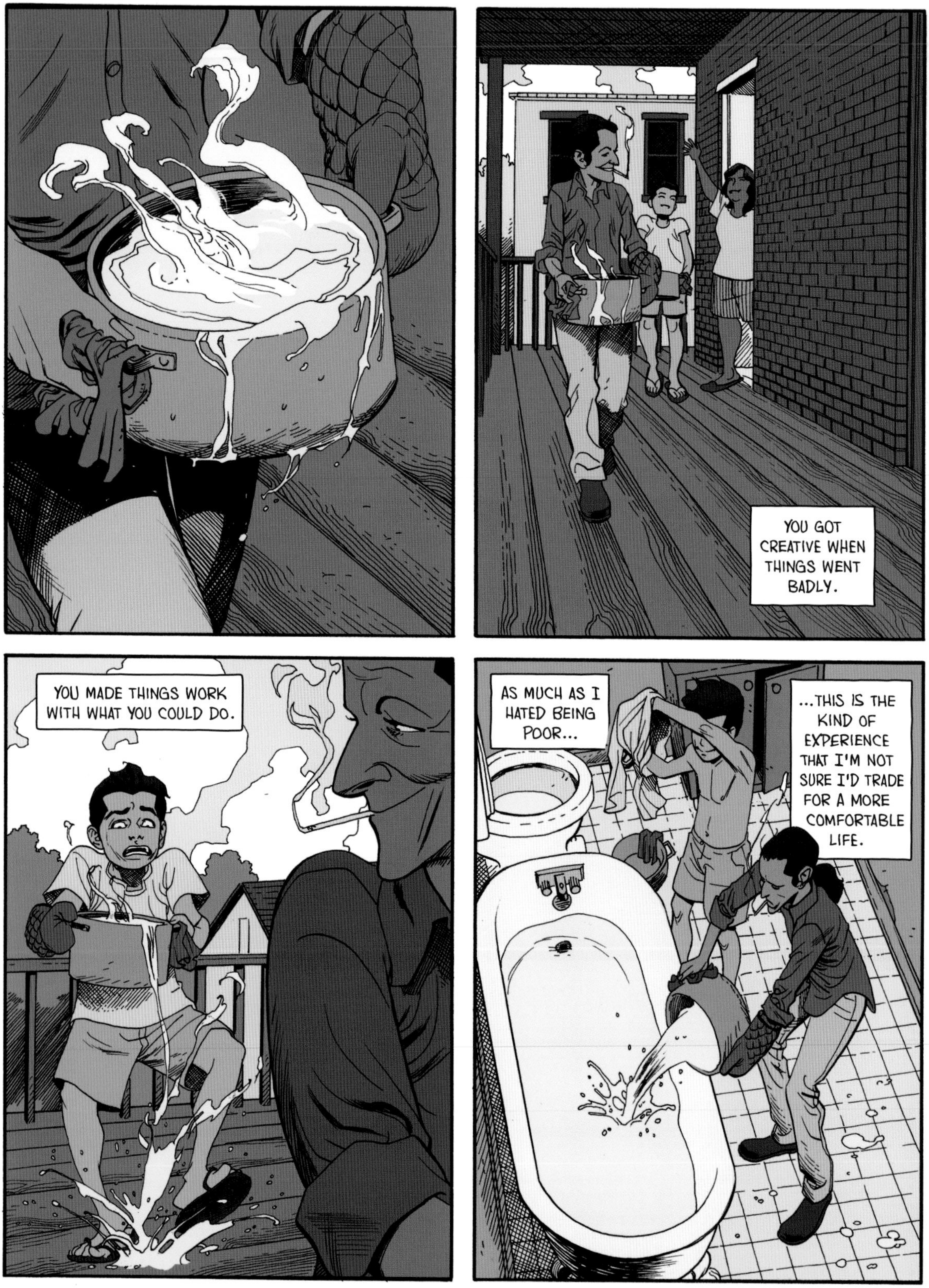
YOU GOT CREATIVE WHEN THINGS WENT BADLY.
YOU MADE THINGS WORK WITH WHAT YOU COULD DO.
AS MUCH AS I HATED BEING POOR...
...THIS IS THE KIND OF EXPERIENCE THAT I'M NOT SURE I'D TRADE FOR A MORE COMFORTABLE LIFE.

I DON'T WANT TO ROMANTICIZE POVERTY. I JUST MEAN THAT THERE WAS, FOR ME, A KIND OF GRACE AND JOY IN IT THAT I CAN'T QUITE DESCRIBE.

I'D HAVE LOVED TO GIVE US ALL ENOUGH TO LIVE BETTER, BUT...

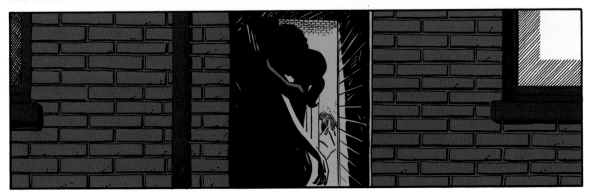

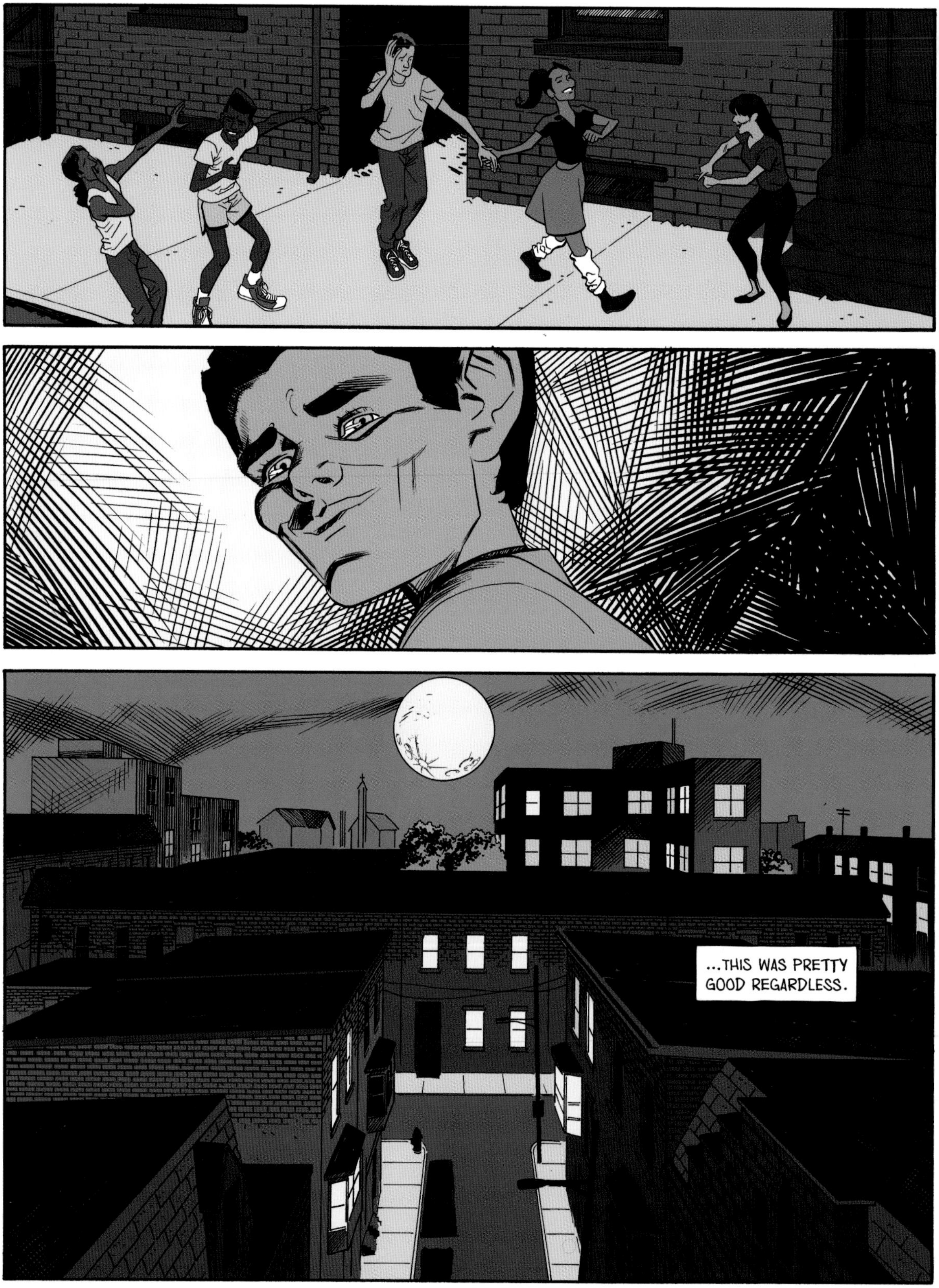
...THIS WAS PRETTY GOOD REGARDLESS.

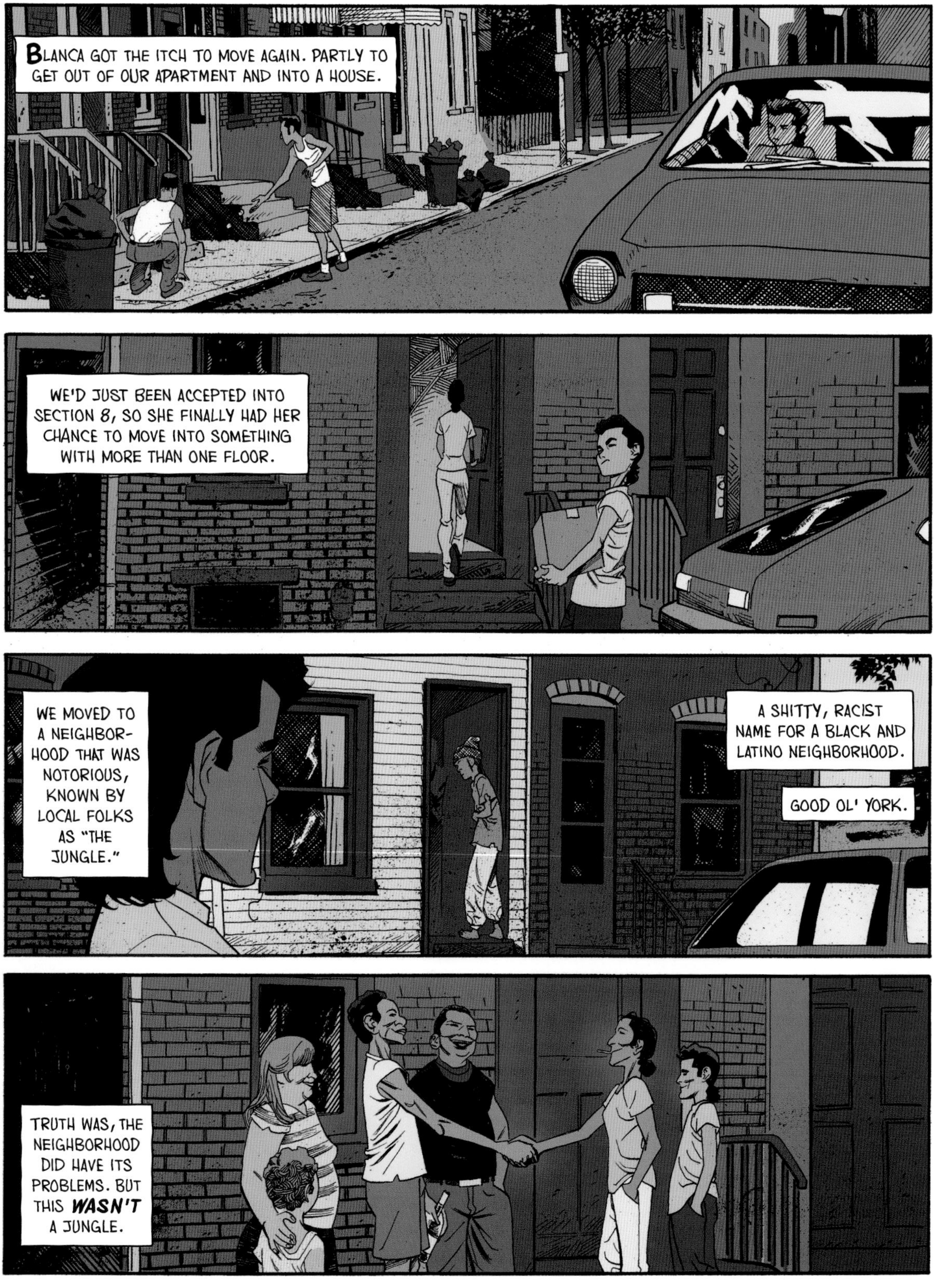
BLANCA GOT THE ITCH TO MOVE AGAIN. PARTLY TO GET OUT OF OUR APARTMENT AND INTO A HOUSE.
WE'D JUST BEEN ACCEPTED INTO SECTION 8, SO SHE FINALLY HAD HER CHANCE TO MOVE INTO SOMETHING WITH MORE THAN ONE FLOOR.
WE MOVED TO A NEIGHBOR-HOOD THAT WAS NOTORIOUS, KNOWN BY LOCAL FOLKS AS "THE JUNGLE."
A SHITTY, RACIST NAME FOR A BLACK AND LATINO NEIGHBORHOOD.
GOOD OL' YORK.
TRUTH WAS, THE NEIGHBORHOOD DID HAVE ITS PROBLEMS. BUT THIS ***WASN'T*** A JUNGLE.

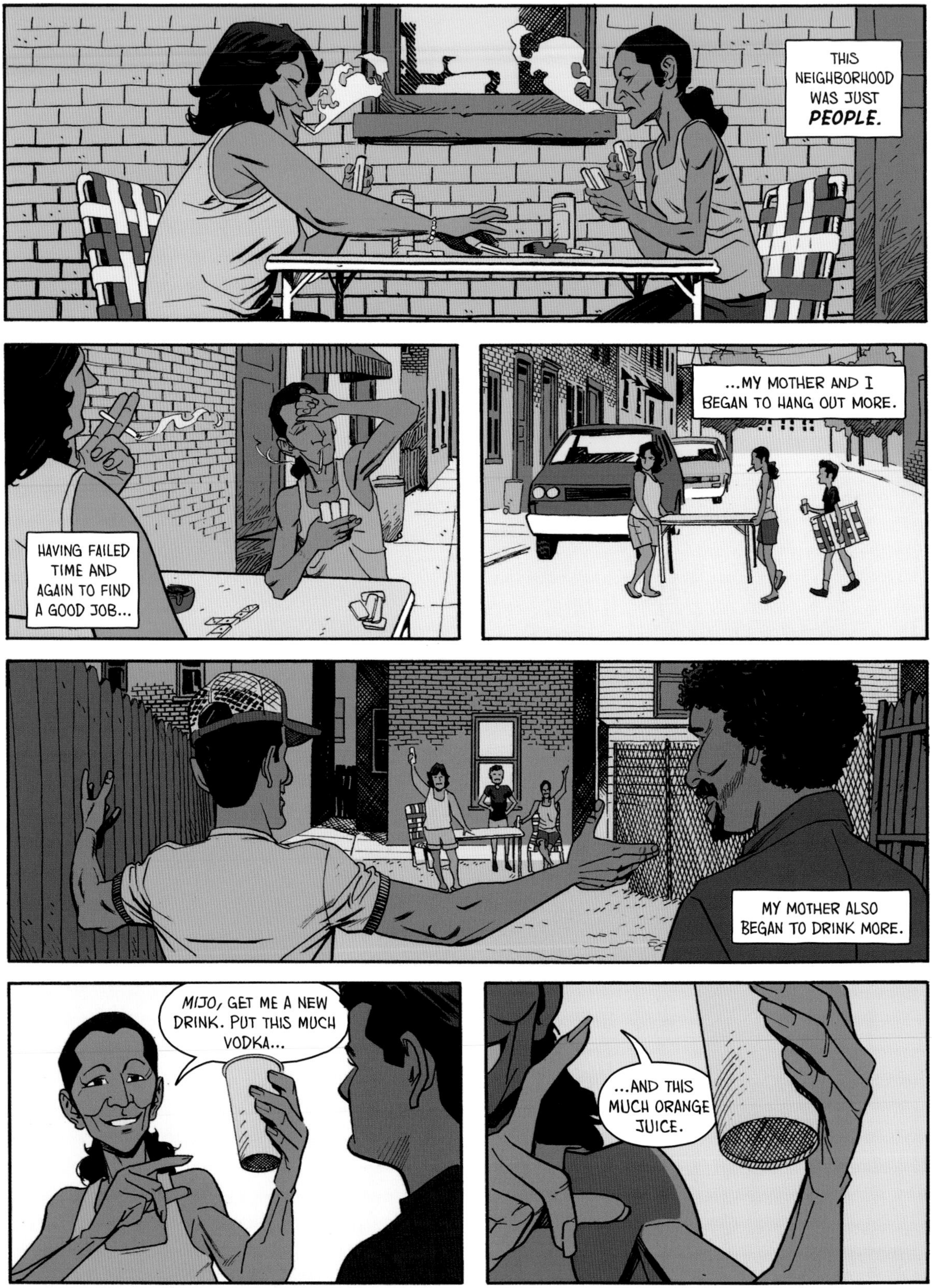
THIS NEIGHBORHOOD WAS JUST ***PEOPLE.***
HAVING FAILED TIME AND AGAIN TO FIND A GOOD JOB...
...MY MOTHER AND I BEGAN TO HANG OUT MORE.
MY MOTHER ALSO BEGAN TO DRINK MORE.
*MIJO,* GET ME A NEW DRINK. PUT THIS MUCH VODKA...
...AND THIS MUCH ORANGE JUICE.

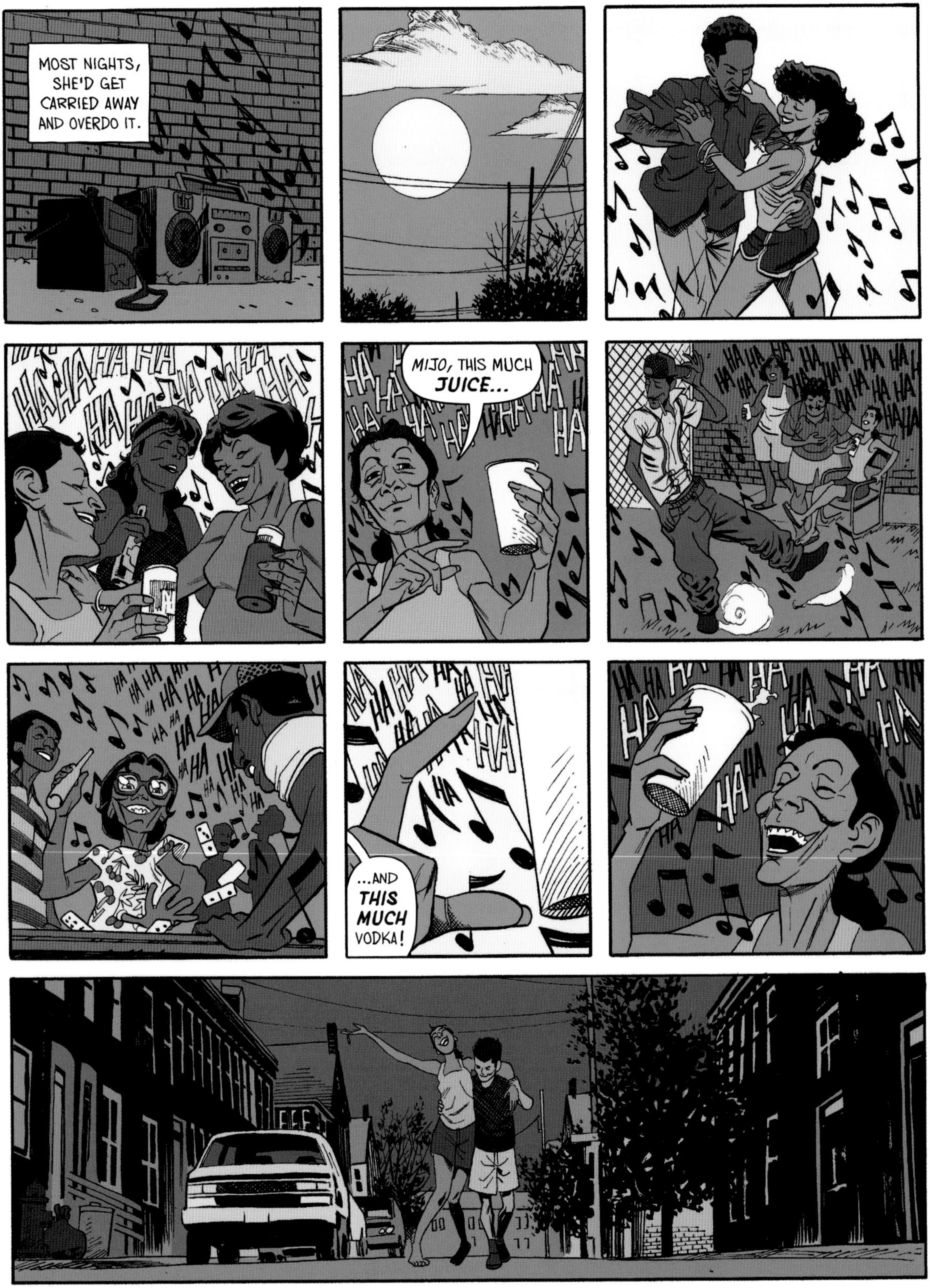
MOST NIGHTS, SHE'D GET CARRIED AWAY AND OVERDO IT.
MIJO, THIS MUCH **JUICE...**
...AND **THIS MUCH** VODKA!

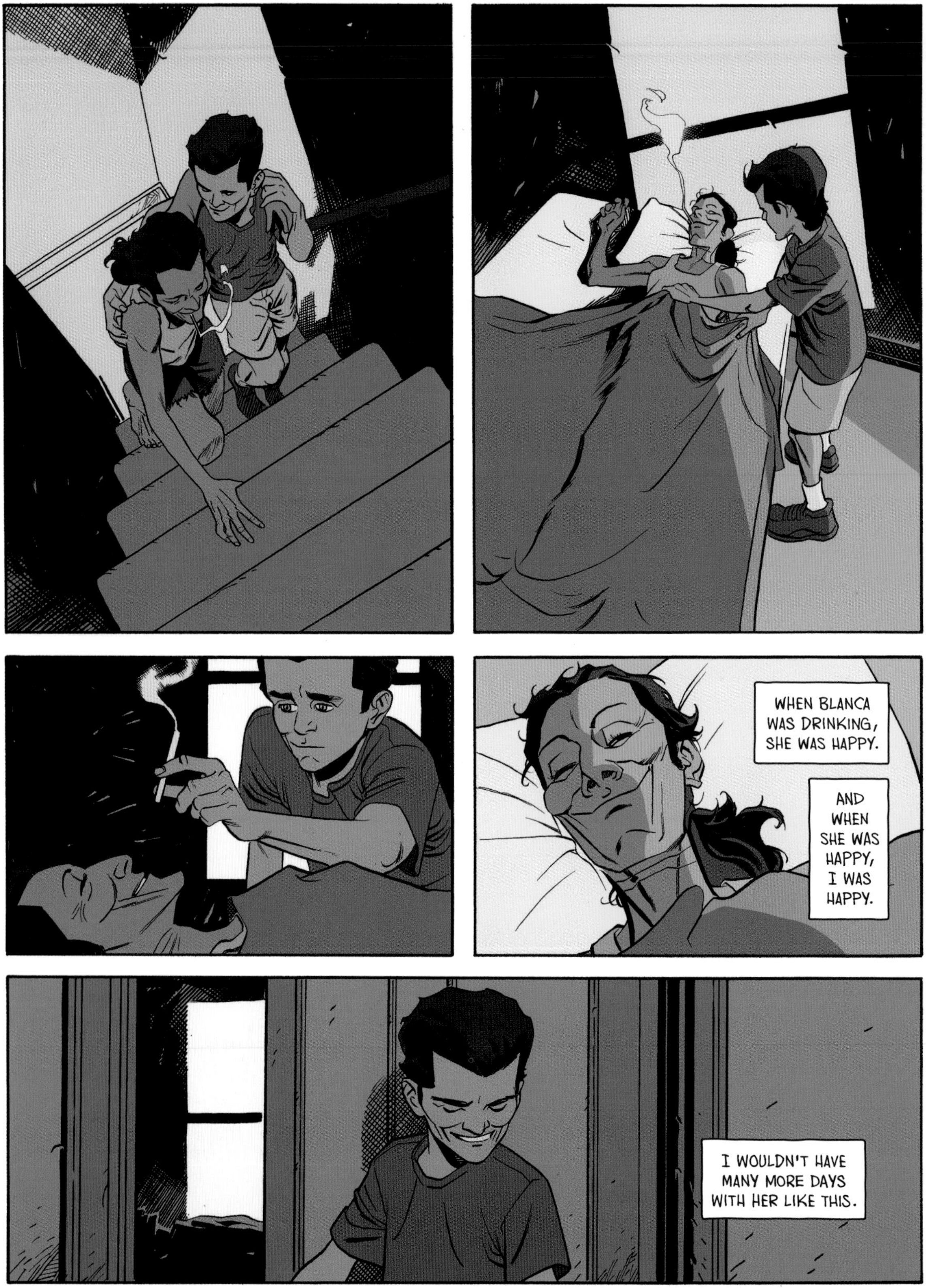
WHEN BLANCA WAS DRINKING, SHE WAS HAPPY.
AND WHEN SHE WAS HAPPY, I WAS HAPPY.
I WOULDN'T HAVE MANY MORE DAYS WITH HER LIKE THIS.

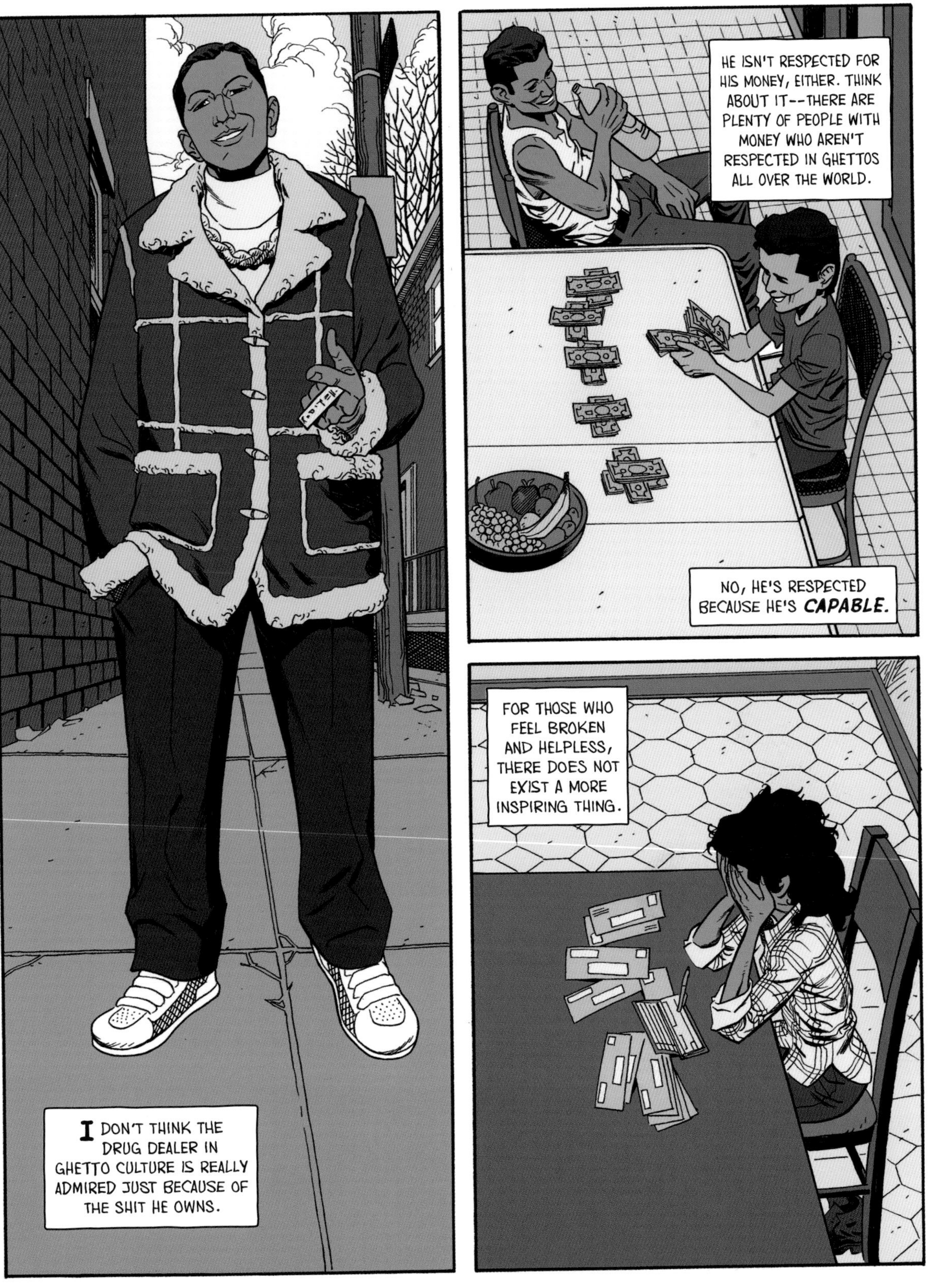
I DON'T THINK THE DRUG DEALER IN GHETTO CULTURE IS REALLY ADMIRED JUST BECAUSE OF THE SHIT HE OWNS.
HE ISN'T RESPECTED FOR HIS MONEY, EITHER. THINK ABOUT IT--THERE ARE PLENTY OF PEOPLE WITH MONEY WHO AREN'T RESPECTED IN GHETTOS ALL OVER THE WORLD.
NO, HE'S RESPECTED BECAUSE HE'S ***CAPABLE.***
FOR THOSE WHO FEEL BROKEN AND HELPLESS, THERE DOES NOT EXIST A MORE INSPIRING THING.

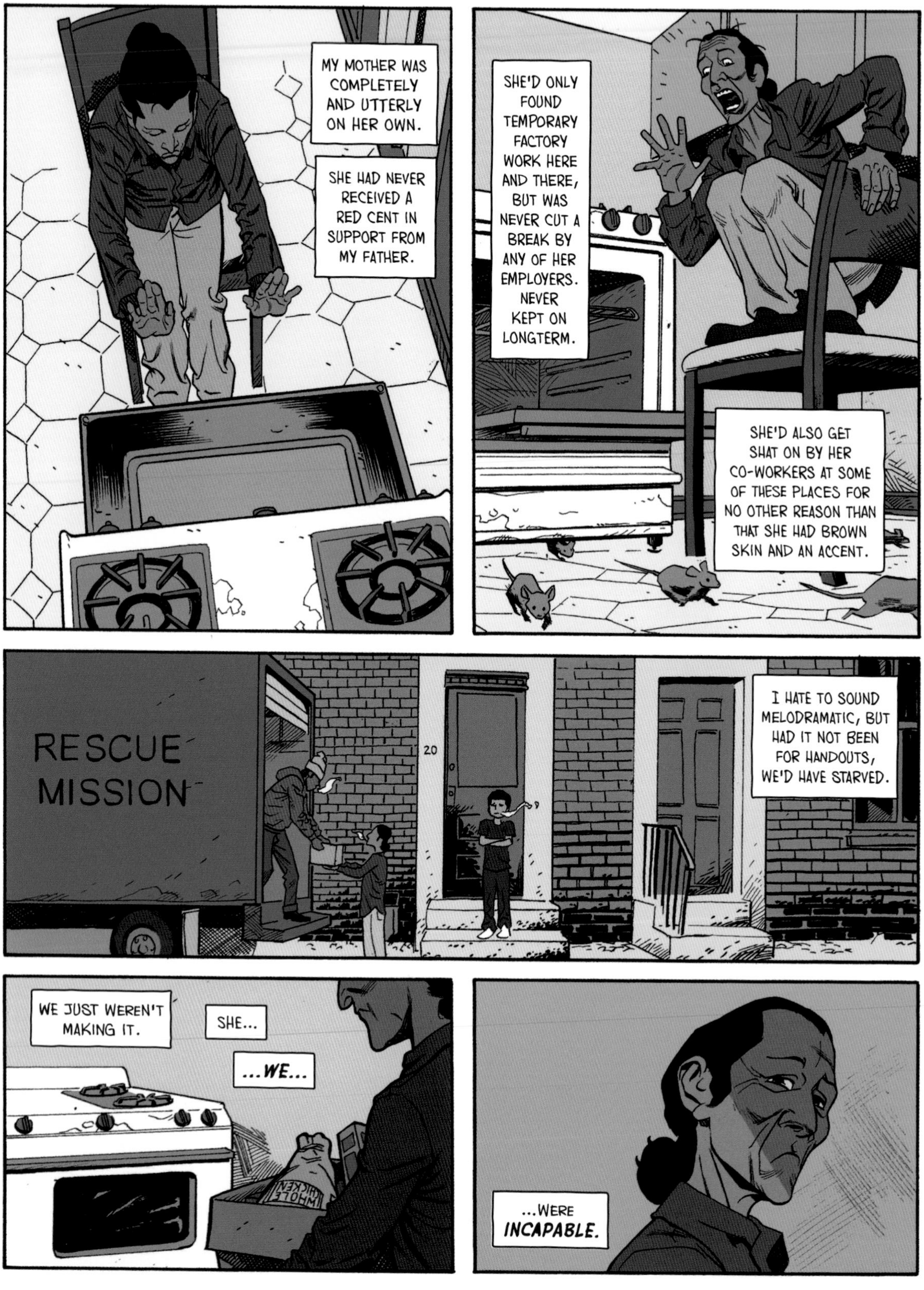
MY MOTHER WAS COMPLETELY AND UTTERLY ON HER OWN.
SHE HAD NEVER RECEIVED A RED CENT IN SUPPORT FROM MY FATHER.
SHE'D ONLY FOUND TEMPORARY FACTORY WORK HERE AND THERE, BUT WAS NEVER CUT A BREAK BY ANY OF HER EMPLOYERS. NEVER KEPT ON LONGTERM.
SHE'D ALSO GET SHAT ON BY HER CO-WORKERS AT SOME OF THESE PLACES FOR NO OTHER REASON THAN THAT SHE HAD BROWN SKIN AND AN ACCENT.
RESCUE MISSION
20
I HATE TO SOUND MELODRAMATIC, BUT HAD IT NOT BEEN FOR HANDOUTS, WE'D HAVE STARVED.
WE JUST WEREN'T MAKING IT.
SHE...
...WE...
...WERE INCAPABLE.

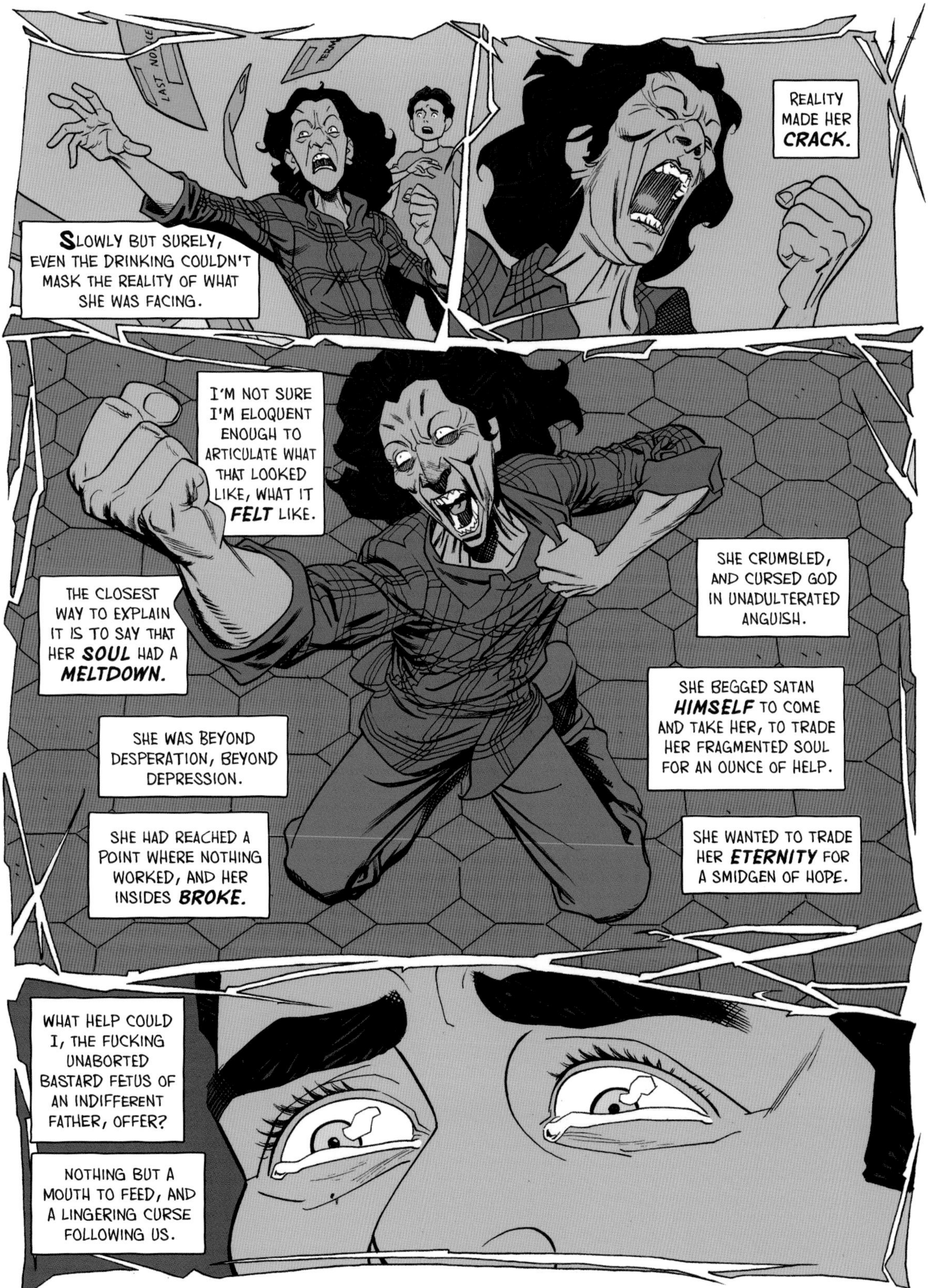
SLOWLY BUT SURELY, EVEN THE DRINKING COULDN'T MASK THE REALITY OF WHAT SHE WAS FACING.
REALITY MADE HER CRACK.
I'M NOT SURE I'M ELOQUENT ENOUGH TO ARTICULATE WHAT THAT LOOKED LIKE, WHAT IT FELT LIKE.
THE CLOSEST WAY TO EXPLAIN IT IS TO SAY THAT HER SOUL HAD A MELTDOWN.
SHE WAS BEYOND DESPERATION, BEYOND DEPRESSION.
SHE HAD REACHED A POINT WHERE NOTHING WORKED, AND HER INSIDES BROKE.
SHE CRUMBLED, AND CURSED GOD IN UNADULTERATED ANGUISH.
SHE BEGGED SATAN HIMSELF TO COME AND TAKE HER, TO TRADE HER FRAGMENTED SOUL FOR AN OUNCE OF HELP.
SHE WANTED TO TRADE HER ETERNITY FOR A SMIDGEN OF HOPE.
WHAT HELP COULD I, THE FUCKING UNABORTED BASTARD FETUS OF AN INDIFFERENT FATHER, OFFER?
NOTHING BUT A MOUTH TO FEED, AND A LINGERING CURSE FOLLOWING US.

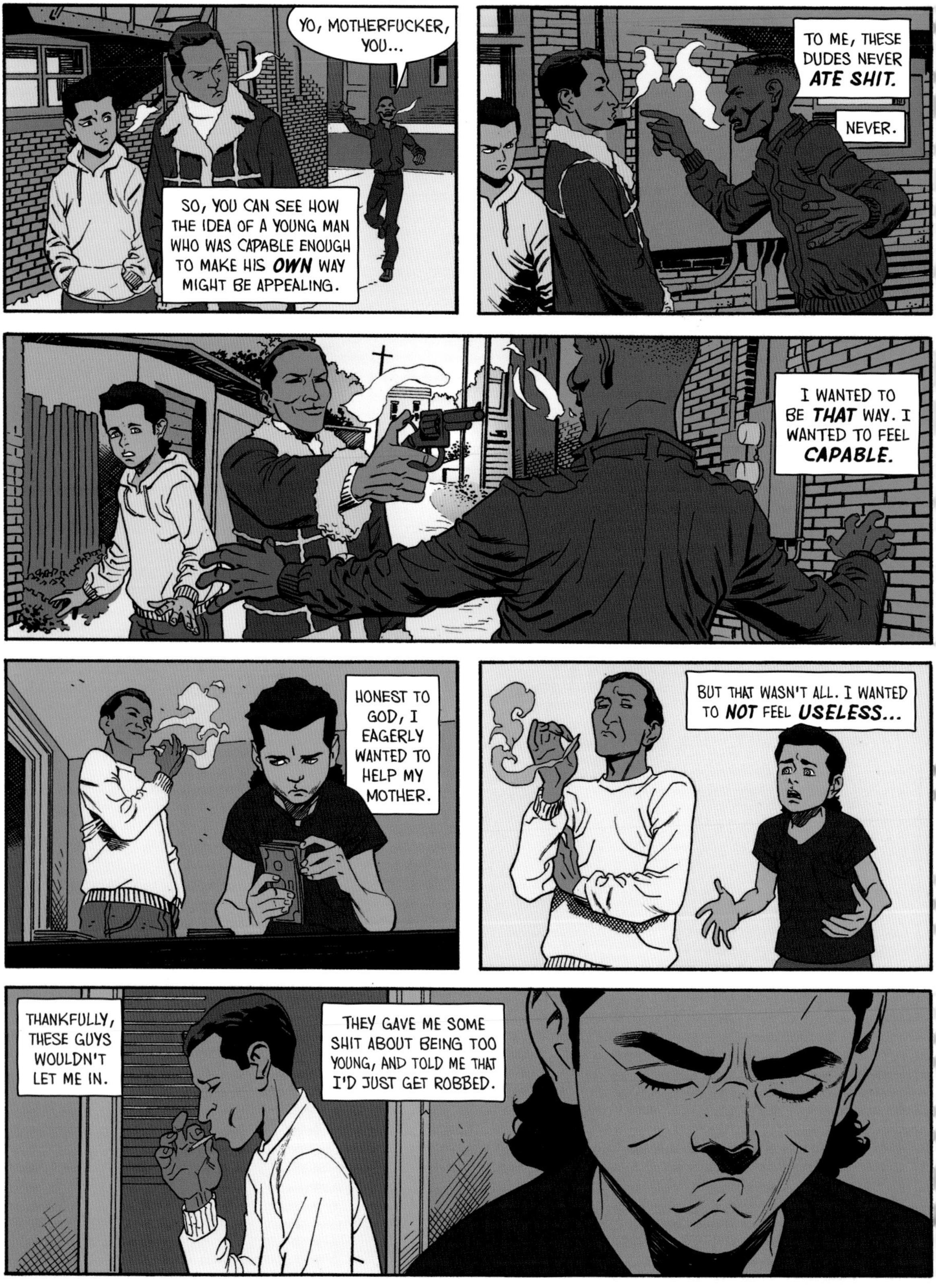
YO, MOTHERFUCKER, YOU...
SO, YOU CAN SEE HOW THE IDEA OF A YOUNG MAN WHO WAS CAPABLE ENOUGH TO MAKE HIS OWN WAY MIGHT BE APPEALING.
TO ME, THESE DUDES NEVER ATE SHIT.
NEVER.
I WANTED TO BE THAT WAY. I WANTED TO FEEL CAPABLE.
HONEST TO GOD, I EAGERLY WANTED TO HELP MY MOTHER.
BUT THAT WASN'T ALL. I WANTED TO NOT FEEL USELESS...
THANKFULLY, THESE GUYS WOULDN'T LET ME IN.
THEY GAVE ME SOME SHIT ABOUT BEING TOO YOUNG, AND TOLD ME THAT I'D JUST GET ROBBED.

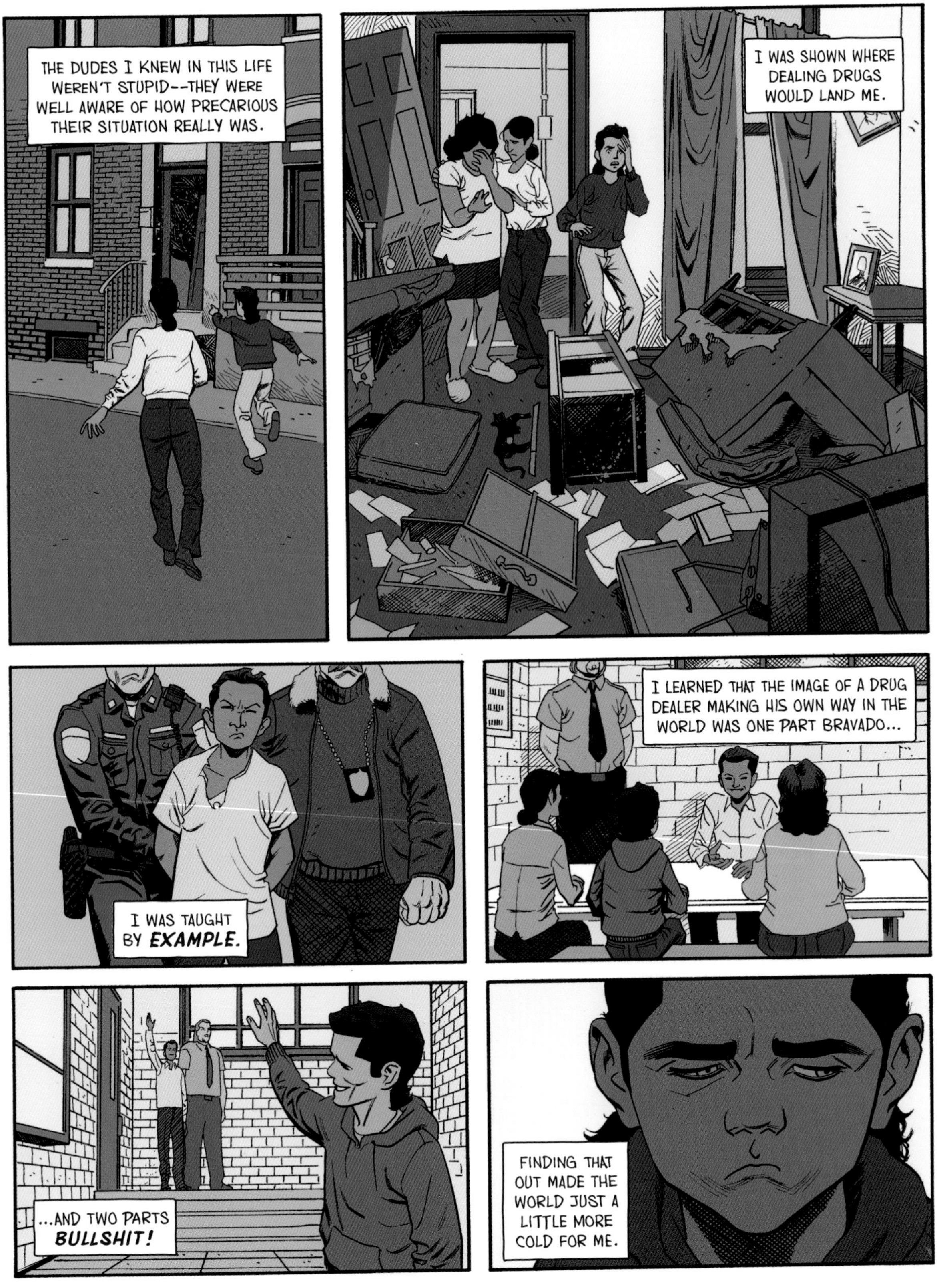
THE DUDES I KNEW IN THIS LIFE WEREN'T STUPID--THEY WERE WELL AWARE OF HOW PRECARIOUS THEIR SITUATION REALLY WAS.
I WAS SHOWN WHERE DEALING DRUGS WOULD LAND ME.
I WAS TAUGHT BY EXAMPLE.
I LEARNED THAT THE IMAGE OF A DRUG DEALER MAKING HIS OWN WAY IN THE WORLD WAS ONE PART BRAVADO...
...AND TWO PARTS BULLSHIT!
FINDING THAT OUT MADE THE WORLD JUST A LITTLE MORE COLD FOR ME.

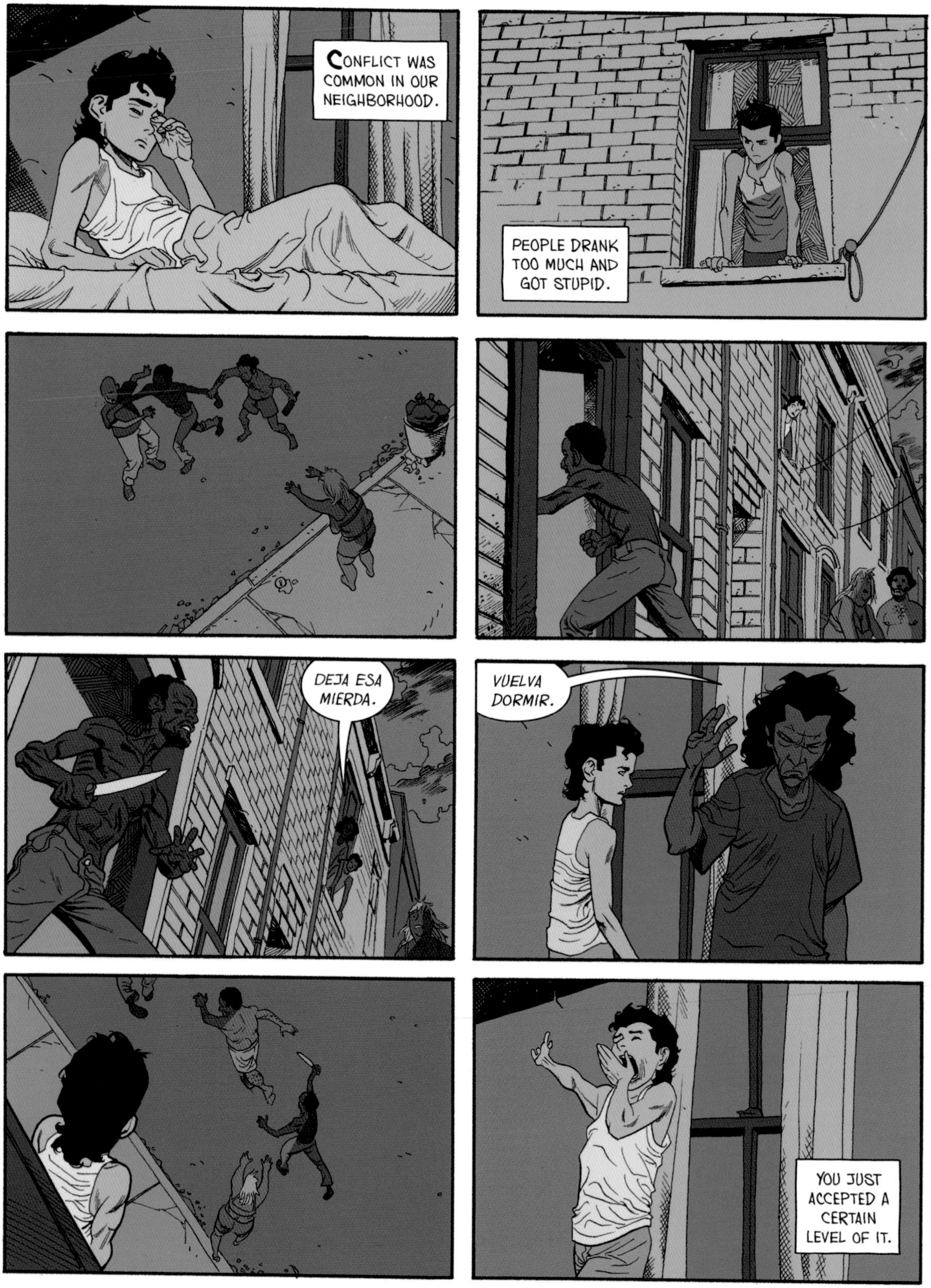

CONFLICT WAS COMMON IN OUR NEIGHBORHOOD.
PEOPLE DRANK TOO MUCH AND GOT STUPID.
DEJA ESA MIERDA.
VUELVA DORMIR.
YOU JUST ACCEPTED A CERTAIN LEVEL OF IT.

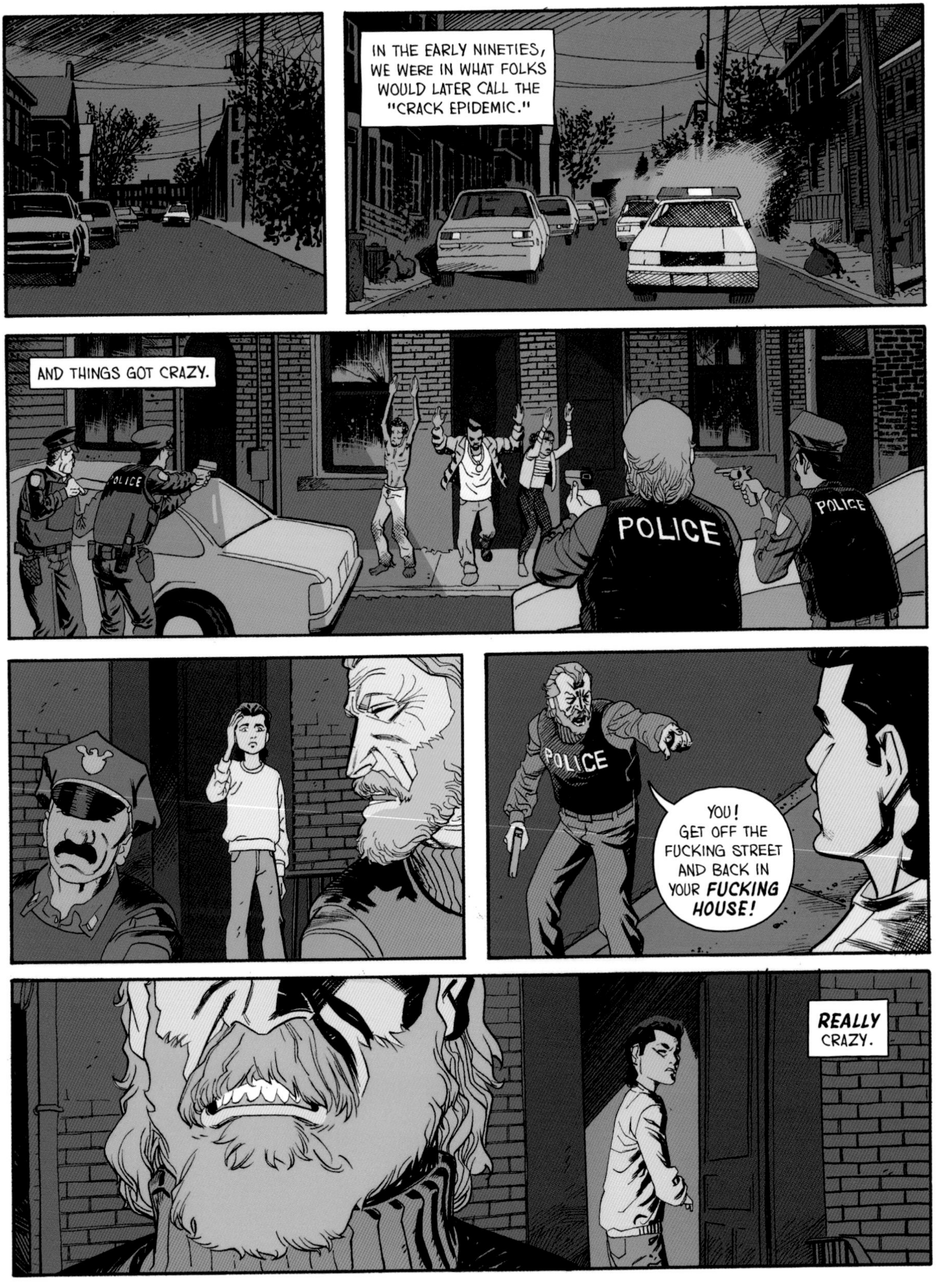
IN THE EARLY NINETIES, WE WERE IN WHAT FOLKS WOULD LATER CALL THE "CRACK EPIDEMIC."
AND THINGS GOT CRAZY.
POLICE
POLICE
POLICE
POLICE
YOU! GET OFF THE FUCKING STREET AND BACK IN YOUR FUCKING HOUSE!
REALLY CRAZY.

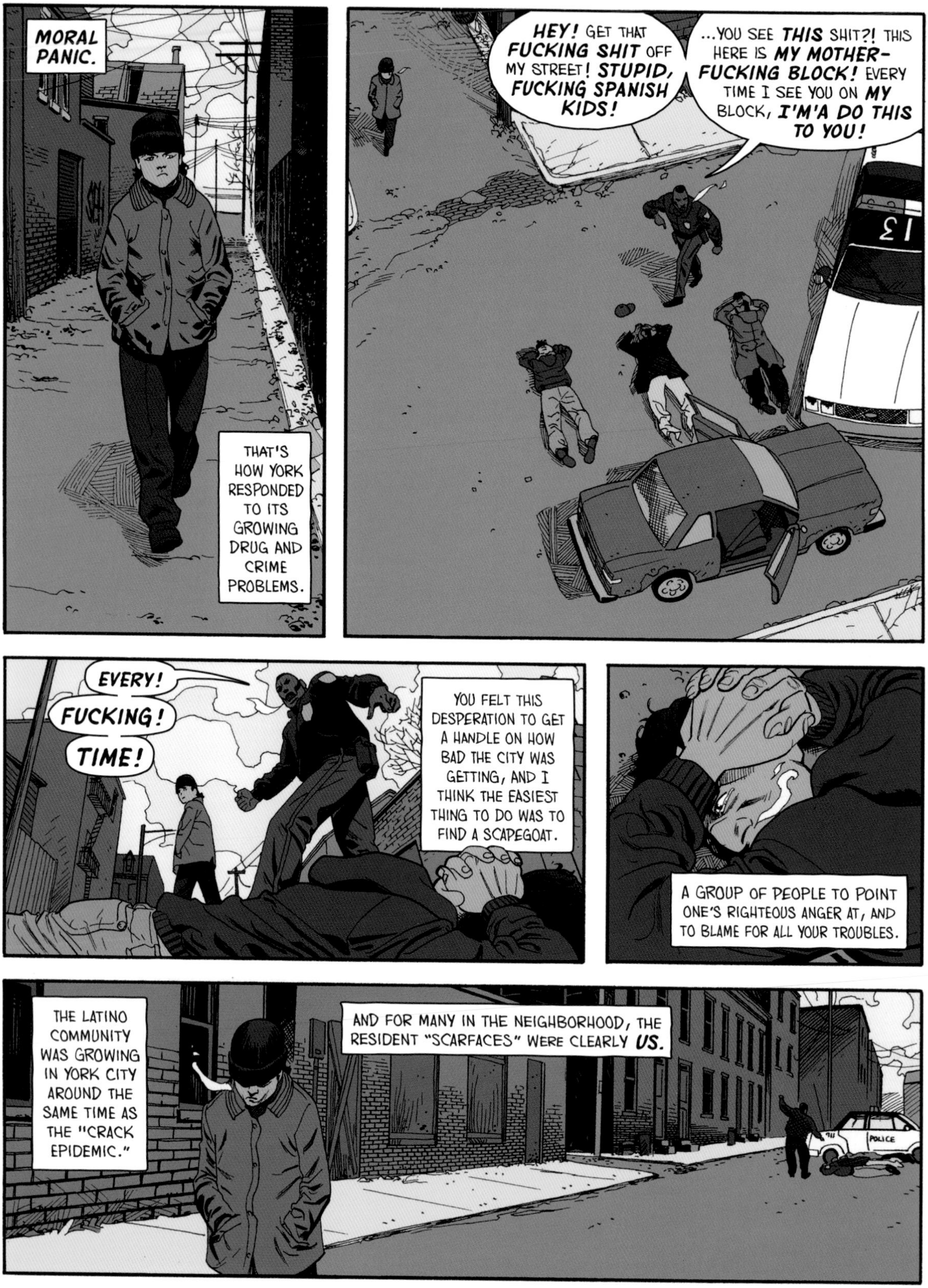
MORAL PANIC.
THAT'S HOW YORK RESPONDED TO ITS GROWING DRUG AND CRIME PROBLEMS.
HEY! GET THAT FUCKING SHIT OFF MY STREET! STUPID, FUCKING SPANISH KIDS!
...YOU SEE THIS SHIT?! THIS HERE IS MY MOTHER-FUCKING BLOCK! EVERY TIME I SEE YOU ON MY BLOCK, I'M'A DO THIS TO YOU!
13
EVERY!
FUCKING!
TIME!
YOU FELT THIS DESPERATION TO GET A HANDLE ON HOW BAD THE CITY WAS GETTING, AND I THINK THE EASIEST THING TO DO WAS TO FIND A SCAPEGOAT.
A GROUP OF PEOPLE TO POINT ONE'S RIGHTEOUS ANGER AT, AND TO BLAME FOR ALL YOUR TROUBLES.
THE LATINO COMMUNITY WAS GROWING IN YORK CITY AROUND THE SAME TIME AS THE "CRACK EPIDEMIC."
AND FOR MANY IN THE NEIGHBORHOOD, THE RESIDENT "SCARFACES" WERE CLEARLY US.
POLICE

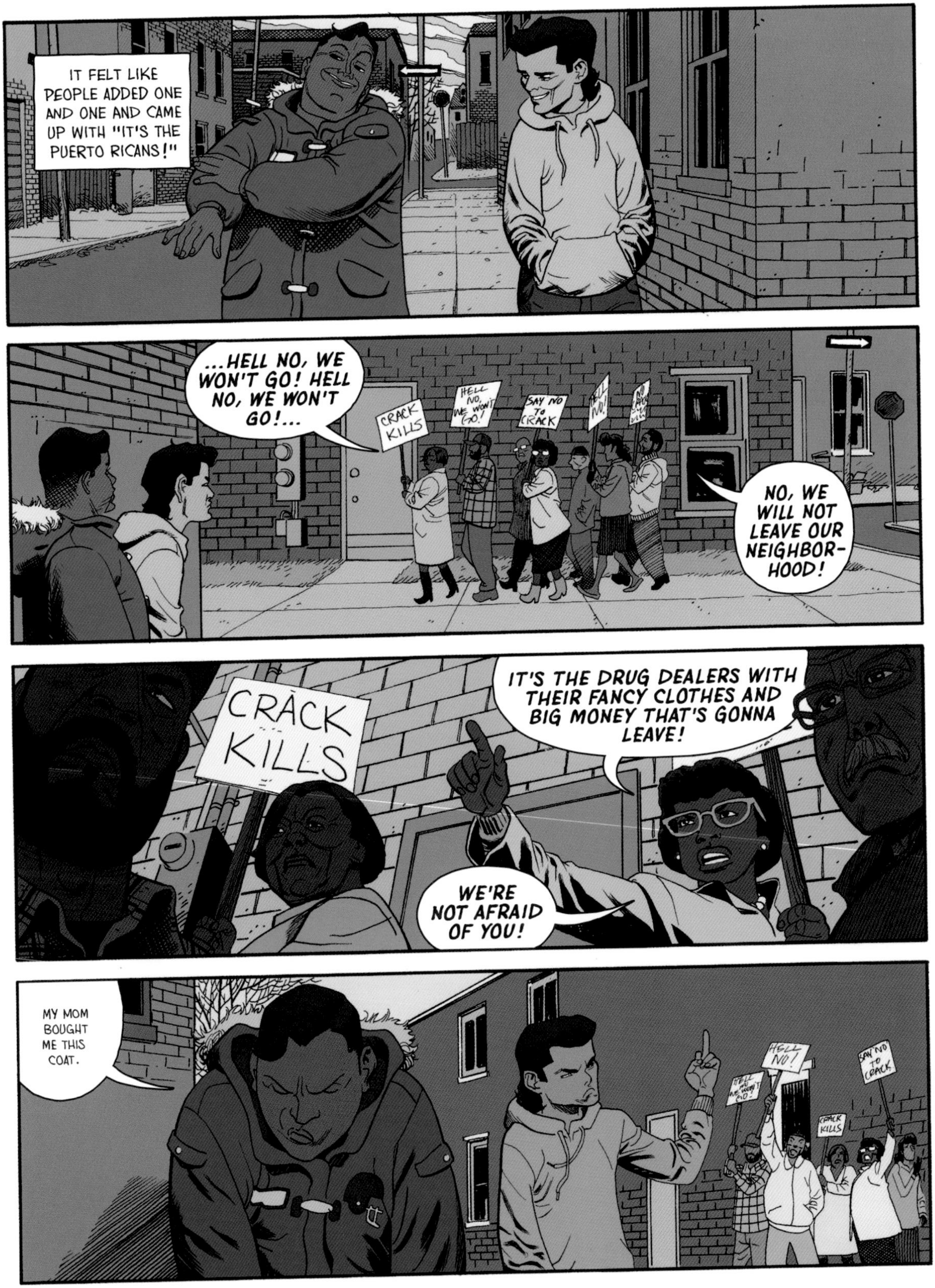
IT FELT LIKE PEOPLE ADDED ONE AND ONE AND CAME UP WITH "IT'S THE PUERTO RICANS!"
...HELL NO, WE WON'T GO! HELL NO, WE WON'T GO!...
CRACK KILLS
HELL NO, WE WON'T GO!
SAY NO TO CRACK
HELL NO!
NO, WE WILL NOT LEAVE OUR NEIGHBOR-HOOD!
CRACK KILLS
IT'S THE DRUG DEALERS WITH THEIR FANCY CLOTHES AND BIG MONEY THAT'S GONNA LEAVE!
WE'RE NOT AFRAID OF YOU!
MY MOM BOUGHT ME THIS COAT.
HELL NO!
HELL NO WE WON'T GO!
SAY NO TO CRACK
CRACK KILLS

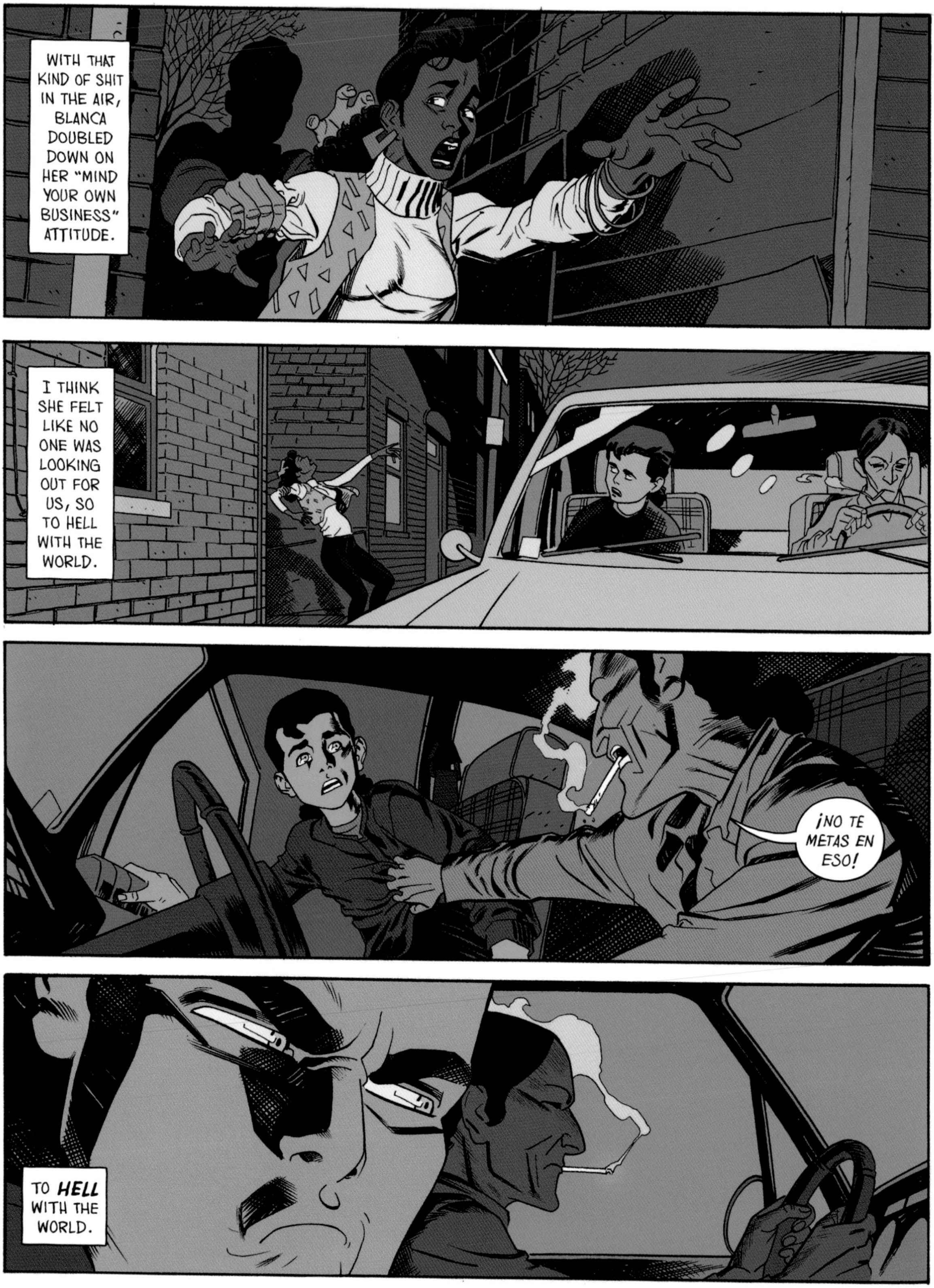
WITH THAT KIND OF SHIT IN THE AIR, BLANCA DOUBLED DOWN ON HER "MIND YOUR OWN BUSINESS" ATTITUDE.
I THINK SHE FELT LIKE NO ONE WAS LOOKING OUT FOR US, SO TO HELL WITH THE WORLD.
¡NO TE METAS EN ESO!
TO HELL WITH THE WORLD.

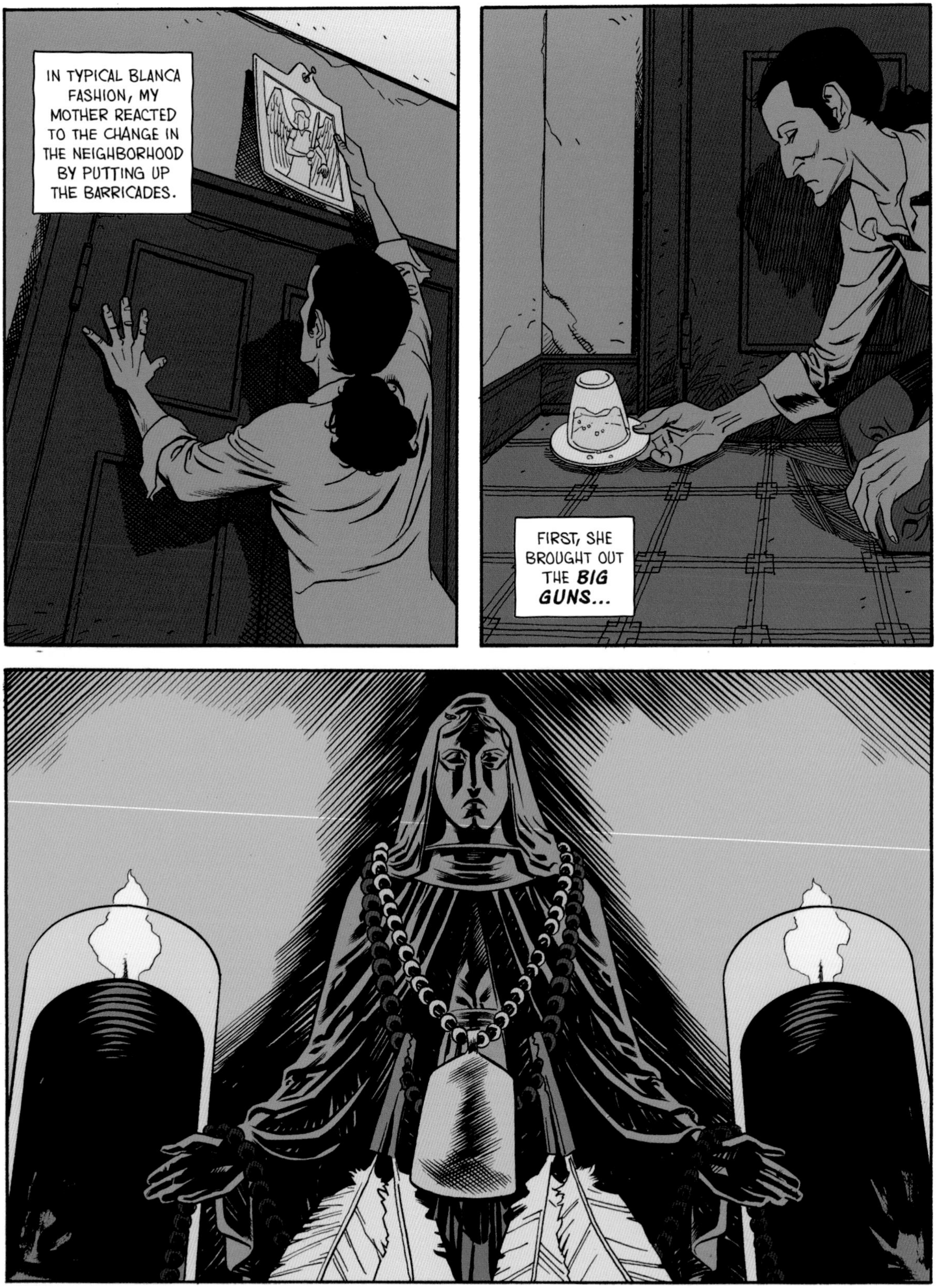
IN TYPICAL BLANCA FASHION, MY MOTHER REACTED TO THE CHANGE IN THE NEIGHBORHOOD BY PUTTING UP THE BARRICADES.
FIRST, SHE BROUGHT OUT THE ***BIG GUNS...***

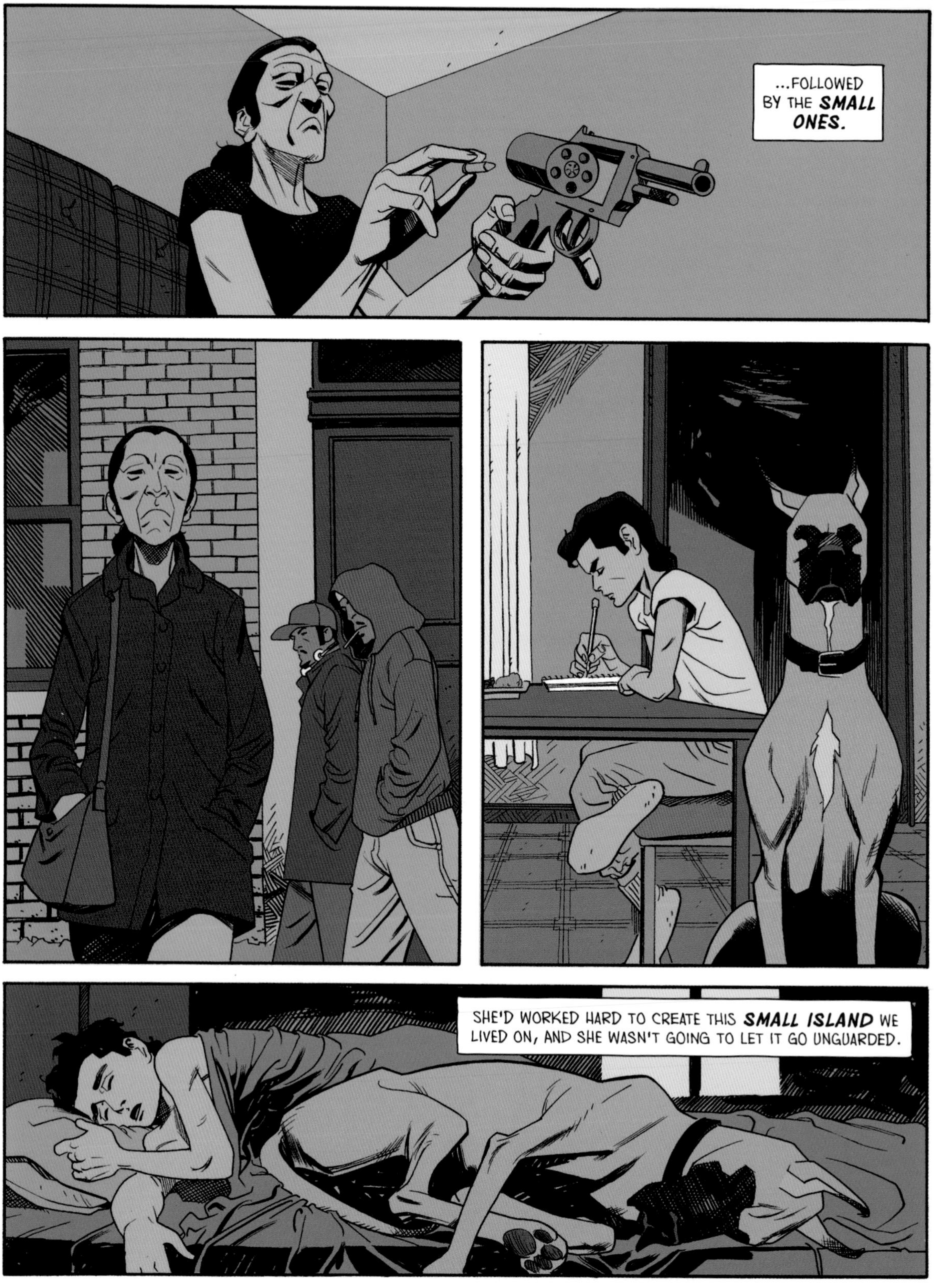
...FOLLOWED BY THE SMALL ONES.
SHE'D WORKED HARD TO CREATE THIS SMALL ISLAND WE LIVED ON, AND SHE WASN'T GOING TO LET IT GO UNGUARDED.

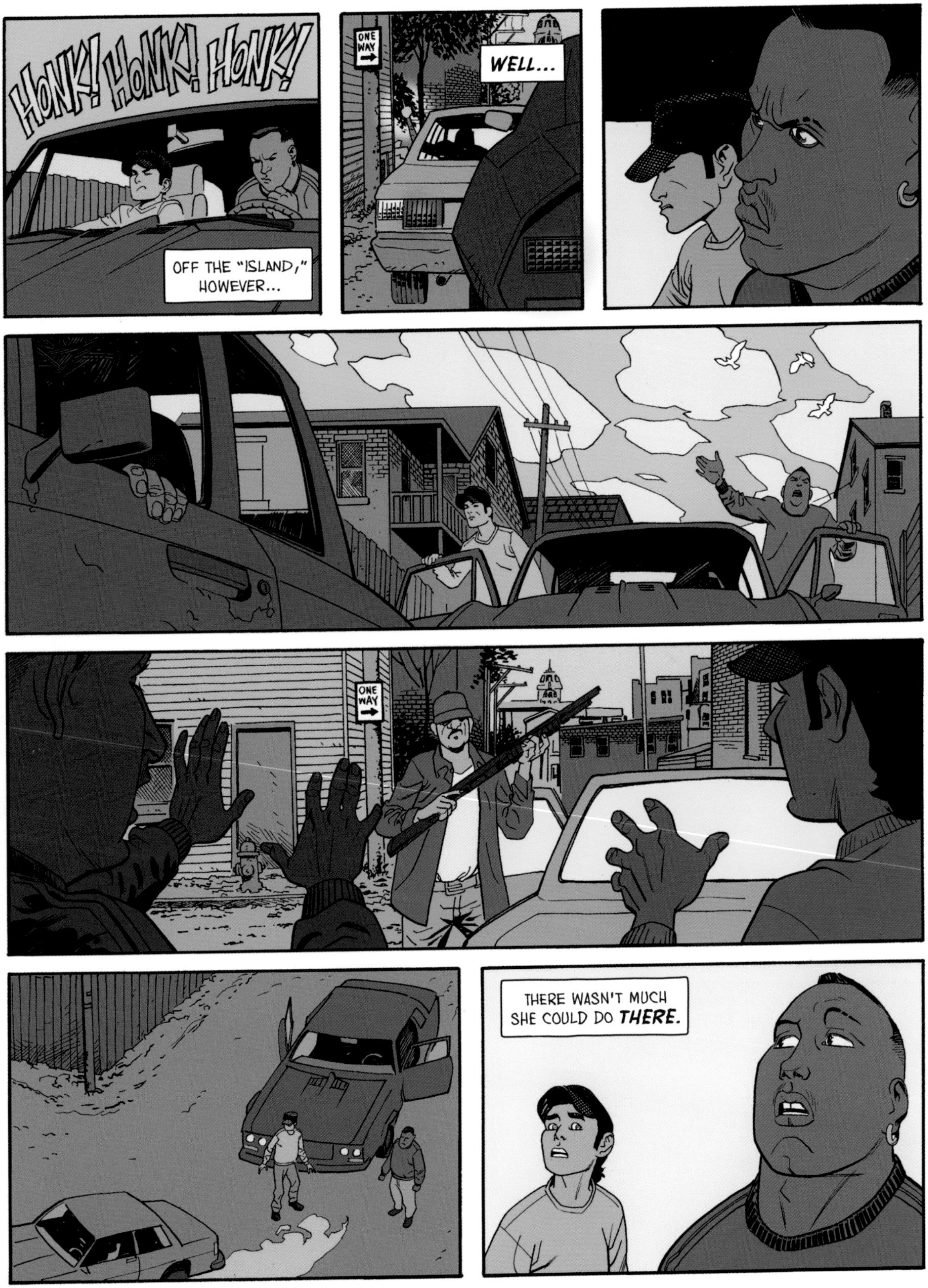
HONK! HONK! HONK!
OFF THE "ISLAND," HOWEVER...
ONE WAY
WELL...
ONE WAY
THERE WASN'T MUCH SHE COULD DO THERE.

A KID ONCE STABBED ME IN THE ARM WITH A PENCIL FOR MAKING FUN OF HIS GIRL-FRIEND'S LOOKS.

HE'D TRIED TO STAB ME IN THE CHEST, BUT I TURNED IN TIME TO SAVE MY ASS.

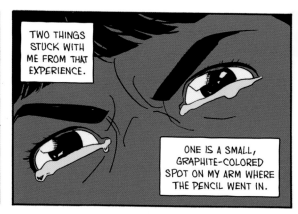

TWO THINGS STUCK WITH ME FROM THAT EXPERIENCE.

ONE IS A SMALL, GRAPHITE-COLORED SPOT ON MY ARM WHERE THE PENCIL WENT IN.

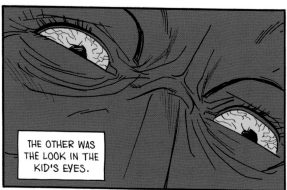

THE OTHER WAS THE LOOK IN THE KID'S EYES.

THEY WERE THE EYES OF SOMEONE WHO TRULY WANTED TO HURT ME.

*THESE* EYES, HOWEVER...

THESE EYES WERE WORSE, BY FAR.

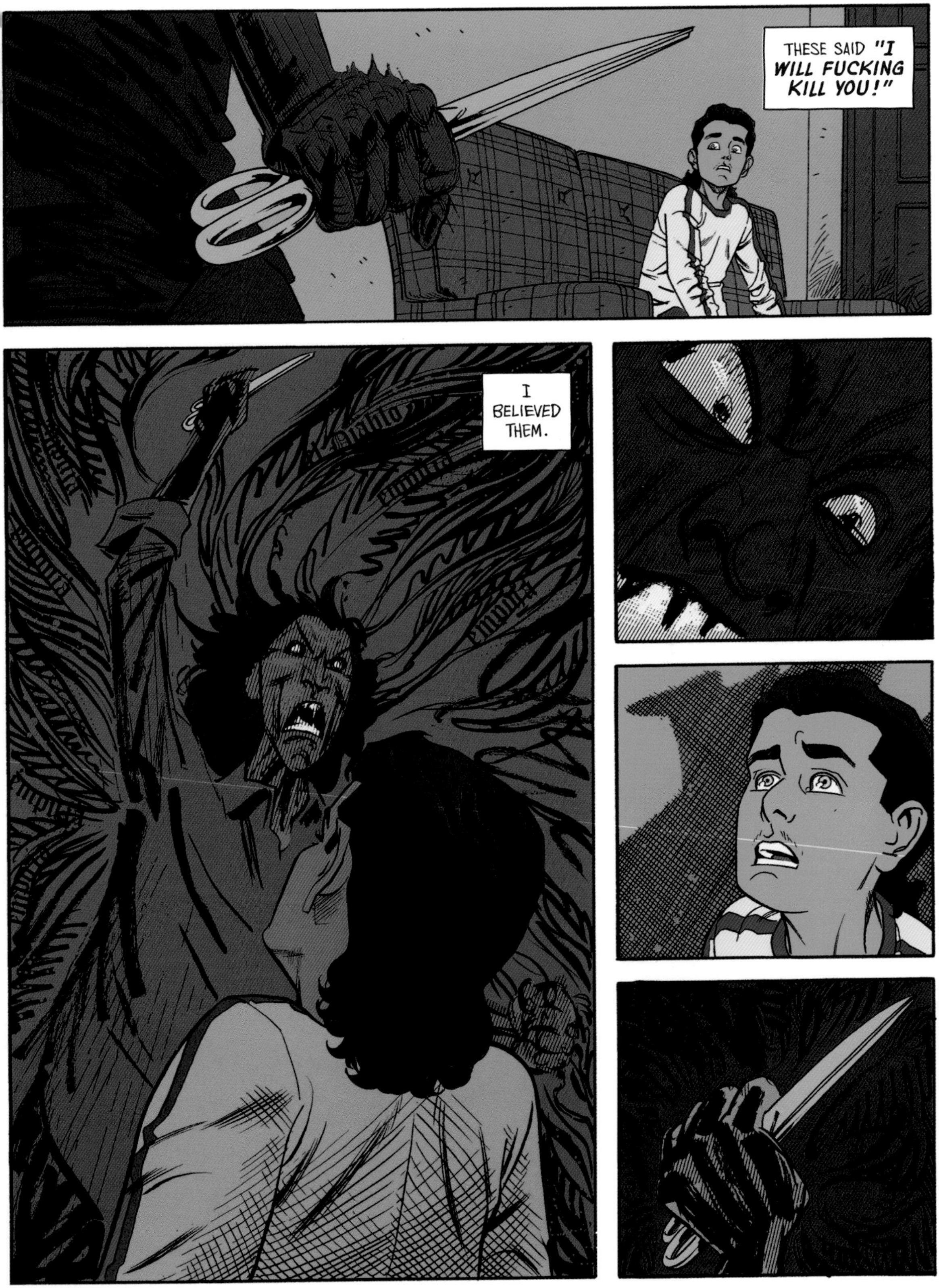
THESE SAID "I WILL FUCKING KILL YOU!"
I BELIEVED THEM.

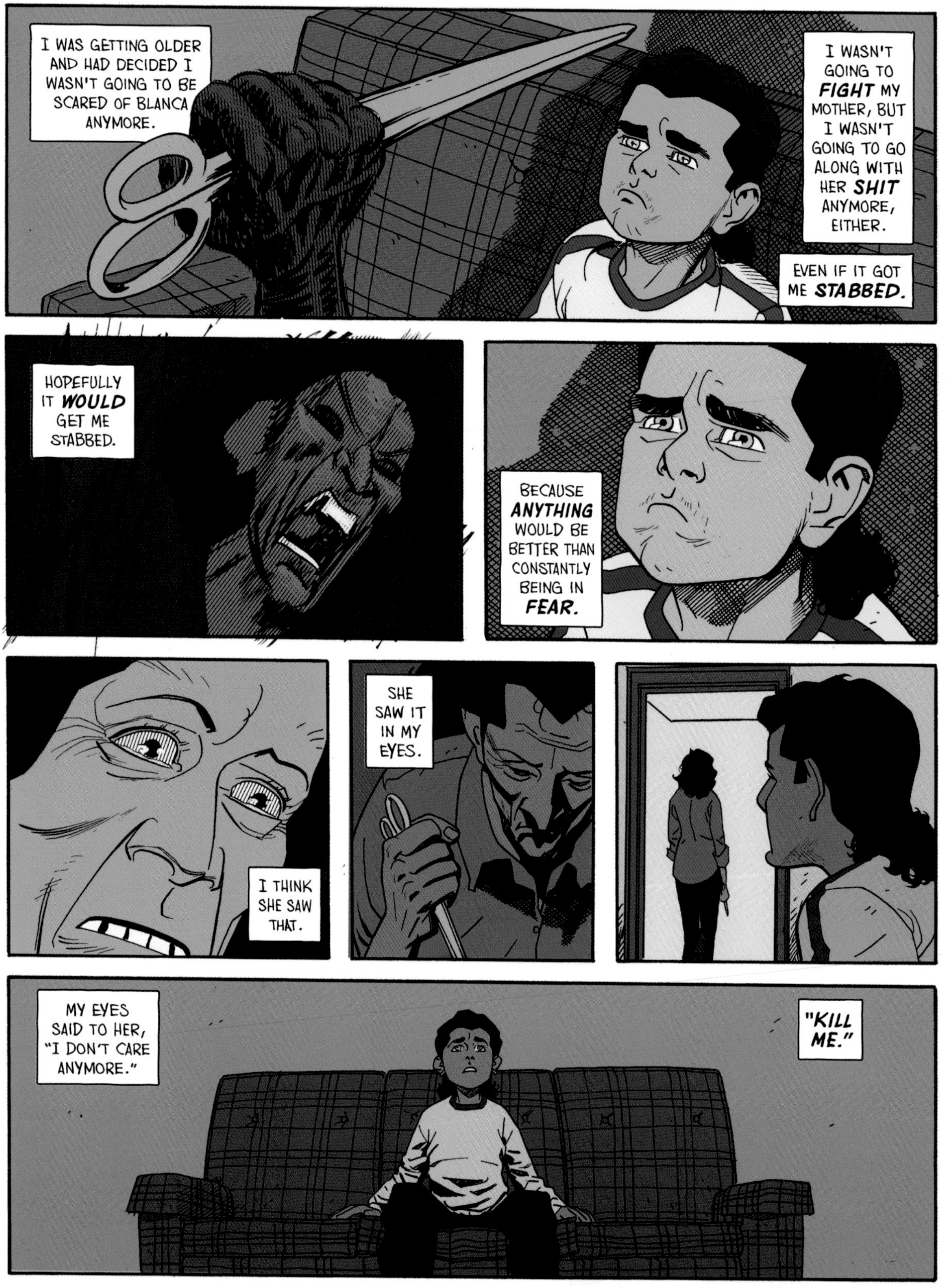
I WAS GETTING OLDER AND HAD DECIDED I WASN'T GOING TO BE SCARED OF BLANCA ANYMORE.
I WASN'T GOING TO FIGHT MY MOTHER, BUT I WASN'T GOING TO GO ALONG WITH HER SHIT ANYMORE, EITHER.
EVEN IF IT GOT ME STABBED.
HOPEFULLY IT WOULD GET ME STABBED.
BECAUSE ANYTHING WOULD BE BETTER THAN CONSTANTLY BEING IN FEAR.
I THINK SHE SAW THAT.
SHE SAW IT IN MY EYES.
MY EYES SAID TO HER, "I DON'T CARE ANYMORE."
"KILL ME."

WHEN HER PHILOSOPHY OF *PUÑOS* BEGAN TO FAIL HER, BLANCA SEEMED TO PICK UP A NEW PHILOSOPHY OF ISOLATION.

SHE FIXATED ON BUILDING HER OWN GREAT WALL TO KEEP OTHERS OUT AND US IN.

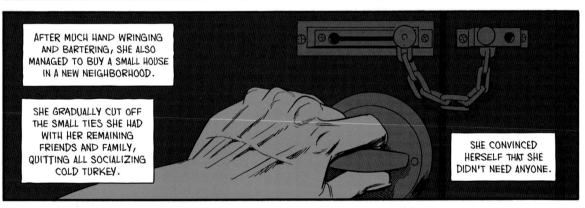

SHE MANAGED TO KEEP A JOB AT A LOCAL FACTORY AND FOCUSED MORE AND MORE ON WORKING.

KITCHEN

AFTER MUCH HAND WRINGING AND BARTERING, SHE ALSO MANAGED TO BUY A SMALL HOUSE IN A NEW NEIGHBORHOOD.

SHE GRADUALLY CUT OFF THE SMALL TIES SHE HAD WITH HER REMAINING FRIENDS AND FAMILY, QUITTING ALL SOCIALIZING COLD TURKEY.

SHE CONVINCED HERSELF THAT SHE DIDN'T NEED ANYONE.

SHE WAS HUNKERING DOWN.

THIS HOUSE MADE BLANCA'S ISLAND OF SOLITUDE COMPLETE.

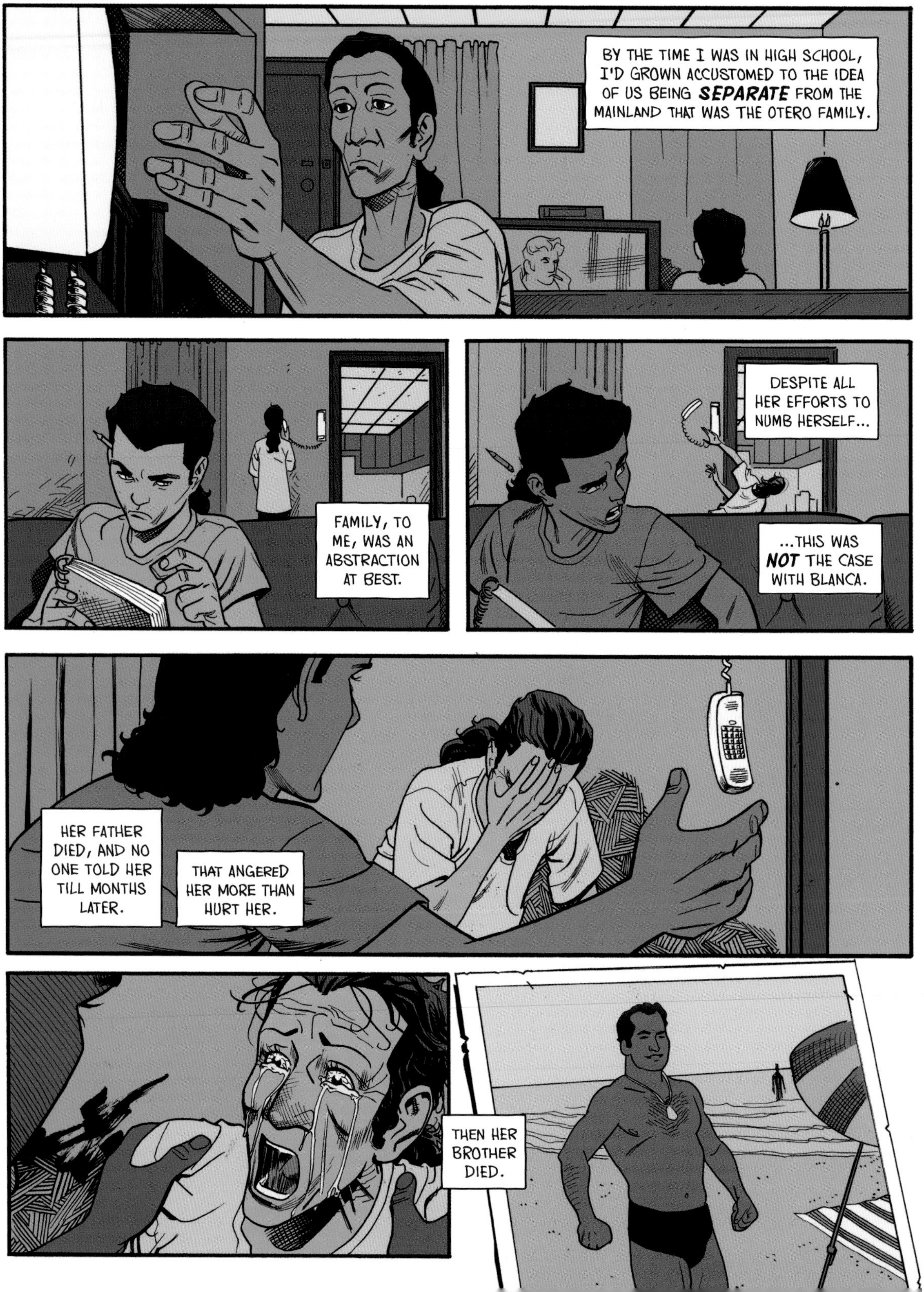
BY THE TIME I WAS IN HIGH SCHOOL, I'D GROWN ACCUSTOMED TO THE IDEA OF US BEING SEPARATE FROM THE MAINLAND THAT WAS THE OTERO FAMILY.
FAMILY, TO ME, WAS AN ABSTRACTION AT BEST.
DESPITE ALL HER EFFORTS TO NUMB HERSELF...
...THIS WAS NOT THE CASE WITH BLANCA.
HER FATHER DIED, AND NO ONE TOLD HER TILL MONTHS LATER.
THAT ANGERED HER MORE THAN HURT HER.
THEN HER BROTHER DIED.

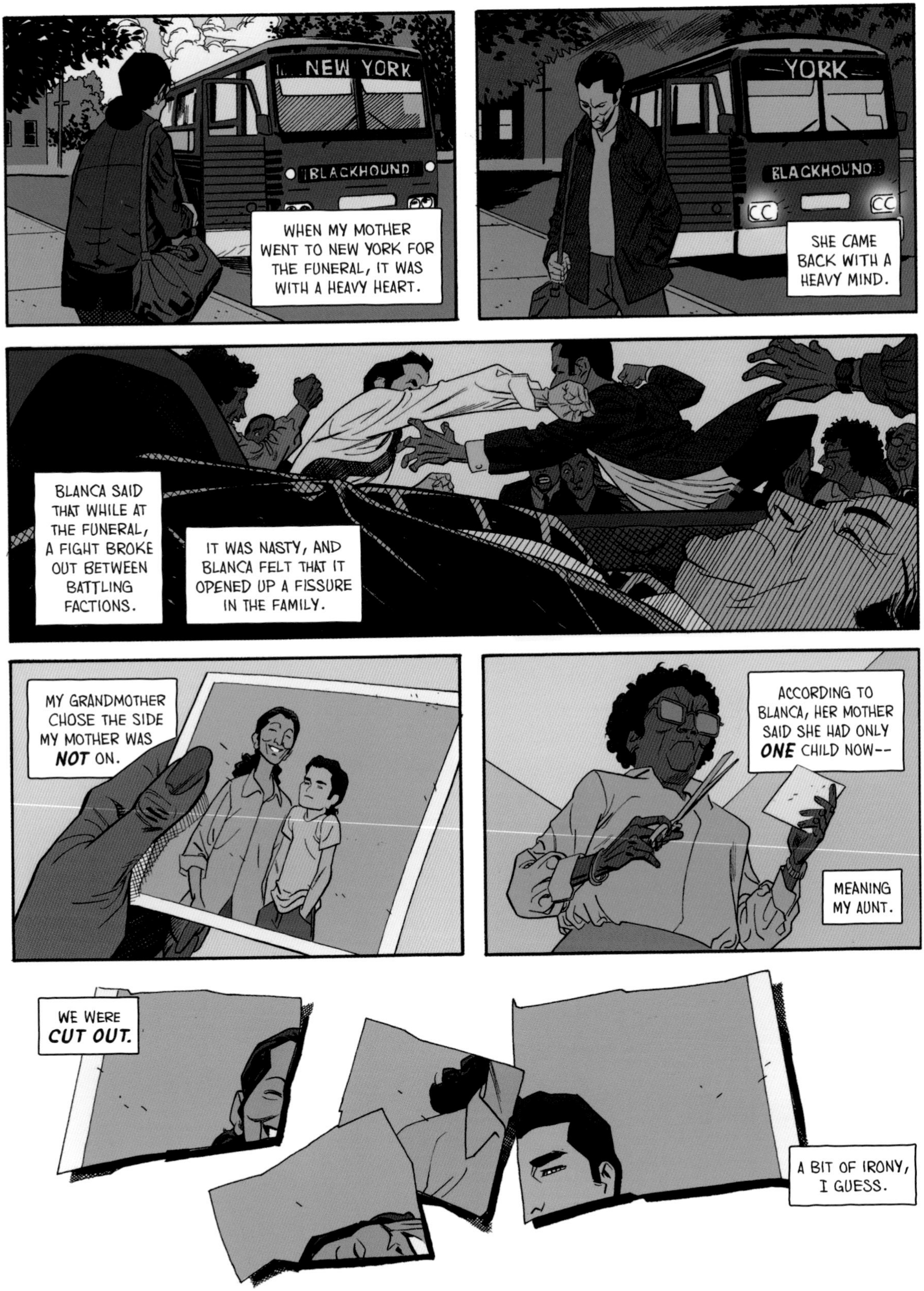
NEW YORK
BLACKHOUND
WHEN MY MOTHER WENT TO NEW YORK FOR THE FUNERAL, IT WAS WITH A HEAVY HEART.
YORK
BLACKHOUND
SHE CAME BACK WITH A HEAVY MIND.
BLANCA SAID THAT WHILE AT THE FUNERAL, A FIGHT BROKE OUT BETWEEN BATTLING FACTIONS.
IT WAS NASTY, AND BLANCA FELT THAT IT OPENED UP A FISSURE IN THE FAMILY.
MY GRANDMOTHER CHOSE THE SIDE MY MOTHER WAS **NOT** ON.
ACCORDING TO BLANCA, HER MOTHER SAID SHE HAD ONLY **ONE** CHILD NOW--
MEANING MY AUNT.
WE WERE **CUT OUT.**
A BIT OF IRONY, I GUESS.

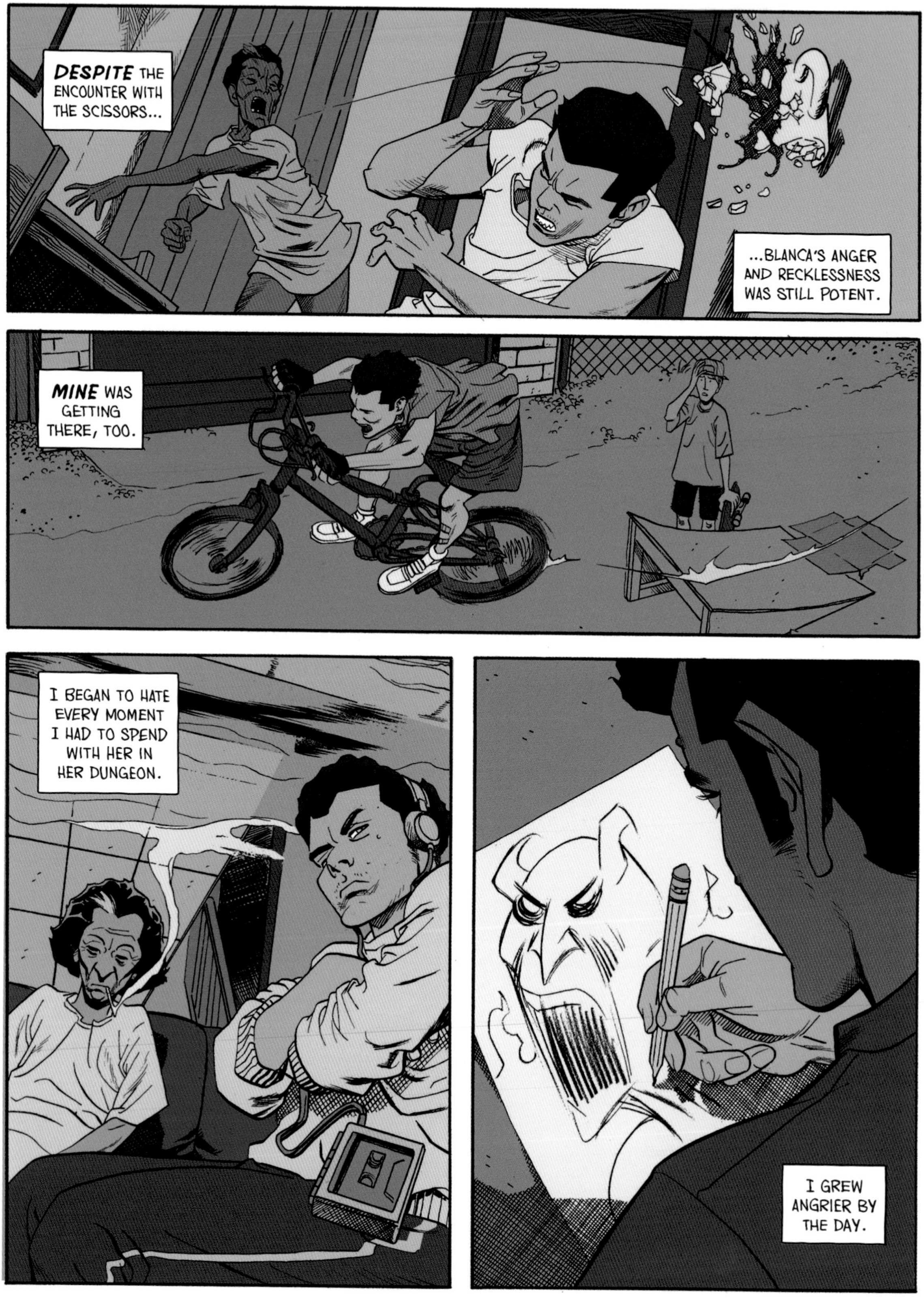
DESPITE THE ENCOUNTER WITH THE SCISSORS...
...BLANCA'S ANGER AND RECKLESSNESS WAS STILL POTENT.
MINE WAS GETTING THERE, TOO.
I BEGAN TO HATE EVERY MOMENT I HAD TO SPEND WITH HER IN HER DUNGEON.
I GREW ANGRIER BY THE DAY.

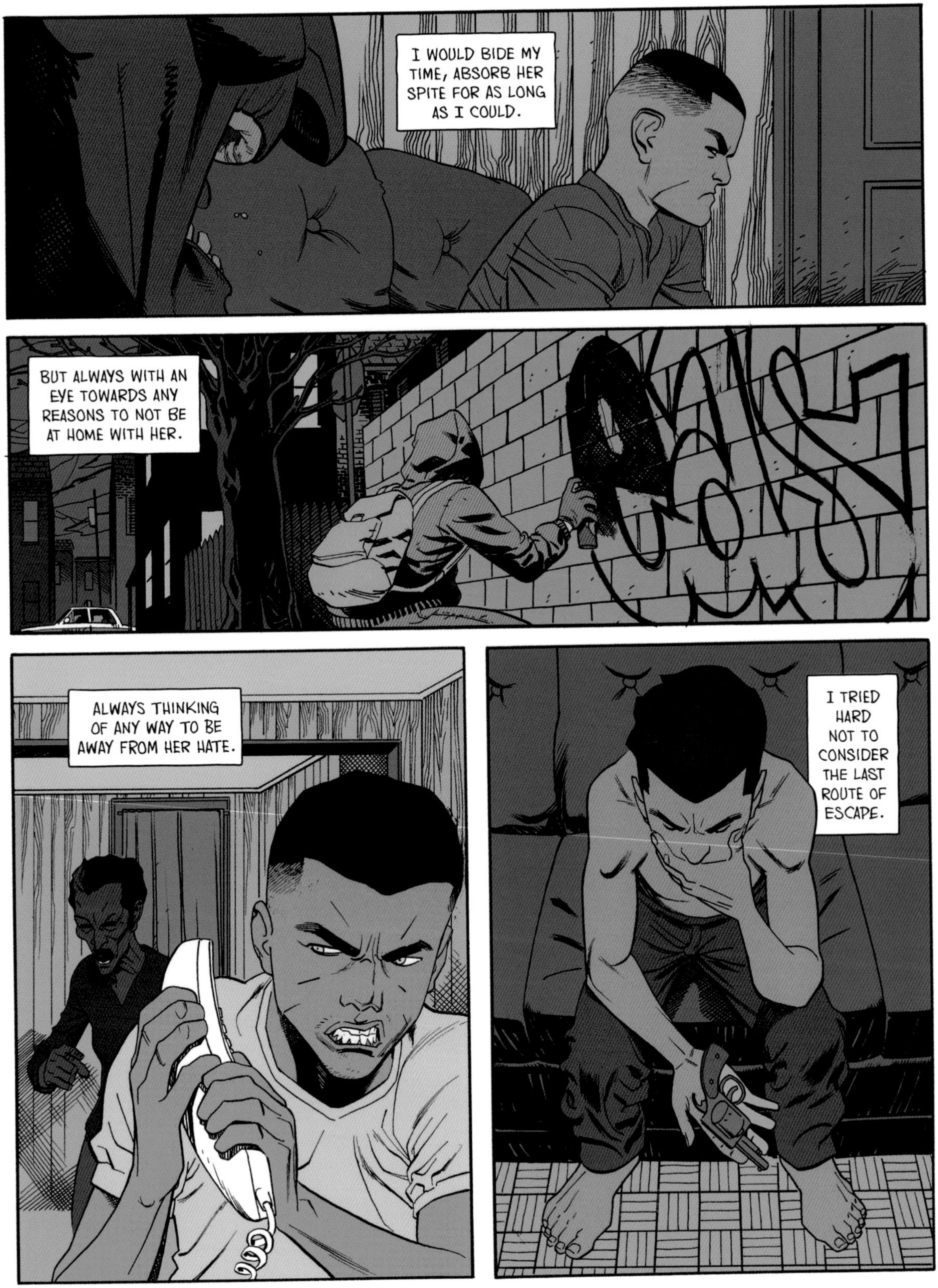
I WOULD BIDE MY TIME, ABSORB HER SPITE FOR AS LONG AS I COULD.
BUT ALWAYS WITH AN EYE TOWARDS ANY REASONS TO NOT BE AT HOME WITH HER.
ALWAYS THINKING OF ANY WAY TO BE AWAY FROM HER HATE.
I TRIED HARD NOT TO CONSIDER THE LAST ROUTE OF ESCAPE.

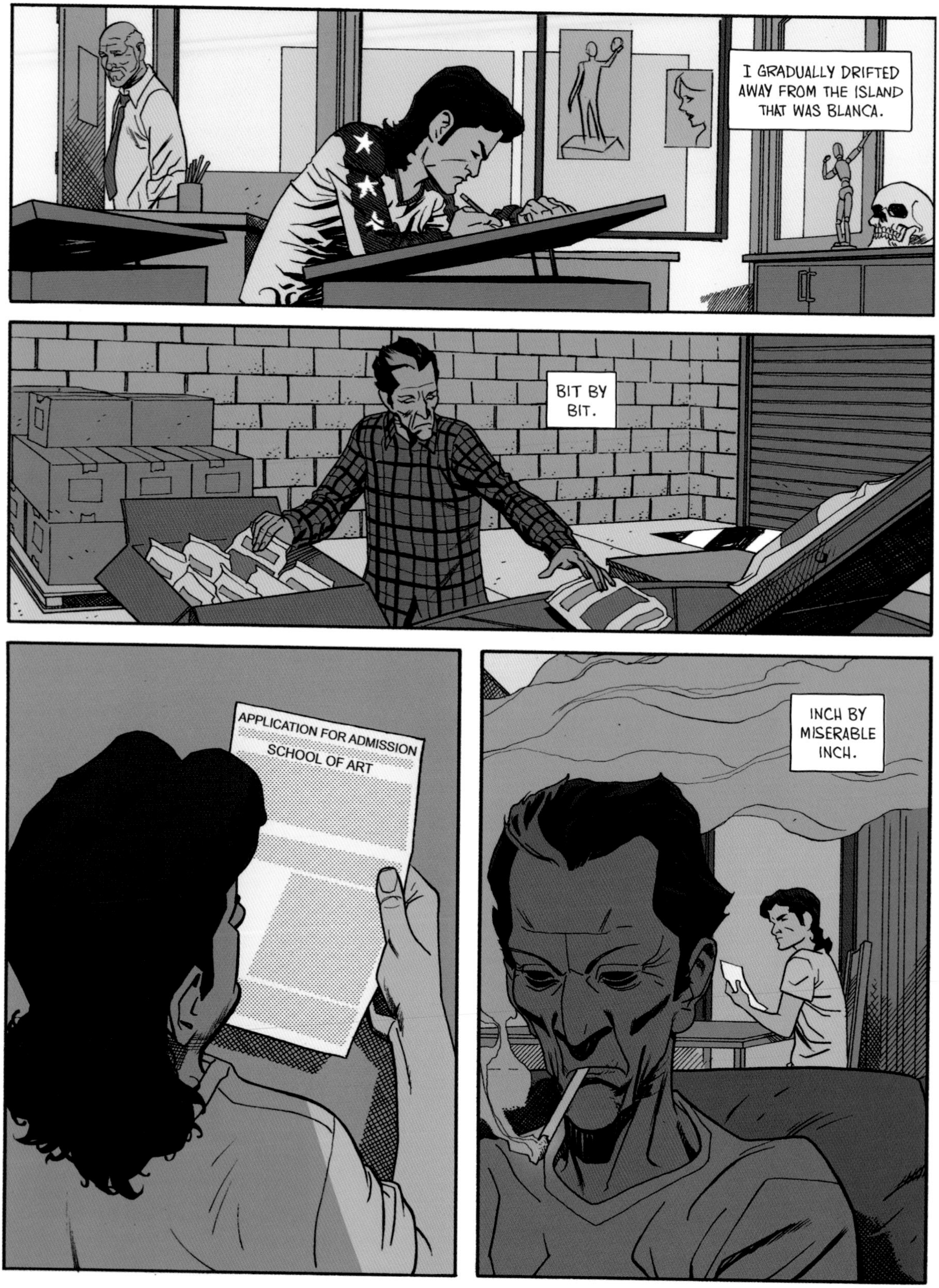
I GRADUALLY DRIFTED AWAY FROM THE ISLAND THAT WAS BLANCA.
BIT BY BIT.
APPLICATION FOR ADMISSION
SCHOOL OF ART
INCH BY MISERABLE INCH.

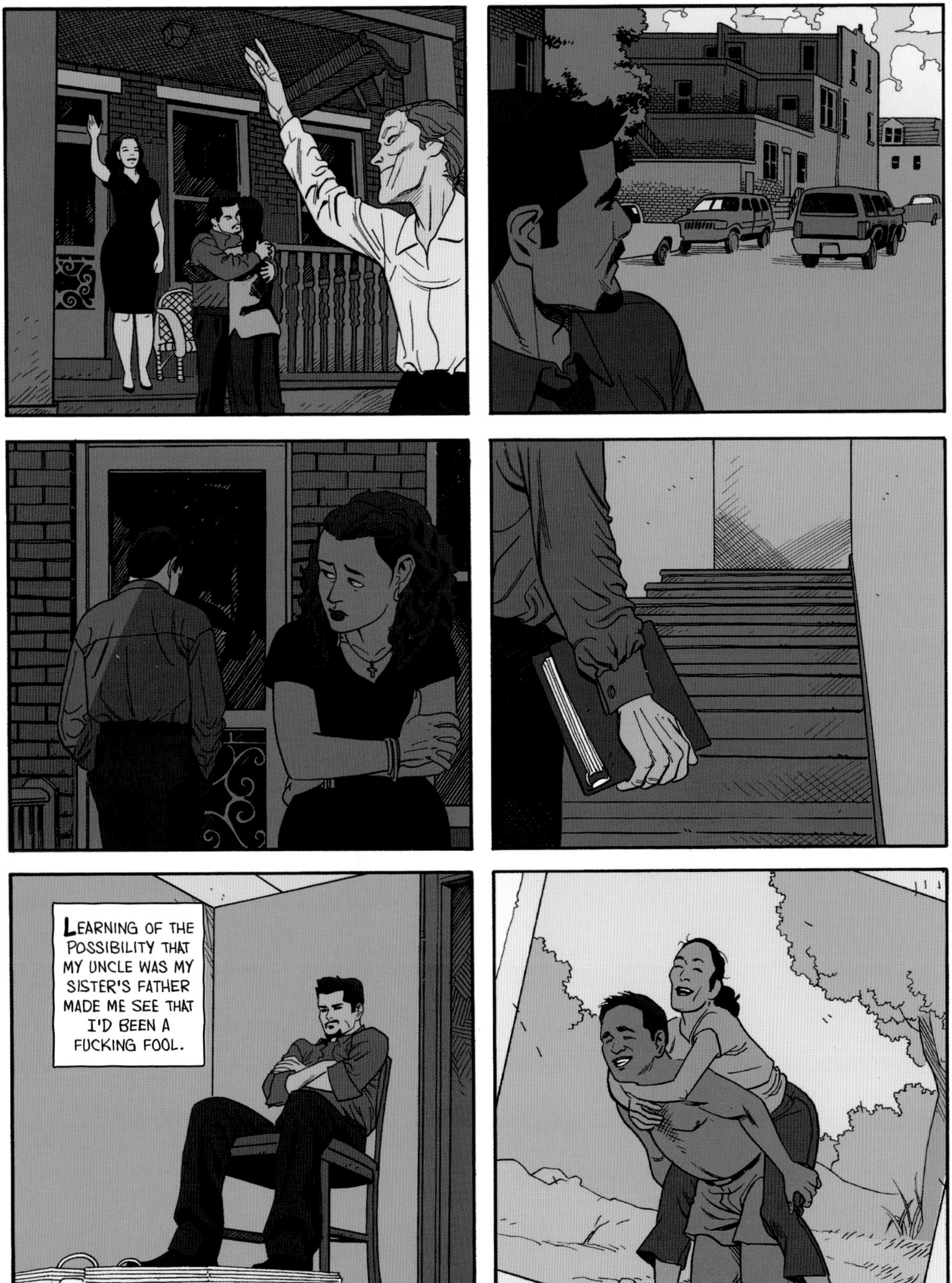
LEARNING OF THE POSSIBILITY THAT MY UNCLE WAS MY SISTER'S FATHER MADE ME SEE THAT I'D BEEN A FUCKING FOOL.

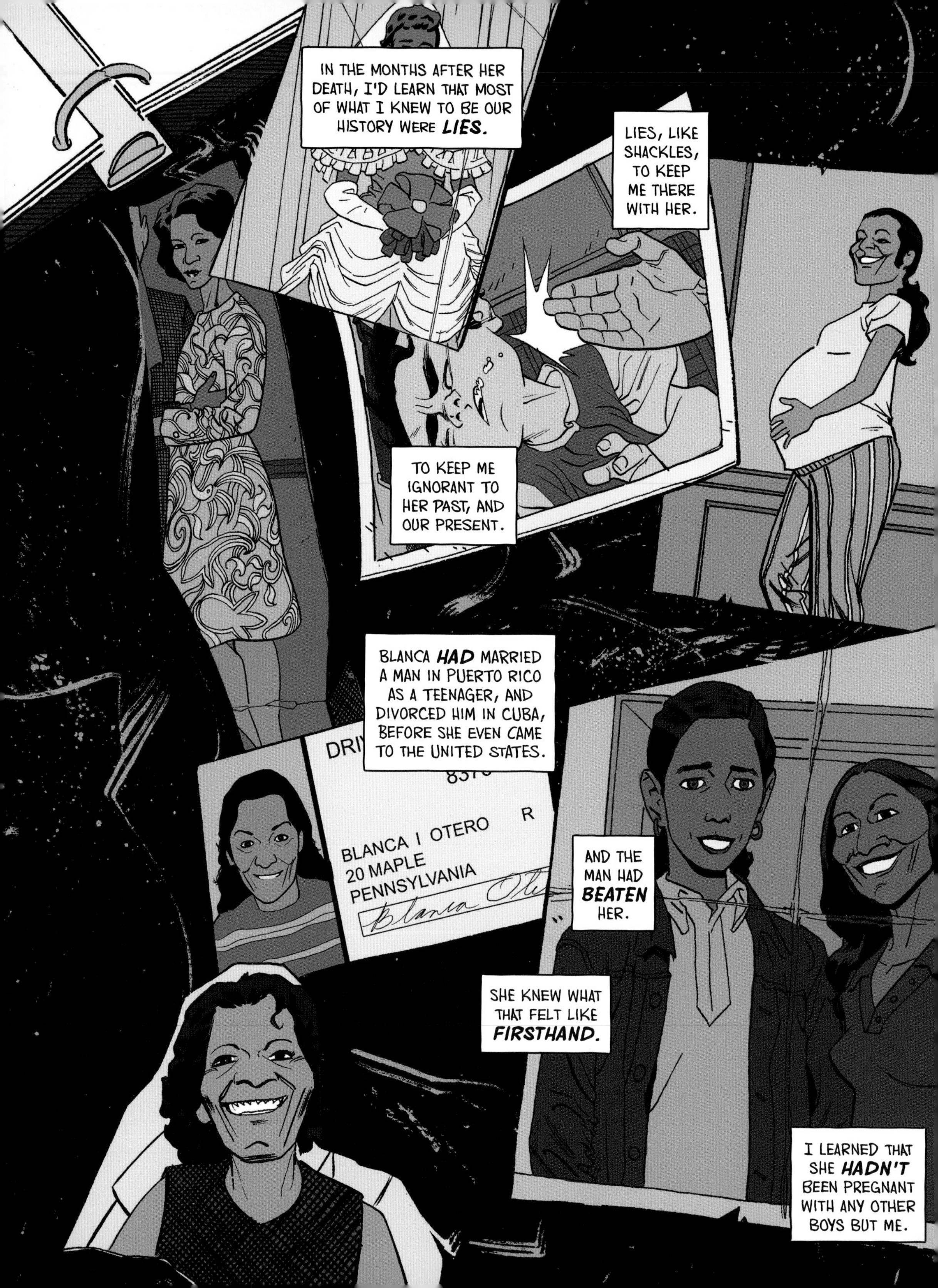
IN THE MONTHS AFTER HER DEATH, I'D LEARN THAT MOST OF WHAT I KNEW TO BE OUR HISTORY WERE LIES.
LIES, LIKE SHACKLES, TO KEEP ME THERE WITH HER.
TO KEEP ME IGNORANT TO HER PAST, AND OUR PRESENT.
BLANCA HAD MARRIED A MAN IN PUERTO RICO AS A TEENAGER, AND DIVORCED HIM IN CUBA, BEFORE SHE EVEN CAME TO THE UNITED STATES.
BLANCA I OTERO
20 MAPLE
PENNSYLVANIA
AND THE MAN HAD BEATEN HER.
SHE KNEW WHAT THAT FELT LIKE FIRSTHAND.
I LEARNED THAT SHE HADN'T BEEN PREGNANT WITH ANY OTHER BOYS BUT ME.

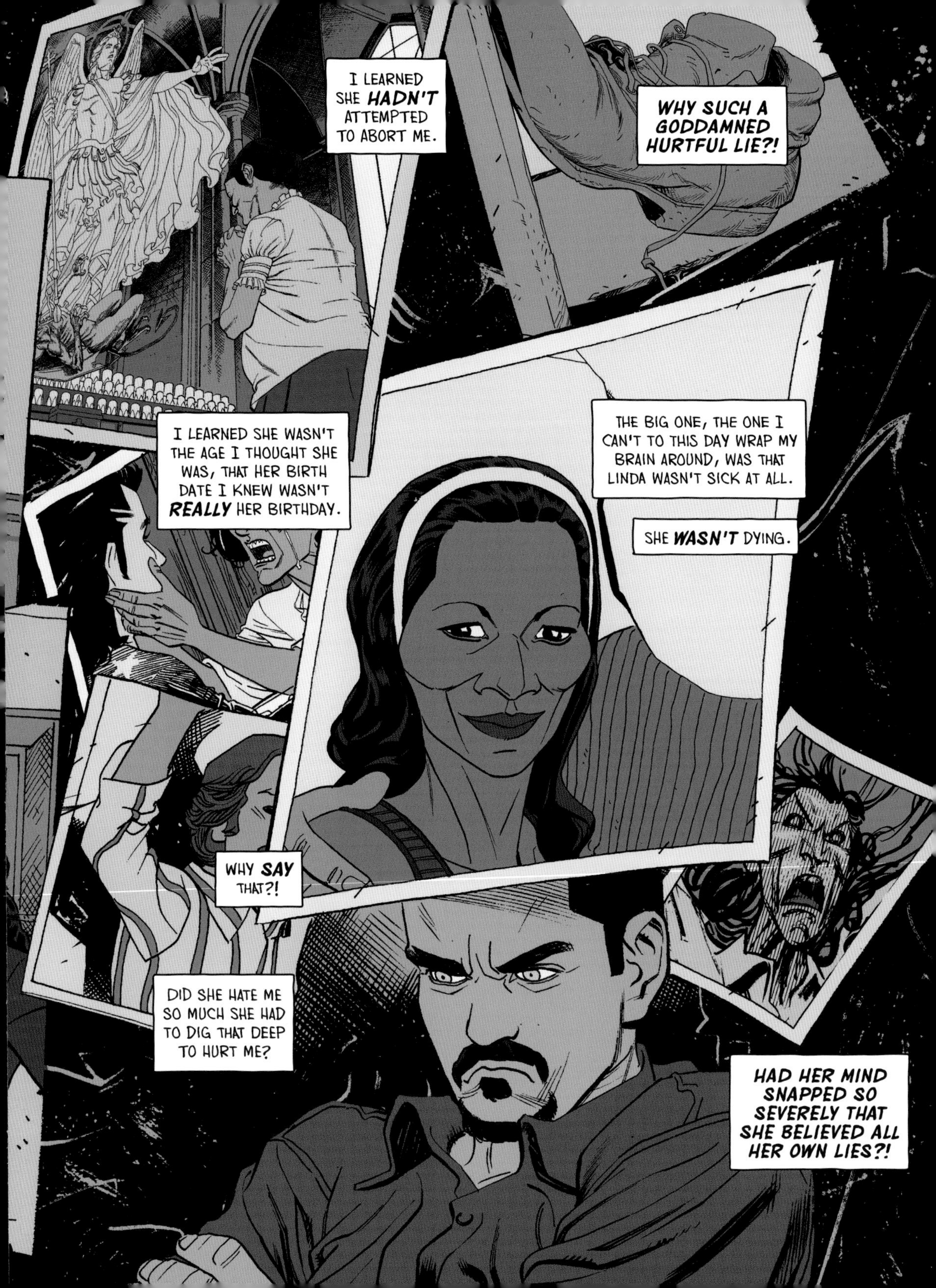
I LEARNED SHE HADN'T ATTEMPTED TO ABORT ME.
WHY SUCH A GODDAMNED HURTFUL LIE?!
I LEARNED SHE WASN'T THE AGE I THOUGHT SHE WAS, THAT HER BIRTH DATE I KNEW WASN'T REALLY HER BIRTHDAY.
THE BIG ONE, THE ONE I CAN'T TO THIS DAY WRAP MY BRAIN AROUND, WAS THAT LINDA WASN'T SICK AT ALL.
SHE WASN'T DYING.
WHY SAY THAT?!
DID SHE HATE ME SO MUCH SHE HAD TO DIG THAT DEEP TO HURT ME?
HAD HER MIND SNAPPED SO SEVERELY THAT SHE BELIEVED ALL HER OWN LIES?!

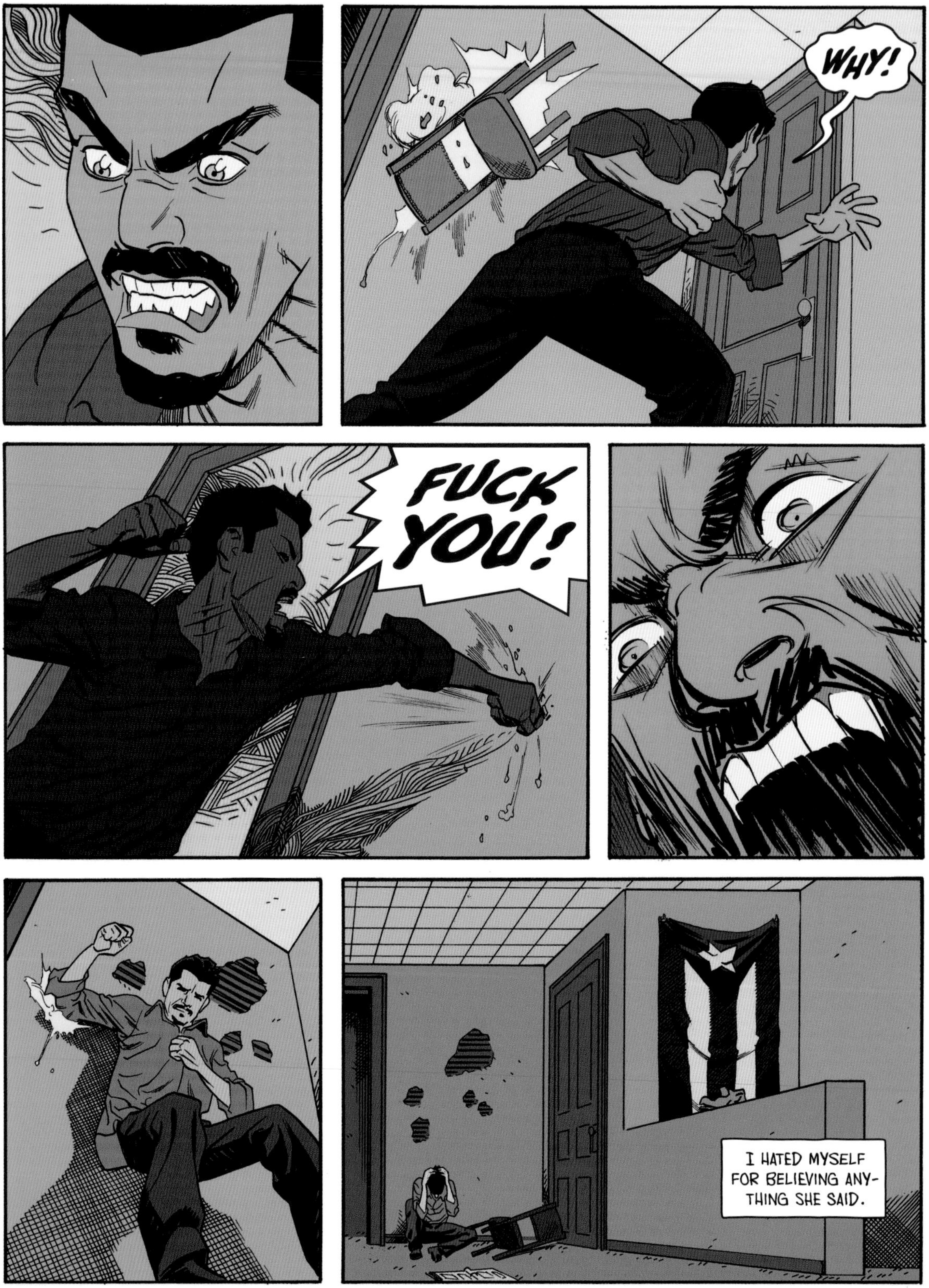
WHY!
FUCK YOU!
I HATED MYSELF FOR BELIEVING ANY-THING SHE SAID.

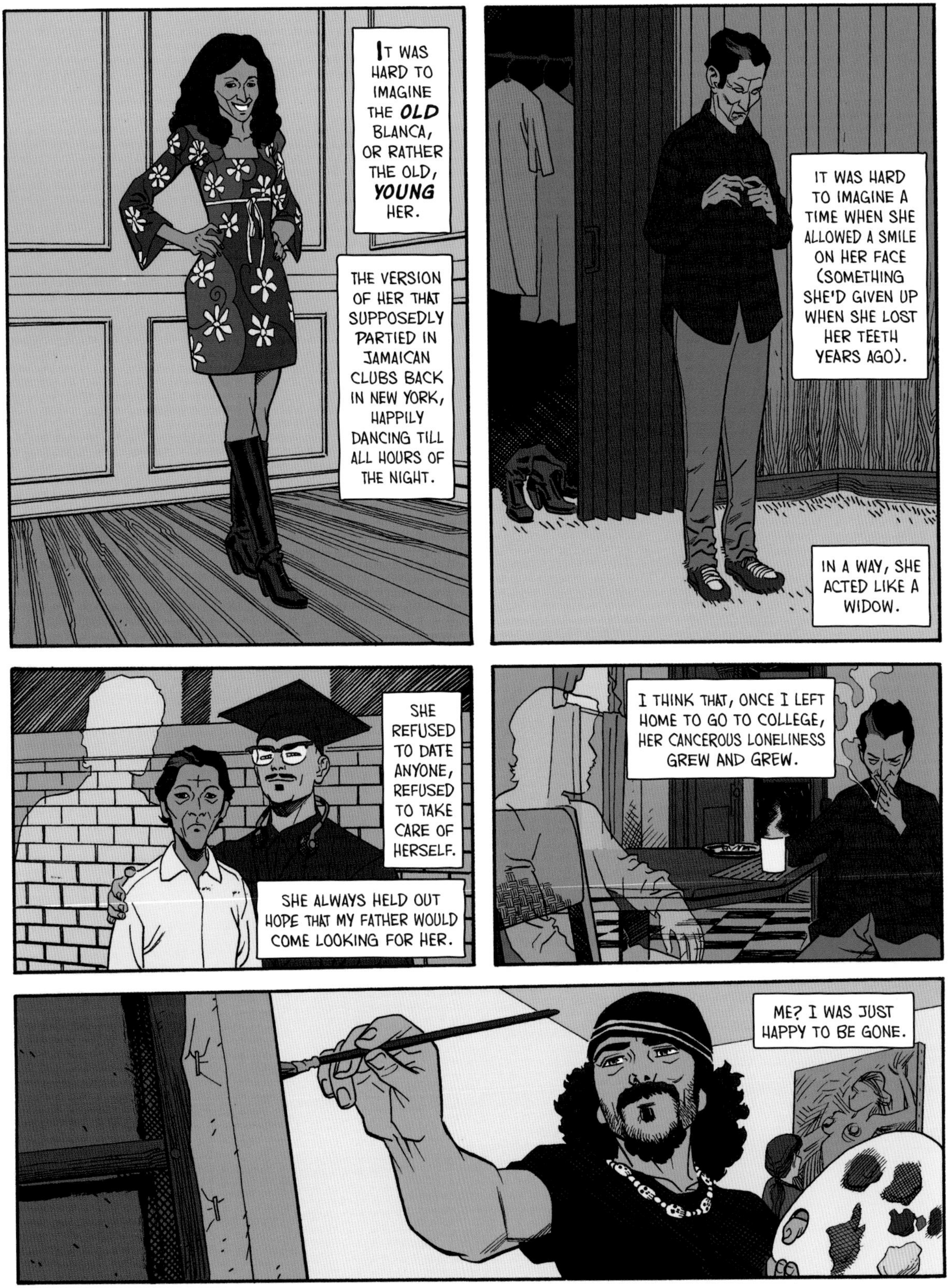
IT WAS HARD TO IMAGINE THE OLD BLANCA, OR RATHER THE OLD, YOUNG HER.
THE VERSION OF HER THAT SUPPOSEDLY PARTIED IN JAMAICAN CLUBS BACK IN NEW YORK, HAPPILY DANCING TILL ALL HOURS OF THE NIGHT.
IT WAS HARD TO IMAGINE A TIME WHEN SHE ALLOWED A SMILE ON HER FACE (SOMETHING SHE'D GIVEN UP WHEN SHE LOST HER TEETH YEARS AGO).
IN A WAY, SHE ACTED LIKE A WIDOW.
SHE REFUSED TO DATE ANYONE, REFUSED TO TAKE CARE OF HERSELF.
SHE ALWAYS HELD OUT HOPE THAT MY FATHER WOULD COME LOOKING FOR HER.
I THINK THAT, ONCE I LEFT HOME TO GO TO COLLEGE, HER CANCEROUS LONELINESS GREW AND GREW.
ME? I WAS JUST HAPPY TO BE GONE.

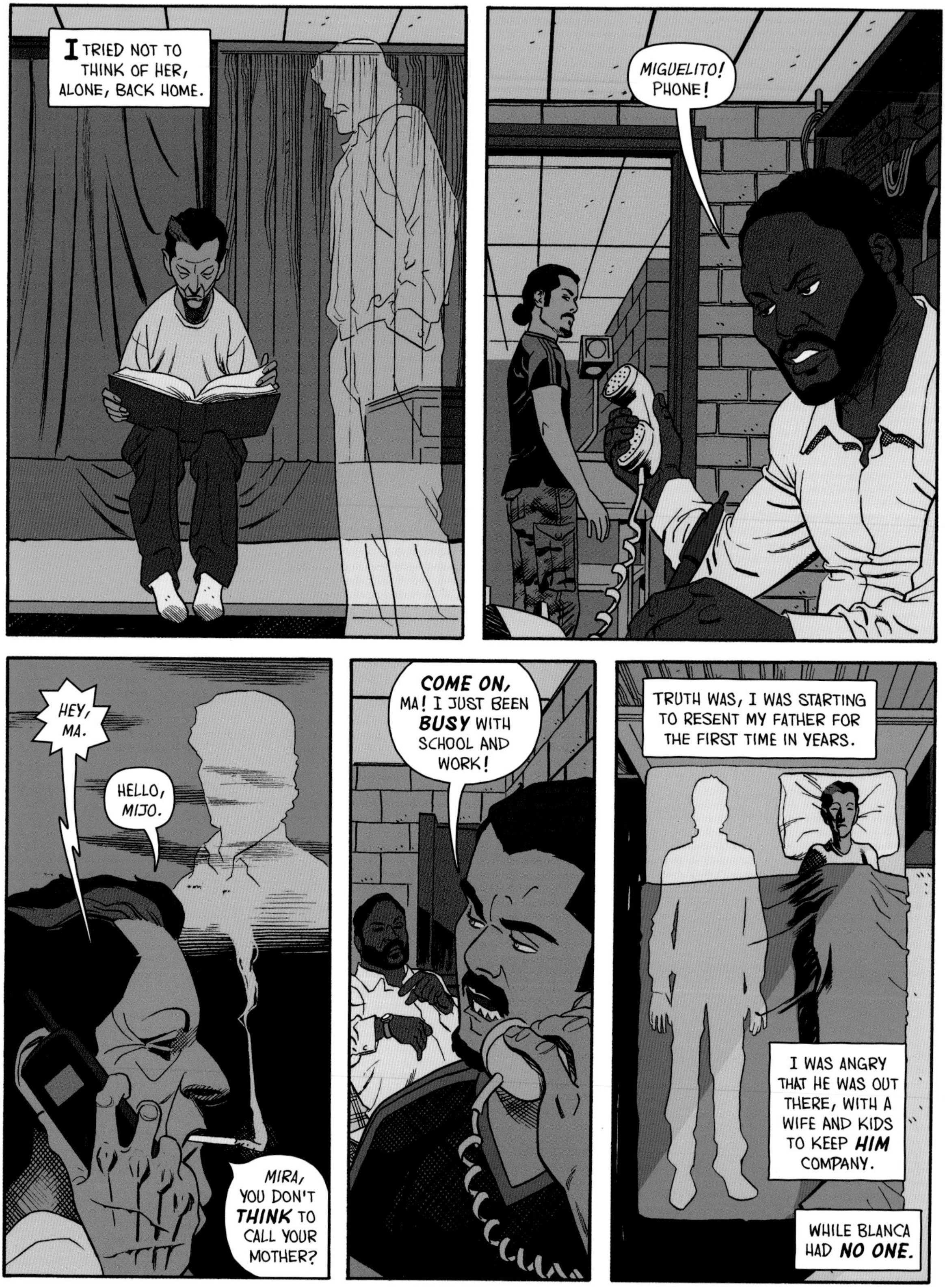
I TRIED NOT TO THINK OF HER, ALONE, BACK HOME.
MIGUELITO! PHONE!
HEY, MA.
HELLO, MIJO.
MIRA, YOU DON'T THINK TO CALL YOUR MOTHER?
COME ON, MA! I JUST BEEN BUSY WITH SCHOOL AND WORK!
TRUTH WAS, I WAS STARTING TO RESENT MY FATHER FOR THE FIRST TIME IN YEARS.
I WAS ANGRY THAT HE WAS OUT THERE, WITH A WIFE AND KIDS TO KEEP HIM COMPANY.
WHILE BLANCA HAD NO ONE.

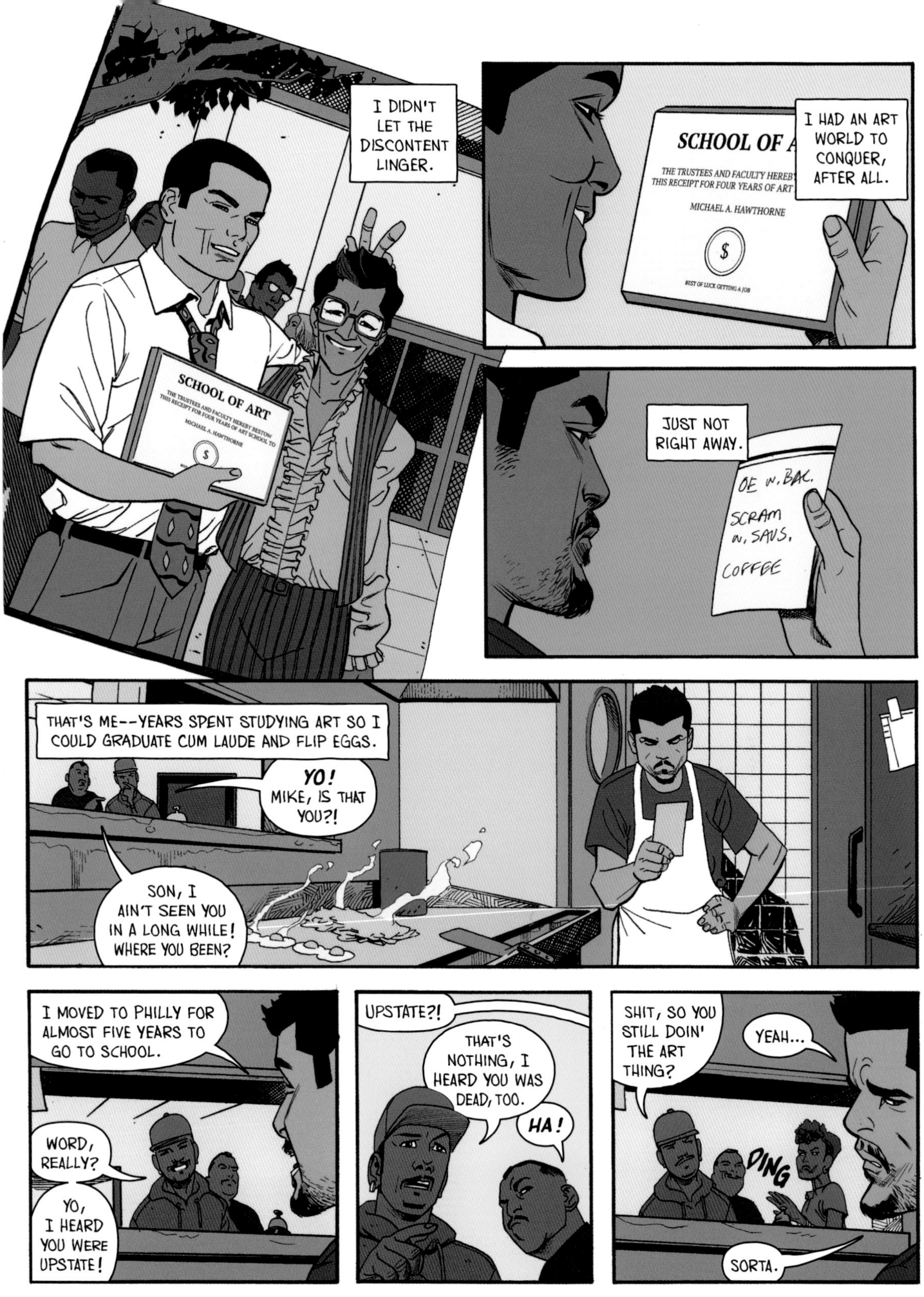

I DIDN'T LET THE DISCONTENT LINGER.
SCHOOL OF ART
THE TRUSTEES AND FACULTY HEREBY BESTOW THIS RECEIPT FOR FOUR YEARS OF ART SCHOOL TO
MICHAEL A. HAWTHORNE
$
I HAD AN ART WORLD TO CONQUER, AFTER ALL.
BEST OF LUCK GETTING A JOB
JUST NOT RIGHT AWAY.
OE W. BAC.
SCRAM W. SAUS.
COFFEE
THAT'S ME--YEARS SPENT STUDYING ART SO I COULD GRADUATE CUM LAUDE AND FLIP EGGS.
YO! MIKE, IS THAT YOU?!
SON, I AIN'T SEEN YOU IN A LONG WHILE! WHERE YOU BEEN?
I MOVED TO PHILLY FOR ALMOST FIVE YEARS TO GO TO SCHOOL.
WORD, REALLY?
YO, I HEARD YOU WERE UPSTATE!
UPSTATE?!
THAT'S NOTHING, I HEARD YOU WAS DEAD, TOO.
HA!
SHIT, SO YOU STILL DOIN' THE ART THING?
YEAH...
DING
SORTA.

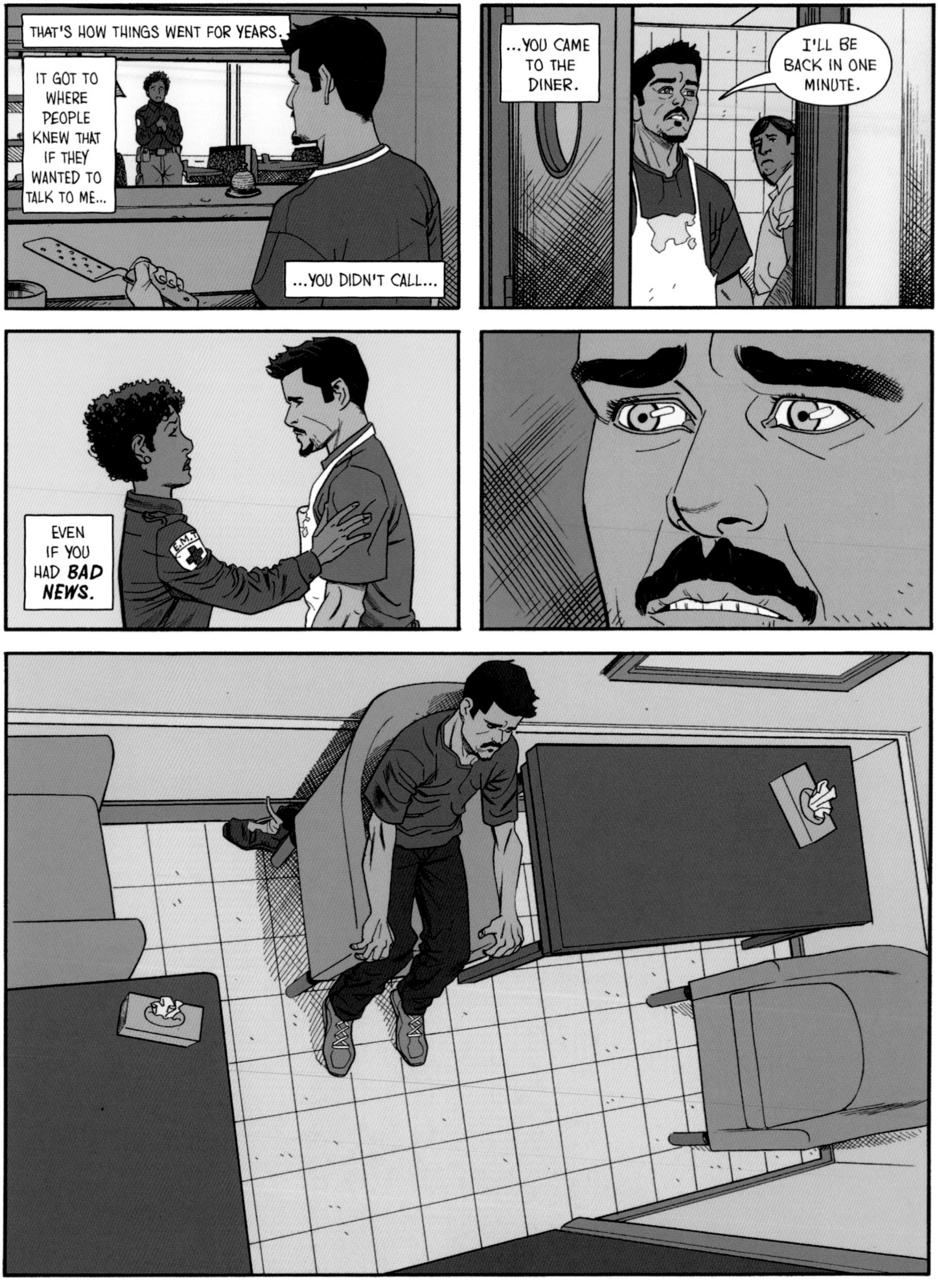
THAT'S HOW THINGS WENT FOR YEARS.
IT GOT TO WHERE PEOPLE KNEW THAT IF THEY WANTED TO TALK TO ME...
...YOU DIDN'T CALL...
...YOU CAME TO THE DINER.
I'LL BE BACK IN ONE MINUTE.
EVEN IF YOU HAD BAD NEWS.
E.M.T.

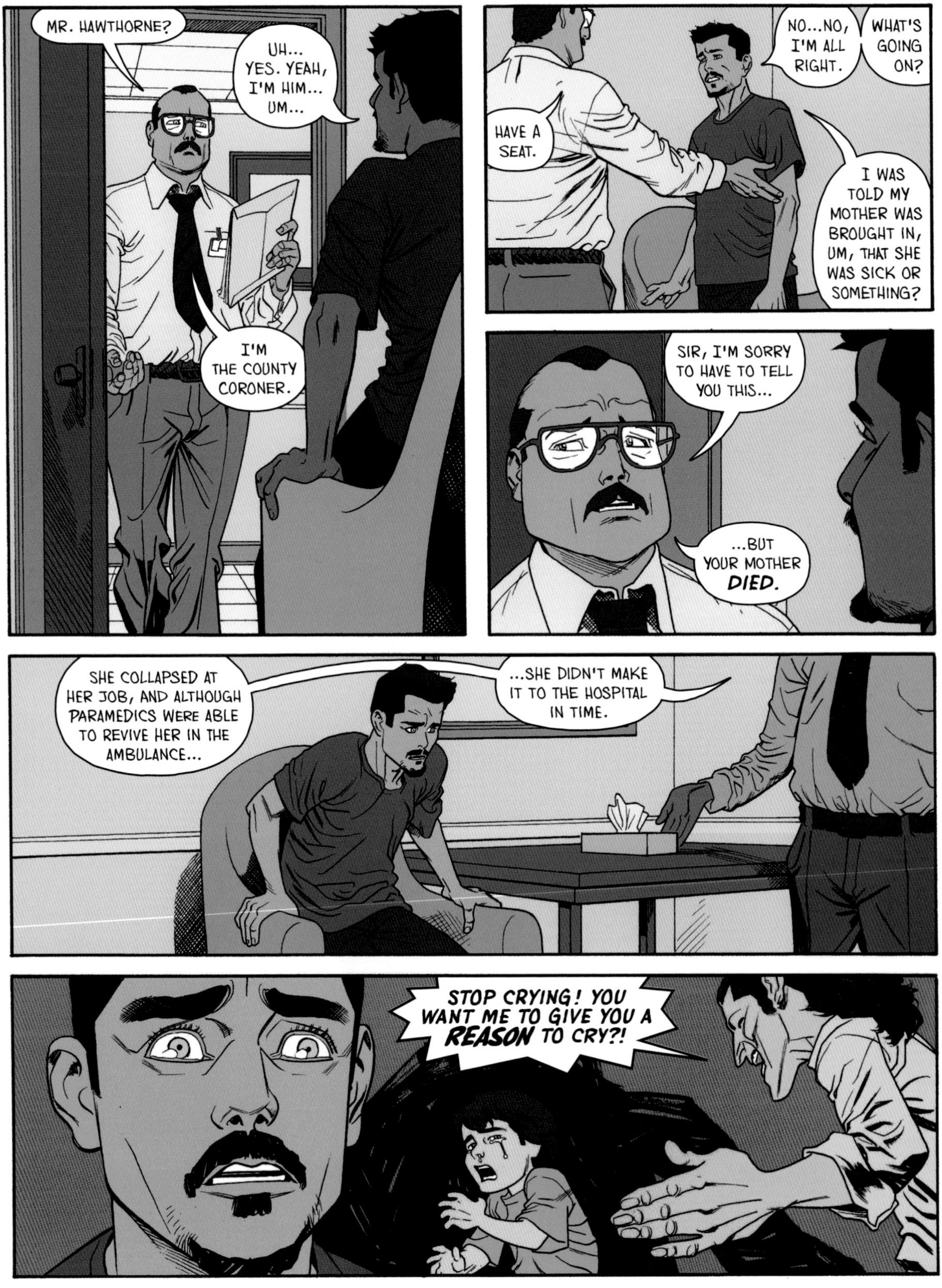
MR. HAWTHORNE?
UH... YES. YEAH, I'M HIM... UM...
I'M THE COUNTY CORONER.
HAVE A SEAT.
NO...NO, I'M ALL RIGHT.
WHAT'S GOING ON?
I WAS TOLD MY MOTHER WAS BROUGHT IN, UM, THAT SHE WAS SICK OR SOMETHING?
SIR, I'M SORRY TO HAVE TO TELL YOU THIS...
...BUT YOUR MOTHER DIED.
SHE COLLAPSED AT HER JOB, AND ALTHOUGH PARAMEDICS WERE ABLE TO REVIVE HER IN THE AMBULANCE...
...SHE DIDN'T MAKE IT TO THE HOSPITAL IN TIME.
STOP CRYING! YOU WANT ME TO GIVE YOU A REASON TO CRY?!

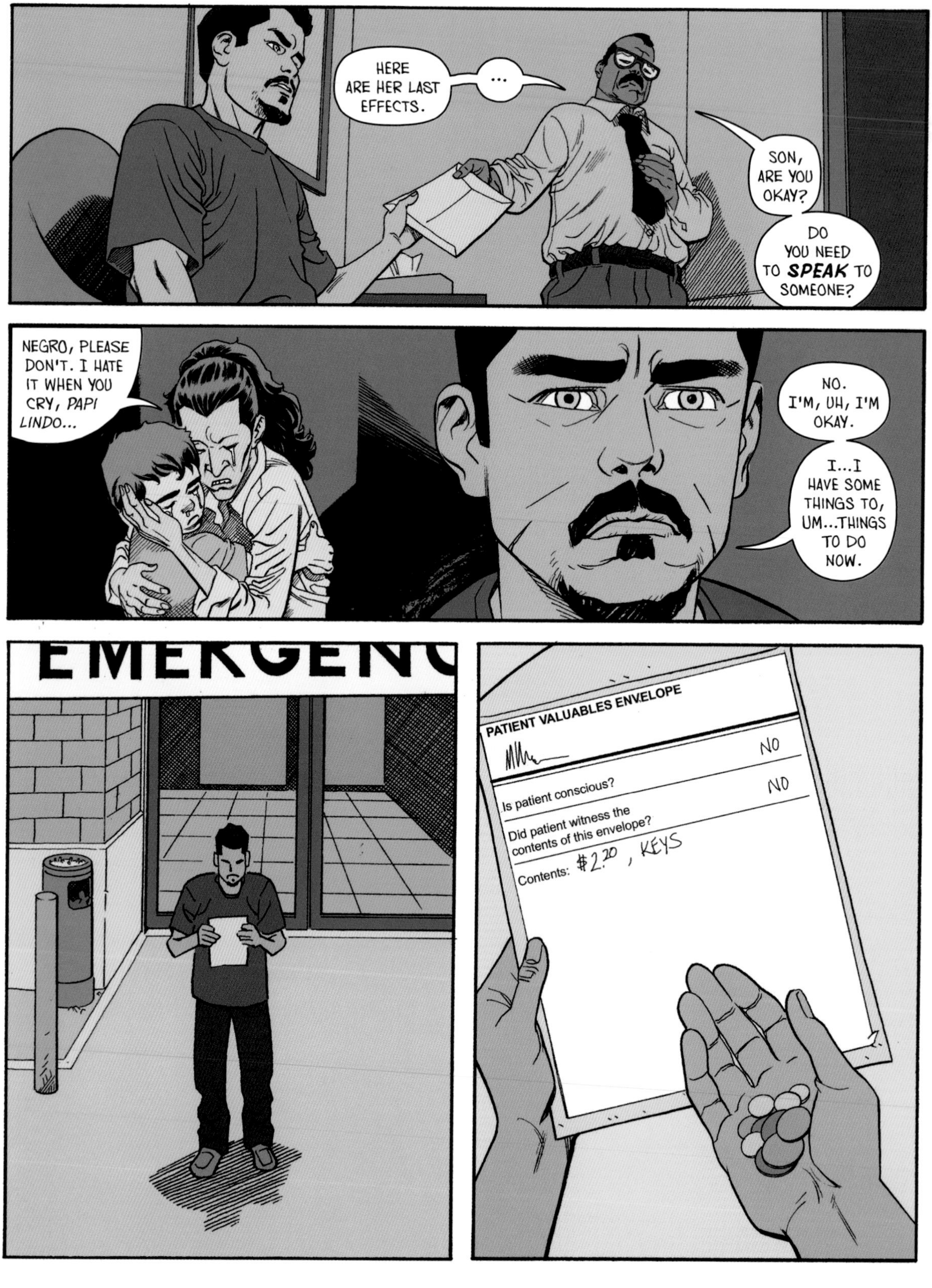
HERE ARE HER LAST EFFECTS.
...
SON, ARE YOU OKAY?
DO YOU NEED TO SPEAK TO SOMEONE?
NEGRO, PLEASE DON'T. I HATE IT WHEN YOU CRY, PAPI LINDO...
NO. I'M, UH, I'M OKAY.
I...I HAVE SOME THINGS TO, UM...THINGS TO DO NOW.
EMERGENC
PATIENT VALUABLES ENVELOPE
NO
Is patient conscious?
NO
Did patient witness the contents of this envelope?
Contents: $2.20, KEYS

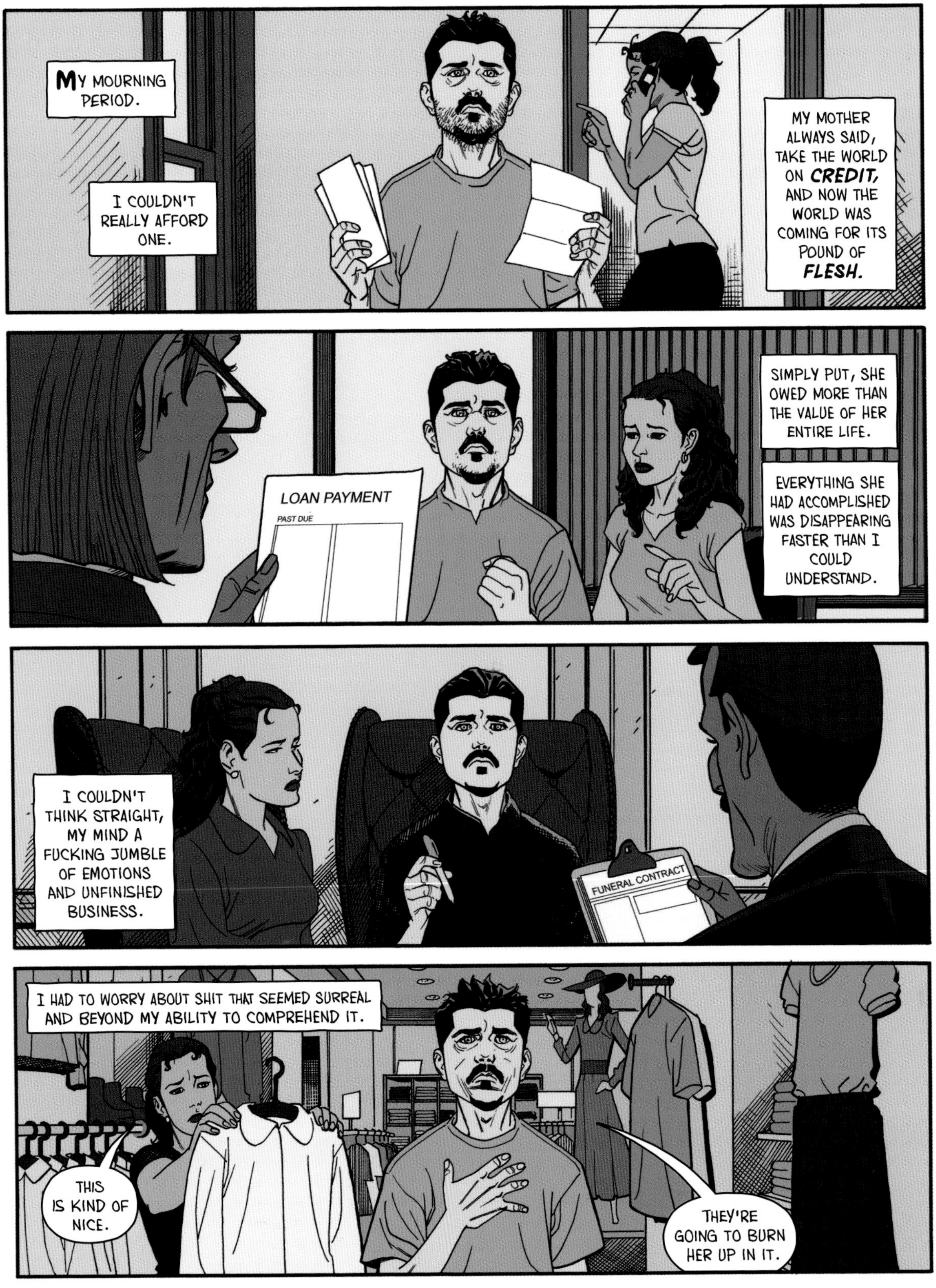
MY MOURNING PERIOD.
I COULDN'T REALLY AFFORD ONE.
MY MOTHER ALWAYS SAID, TAKE THE WORLD ON CREDIT, AND NOW THE WORLD WAS COMING FOR ITS POUND OF FLESH.
LOAN PAYMENT
PAST DUE
SIMPLY PUT, SHE OWED MORE THAN THE VALUE OF HER ENTIRE LIFE.
EVERYTHING SHE HAD ACCOMPLISHED WAS DISAPPEARING FASTER THAN I COULD UNDERSTAND.
I COULDN'T THINK STRAIGHT, MY MIND A FUCKING JUMBLE OF EMOTIONS AND UNFINISHED BUSINESS.
FUNERAL CONTRACT
I HAD TO WORRY ABOUT SHIT THAT SEEMED SURREAL AND BEYOND MY ABILITY TO COMPREHEND IT.
THIS IS KIND OF NICE.
THEY'RE GOING TO BURN HER UP IN IT.

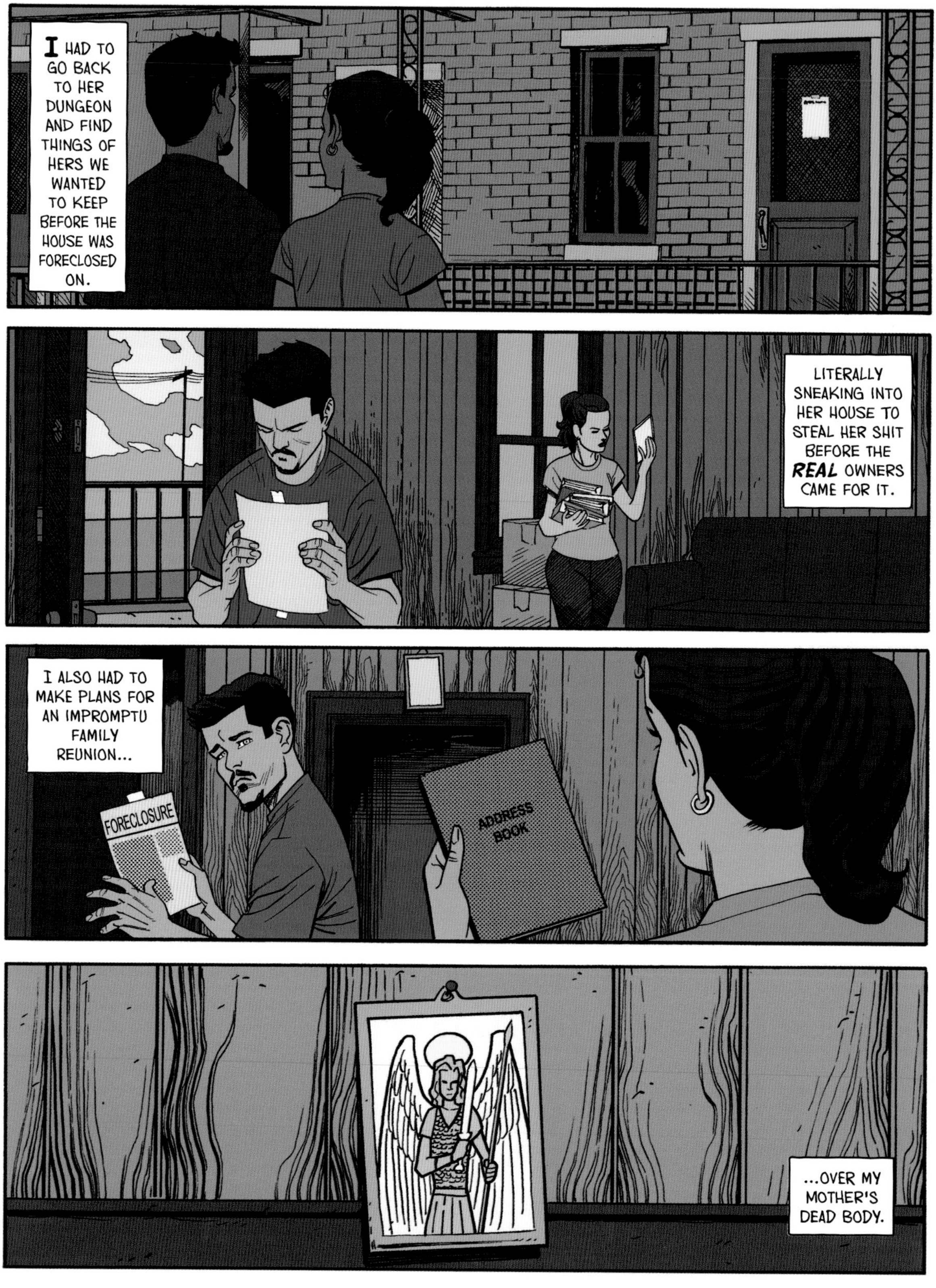
I HAD TO GO BACK TO HER DUNGEON AND FIND THINGS OF HERS WE WANTED TO KEEP BEFORE THE HOUSE WAS FORECLOSED ON.
LITERALLY SNEAKING INTO HER HOUSE TO STEAL HER SHIT BEFORE THE REAL OWNERS CAME FOR IT.
I ALSO HAD TO MAKE PLANS FOR AN IMPROMPTU FAMILY REUNION...
FORECLOSURE
ADDRESS BOOK
...OVER MY MOTHER'S DEAD BODY.

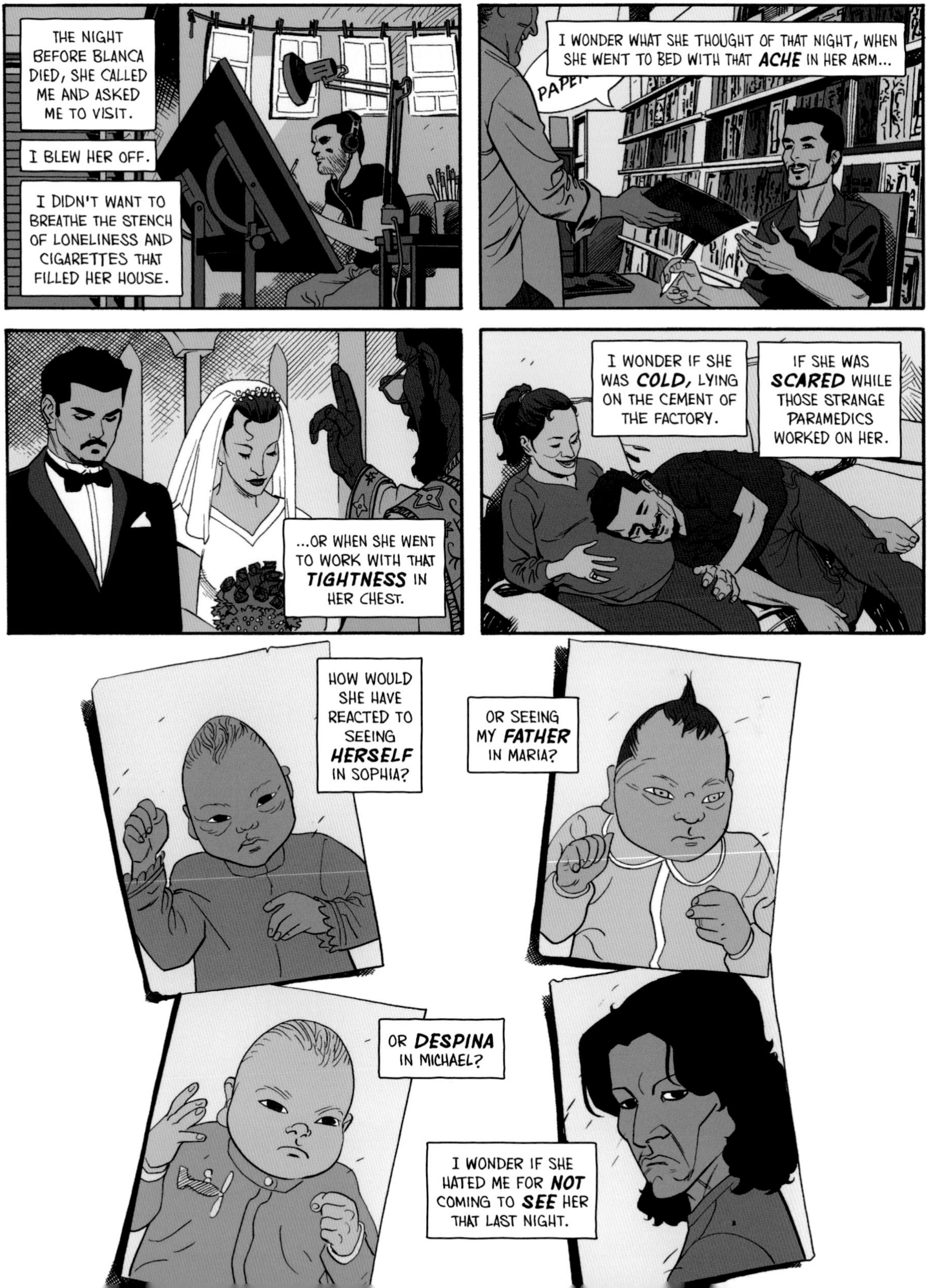
THE NIGHT BEFORE BLANCA DIED, SHE CALLED ME AND ASKED ME TO VISIT.
I BLEW HER OFF.
I DIDN'T WANT TO BREATHE THE STENCH OF LONELINESS AND CIGARETTES THAT FILLED HER HOUSE.
I WONDER WHAT SHE THOUGHT OF THAT NIGHT, WHEN SHE WENT TO BED WITH THAT ACHE IN HER ARM...
...OR WHEN SHE WENT TO WORK WITH THAT TIGHTNESS IN HER CHEST.
I WONDER IF SHE WAS COLD, LYING ON THE CEMENT OF THE FACTORY.
IF SHE WAS SCARED WHILE THOSE STRANGE PARAMEDICS WORKED ON HER.
HOW WOULD SHE HAVE REACTED TO SEEING HERSELF IN SOPHIA?
OR SEEING MY FATHER IN MARIA?
OR DESPINA IN MICHAEL?
I WONDER IF SHE HATED ME FOR NOT COMING TO SEE HER THAT LAST NIGHT.

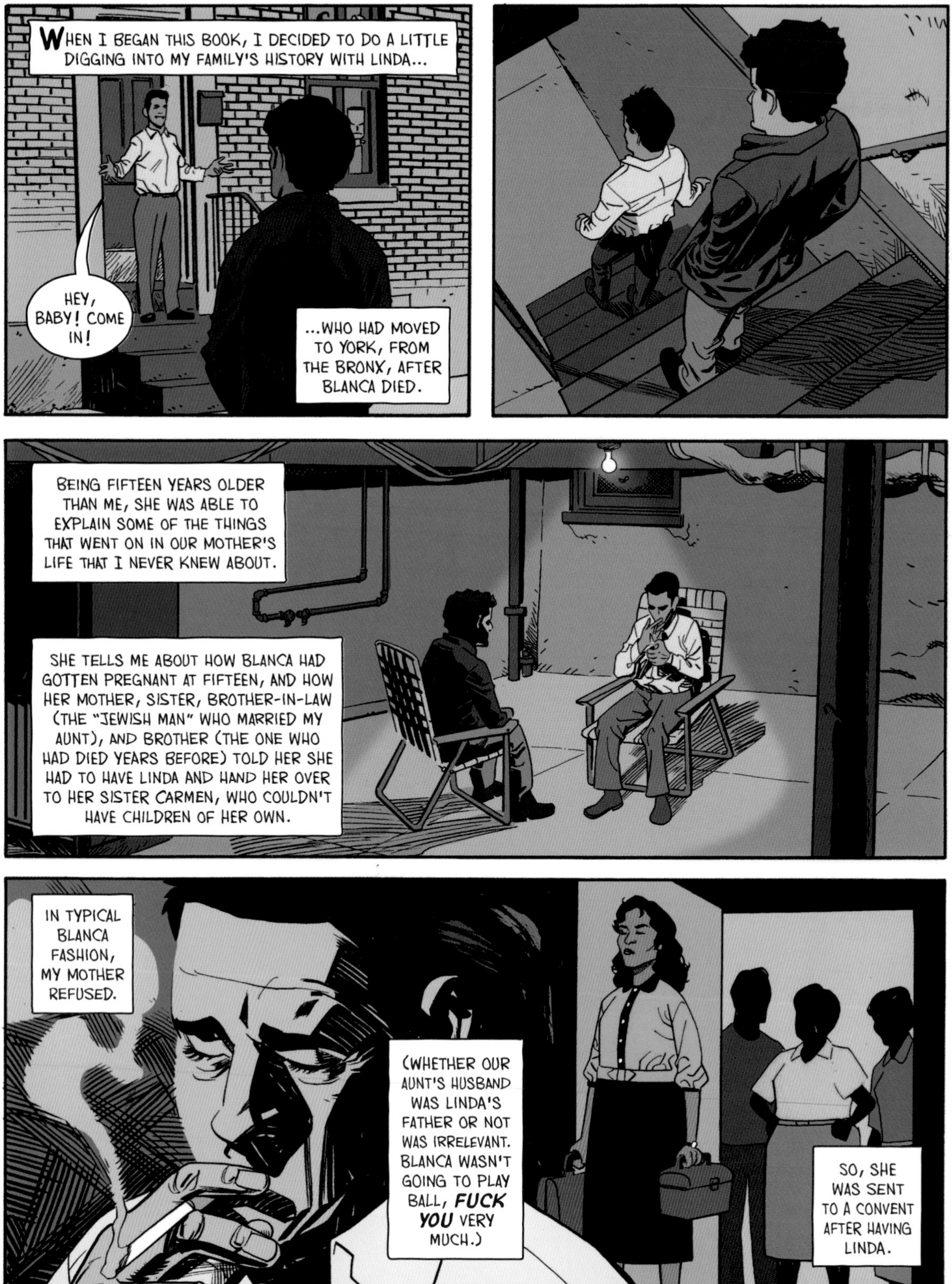
WHEN I BEGAN THIS BOOK, I DECIDED TO DO A LITTLE DIGGING INTO MY FAMILY'S HISTORY WITH LINDA...
HEY, BABY! COME IN!
...WHO HAD MOVED TO YORK, FROM THE BRONX, AFTER BLANCA DIED.
BEING FIFTEEN YEARS OLDER THAN ME, SHE WAS ABLE TO EXPLAIN SOME OF THE THINGS THAT WENT ON IN OUR MOTHER'S LIFE THAT I NEVER KNEW ABOUT.
SHE TELLS ME ABOUT HOW BLANCA HAD GOTTEN PREGNANT AT FIFTEEN, AND HOW HER MOTHER, SISTER, BROTHER-IN-LAW (THE "JEWISH MAN" WHO MARRIED MY AUNT), AND BROTHER (THE ONE WHO HAD DIED YEARS BEFORE) TOLD HER SHE HAD TO HAVE LINDA AND HAND HER OVER TO HER SISTER CARMEN, WHO COULDN'T HAVE CHILDREN OF HER OWN.
IN TYPICAL BLANCA FASHION, MY MOTHER REFUSED.
(WHETHER OUR AUNT'S HUSBAND WAS LINDA'S FATHER OR NOT WAS IRRELEVANT. BLANCA WASN'T GOING TO PLAY BALL, ***FUCK YOU*** VERY MUCH.)
SO, SHE WAS SENT TO A CONVENT AFTER HAVING LINDA.

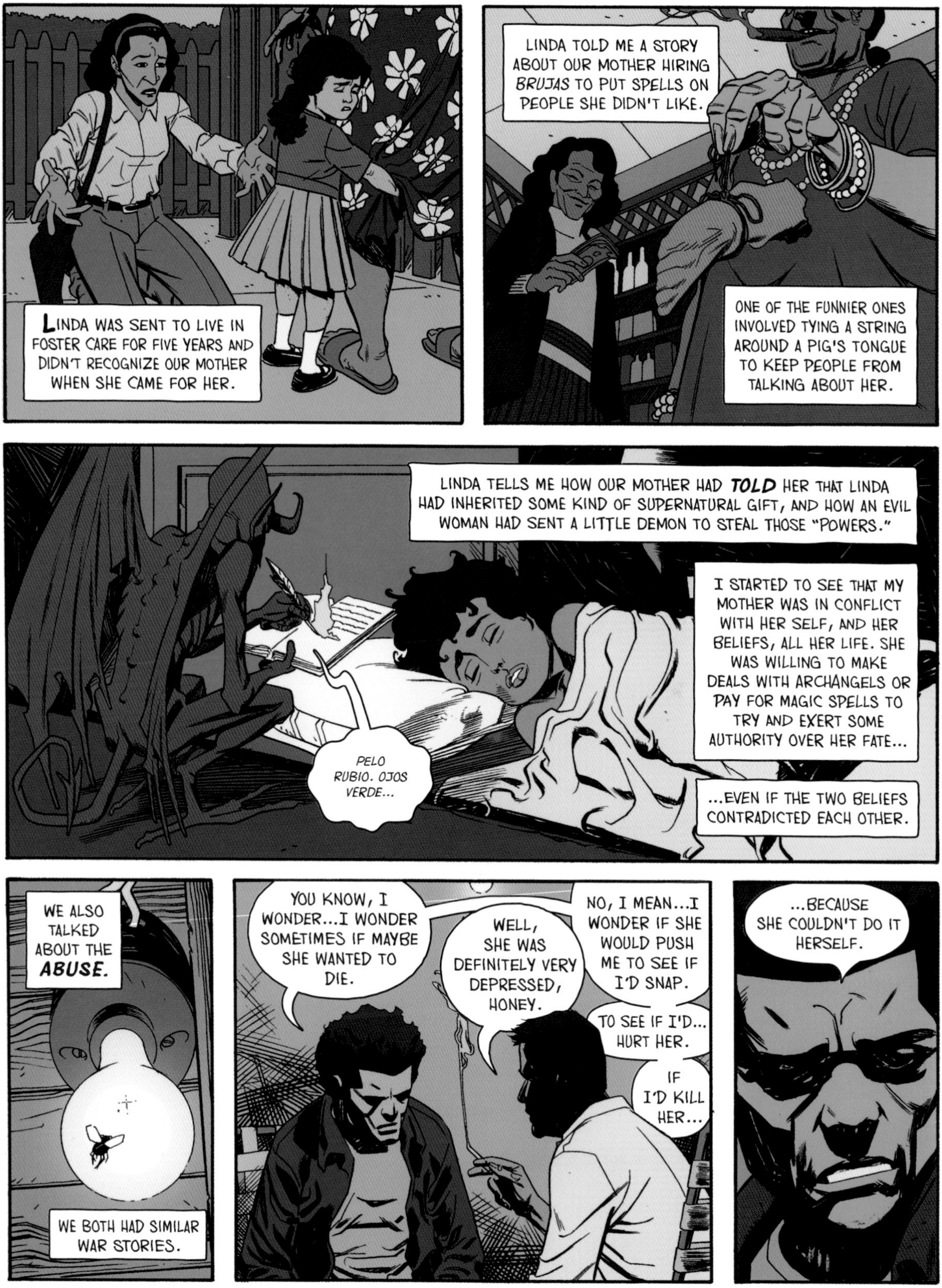
LINDA WAS SENT TO LIVE IN FOSTER CARE FOR FIVE YEARS AND DIDN'T RECOGNIZE OUR MOTHER WHEN SHE CAME FOR HER.
LINDA TOLD ME A STORY ABOUT OUR MOTHER HIRING *BRUJAS* TO PUT SPELLS ON PEOPLE SHE DIDN'T LIKE.
ONE OF THE FUNNIER ONES INVOLVED TYING A STRING AROUND A PIG'S TONGUE TO KEEP PEOPLE FROM TALKING ABOUT HER.
LINDA TELLS ME HOW OUR MOTHER HAD **TOLD** HER THAT LINDA HAD INHERITED SOME KIND OF SUPERNATURAL GIFT, AND HOW AN EVIL WOMAN HAD SENT A LITTLE DEMON TO STEAL THOSE "POWERS."
*PELO RUBIO. OJOS VERDE...*
I STARTED TO SEE THAT MY MOTHER WAS IN CONFLICT WITH HER SELF, AND HER BELIEFS, ALL HER LIFE. SHE WAS WILLING TO MAKE DEALS WITH ARCHANGELS OR PAY FOR MAGIC SPELLS TO TRY AND EXERT SOME AUTHORITY OVER HER FATE...
...EVEN IF THE TWO BELIEFS CONTRADICTED EACH OTHER.
WE ALSO TALKED ABOUT THE ***ABUSE.***
WE BOTH HAD SIMILAR WAR STORIES.
YOU KNOW, I WONDER...I WONDER SOMETIMES IF MAYBE SHE WANTED TO DIE.
WELL, SHE WAS DEFINITELY VERY DEPRESSED, HONEY.
NO, I MEAN...I WONDER IF SHE WOULD PUSH ME TO SEE IF I'D SNAP.
TO SEE IF I'D... HURT HER.
IF I'D KILL HER...
...BECAUSE SHE COULDN'T DO IT HERSELF.

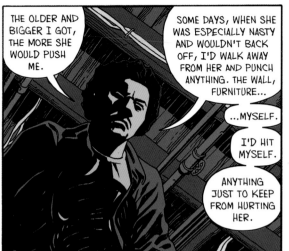

THE OLDER AND BIGGER I GOT, THE MORE SHE WOULD PUSH ME.

SOME DAYS, WHEN SHE WAS ESPECIALLY NASTY AND WOULDN'T BACK OFF, I'D WALK AWAY FROM HER AND PUNCH ANYTHING. THE WALL, FURNITURE...

...MYSELF.

I'D HIT MYSELF.

ANYTHING JUST TO KEEP FROM HURTING HER.

I EXPECT LINDA TO THINK I'M CRAZY. I THOUGHT I WAS CRAZY.

*INSTEAD,* SHE TELLS ME A STORY...

ONE NIGHT, LINDA SAID, BLANCA WAS STARTING A FIGHT WITH HER FOR GOD KNOWS WHAT REASON.

SHE WAS HITTING HER, BUT LINDA WAS OLD ENOUGH AT THIS POINT TO PROTECT HERSELF AND WAS KEEPING OUR MOTHER AT BAY.

OUR MOTHER MANAGED TO KNOCK LINDA TO THE FLOOR, AND *WRAPPED HER HANDS* AROUND HER THROAT.

LINDA DECIDED, THEN AND THERE, TO NOT GIVE IN ANYMORE.

SHE DECIDED TO NOT BE SCARED.

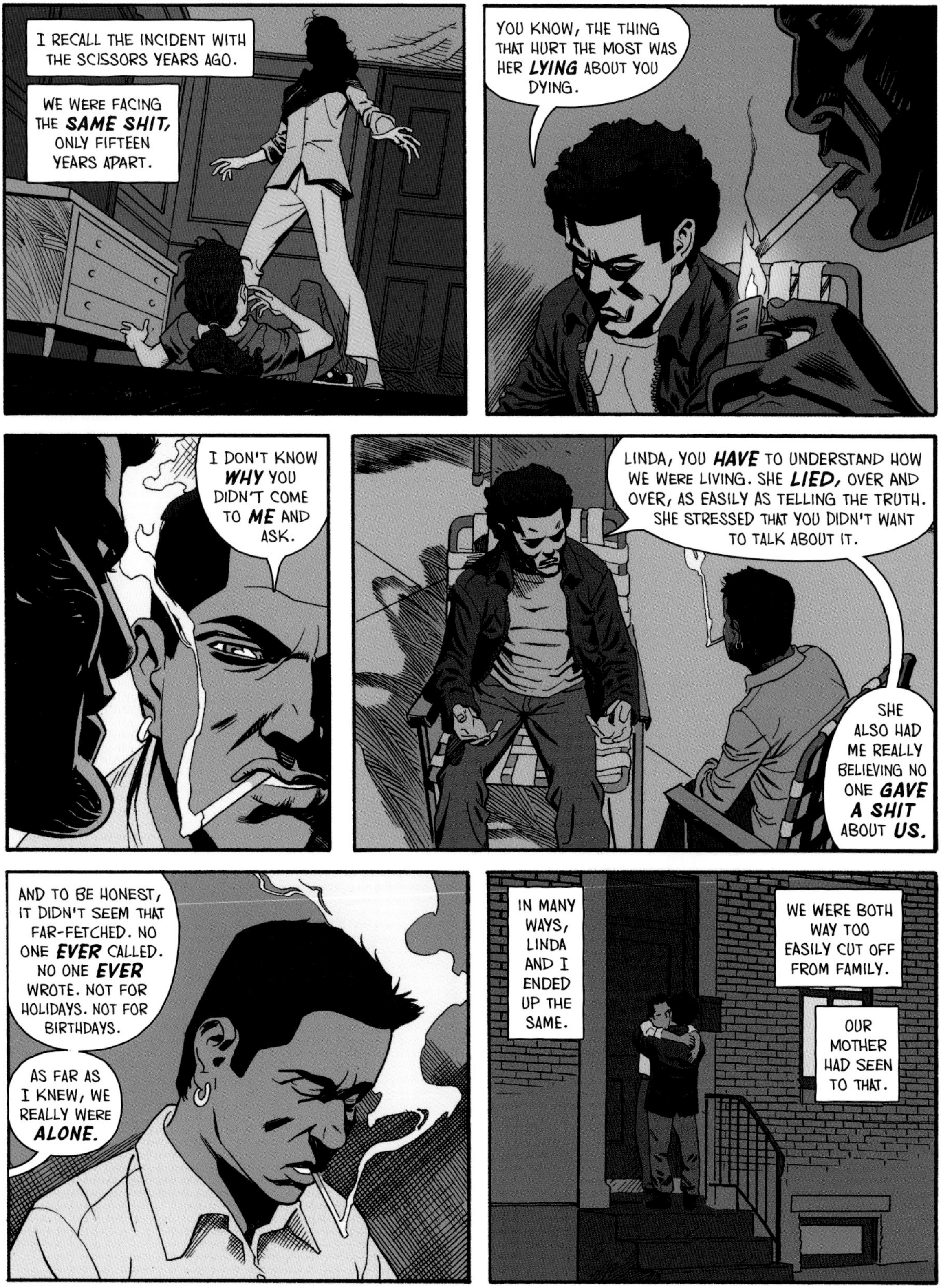
I RECALL THE INCIDENT WITH THE SCISSORS YEARS AGO.
WE WERE FACING THE SAME SHIT, ONLY FIFTEEN YEARS APART.
YOU KNOW, THE THING THAT HURT THE MOST WAS HER LYING ABOUT YOU DYING.
I DON'T KNOW WHY YOU DIDN'T COME TO ME AND ASK.
LINDA, YOU HAVE TO UNDERSTAND HOW WE WERE LIVING. SHE LIED, OVER AND OVER, AS EASILY AS TELLING THE TRUTH. SHE STRESSED THAT YOU DIDN'T WANT TO TALK ABOUT IT.
SHE ALSO HAD ME REALLY BELIEVING NO ONE GAVE A SHIT ABOUT US.
AND TO BE HONEST, IT DIDN'T SEEM THAT FAR-FETCHED. NO ONE EVER CALLED. NO ONE EVER WROTE. NOT FOR HOLIDAYS. NOT FOR BIRTHDAYS.
AS FAR AS I KNEW, WE REALLY WERE ALONE.
IN MANY WAYS, LINDA AND I ENDED UP THE SAME.
WE WERE BOTH WAY TOO EASILY CUT OFF FROM FAMILY.
OUR MOTHER HAD SEEN TO THAT.

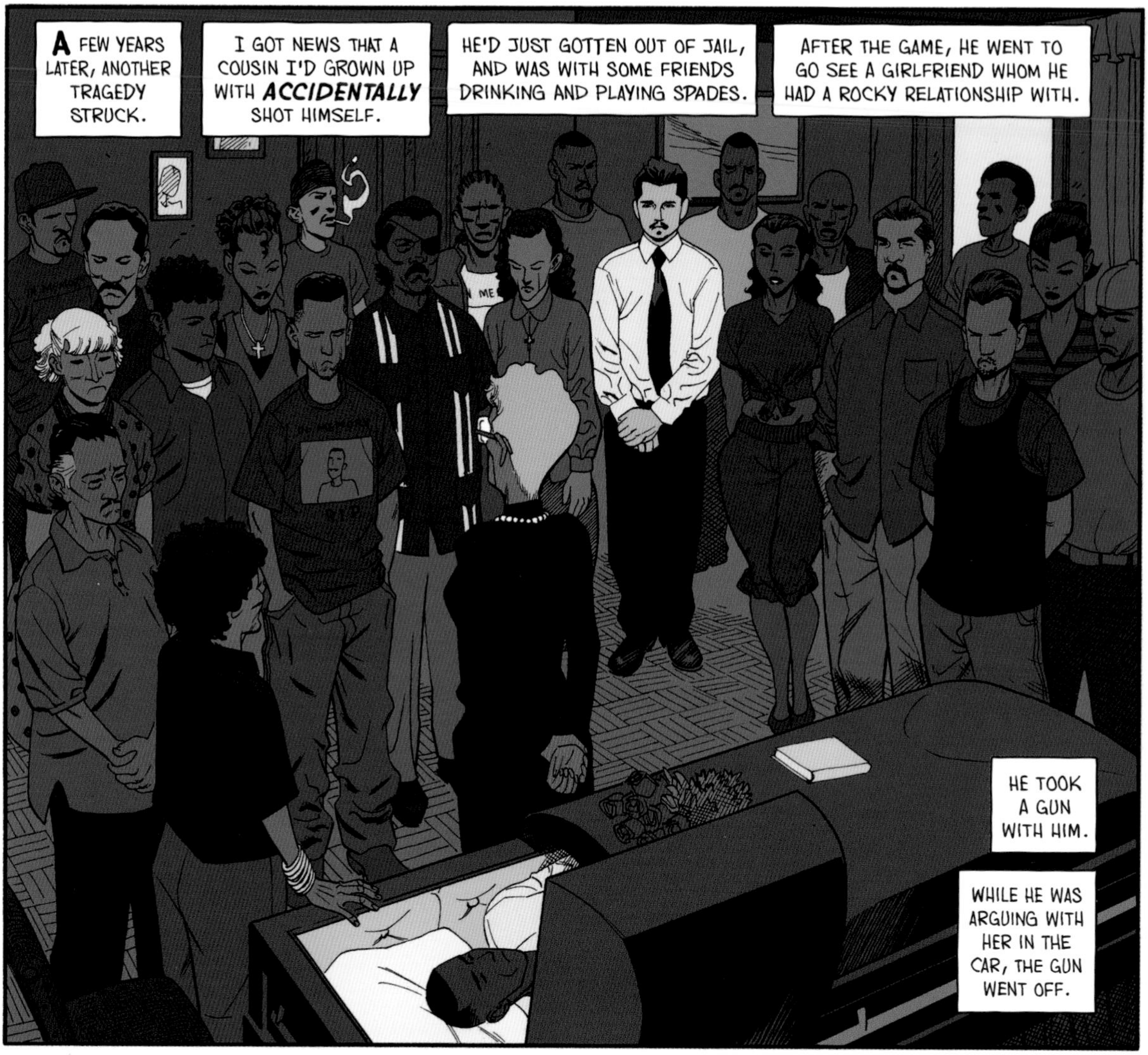
A FEW YEARS LATER, ANOTHER TRAGEDY STRUCK.
I GOT NEWS THAT A COUSIN I'D GROWN UP WITH ACCIDENTALLY SHOT HIMSELF.
HE'D JUST GOTTEN OUT OF JAIL, AND WAS WITH SOME FRIENDS DRINKING AND PLAYING SPADES.
AFTER THE GAME, HE WENT TO GO SEE A GIRLFRIEND WHOM HE HAD A ROCKY RELATIONSHIP WITH.
HE TOOK A GUN WITH HIM.
WHILE HE WAS ARGUING WITH HER IN THE CAR, THE GUN WENT OFF.

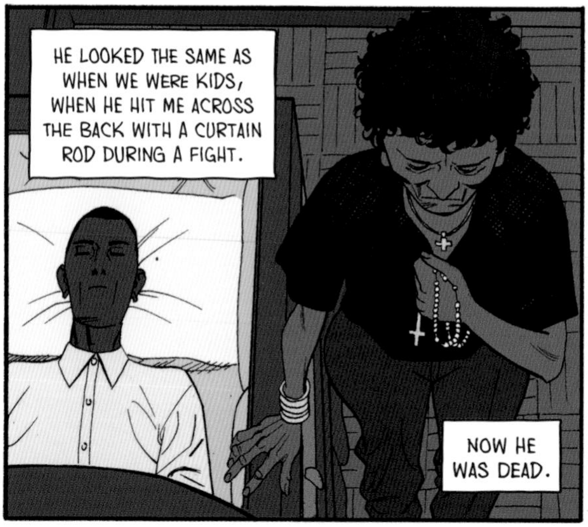
HE LOOKED THE SAME AS WHEN WE WERE KIDS, WHEN HE HIT ME ACROSS THE BACK WITH A CURTAIN ROD DURING A FIGHT.
NOW HE WAS DEAD.

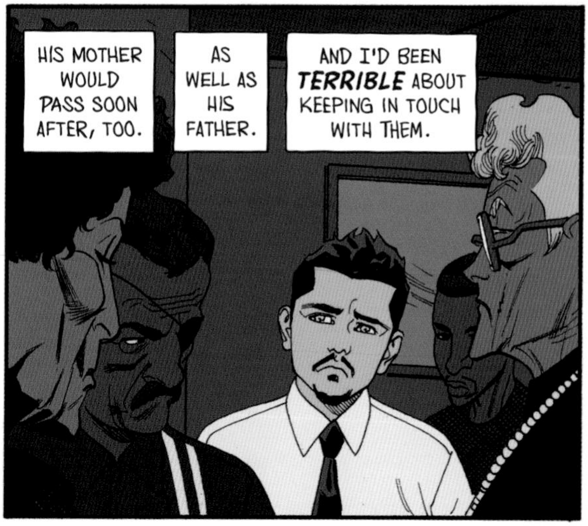
HIS MOTHER WOULD PASS SOON AFTER, TOO.
AS WELL AS HIS FATHER.
AND I'D BEEN TERRIBLE ABOUT KEEPING IN TOUCH WITH THEM.

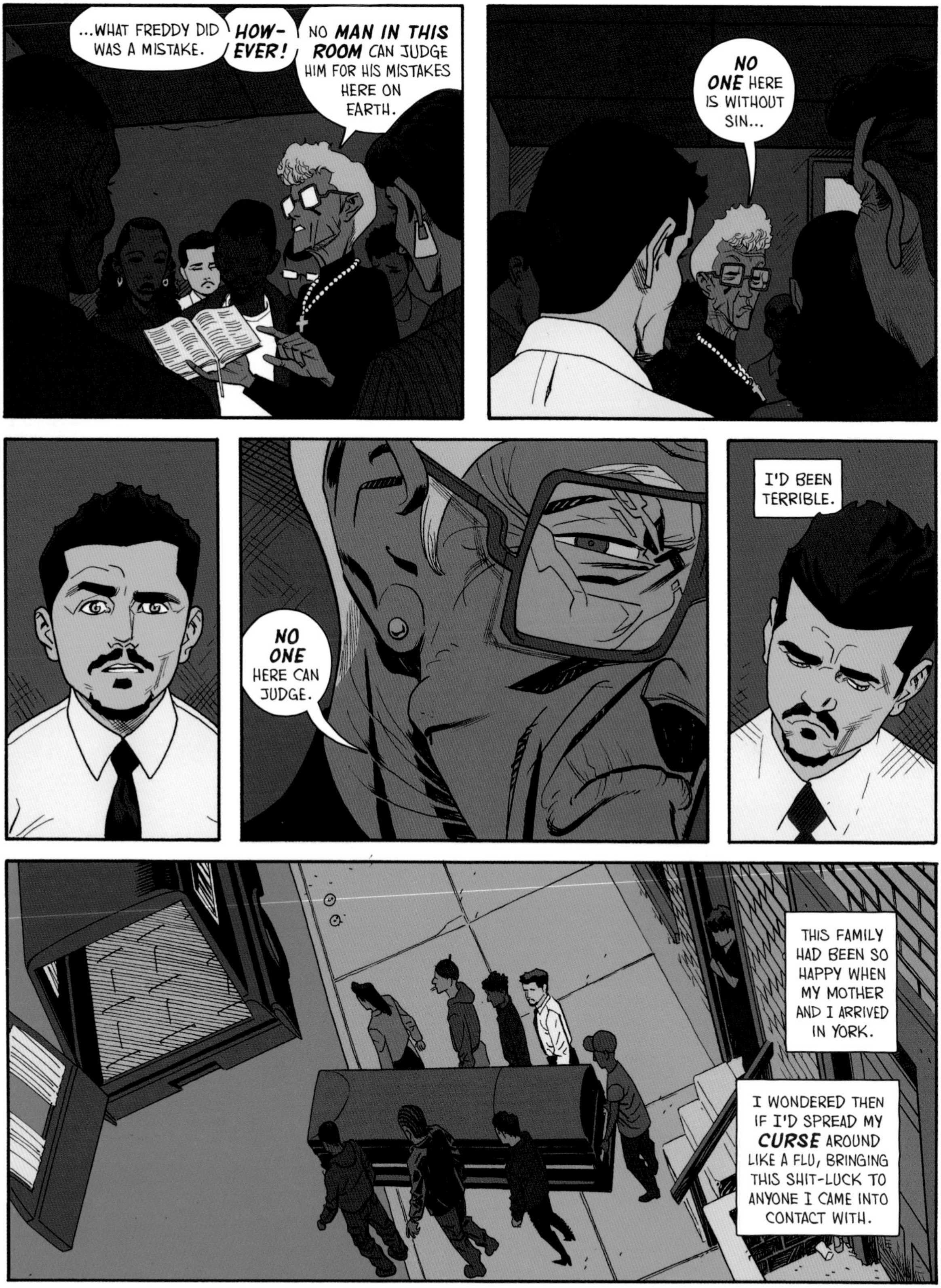
...WHAT FREDDY DID WAS A MISTAKE.
HOW-EVER!
NO **MAN IN THIS ROOM** CAN JUDGE HIM FOR HIS MISTAKES HERE ON EARTH.
**NO ONE** HERE IS WITHOUT SIN...
**NO ONE** HERE CAN JUDGE.
I'D BEEN TERRIBLE.
THIS FAMILY HAD BEEN SO HAPPY WHEN MY MOTHER AND I ARRIVED IN YORK.
I WONDERED THEN IF I'D SPREAD MY **CURSE** AROUND LIKE A FLU, BRINGING THIS SHIT-LUCK TO ANYONE I CAME INTO CONTACT WITH.

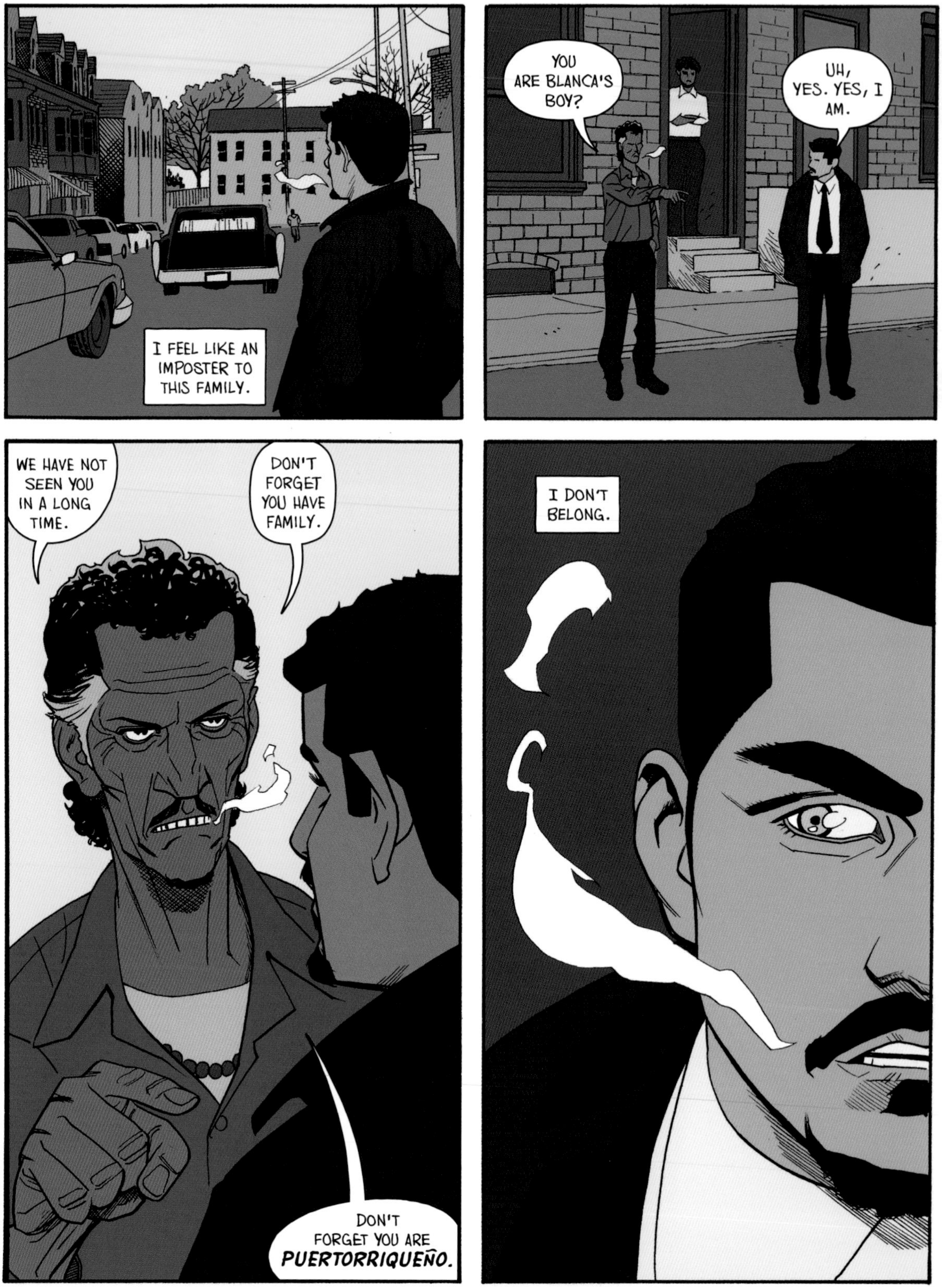
I FEEL LIKE AN IMPOSTER TO THIS FAMILY.
YOU ARE BLANCA'S BOY?
UH, YES. YES, I AM.
WE HAVE NOT SEEN YOU IN A LONG TIME.
DON'T FORGET YOU HAVE FAMILY.
DON'T FORGET YOU ARE *PUERTORRIQUEÑO.*
I DON'T BELONG.

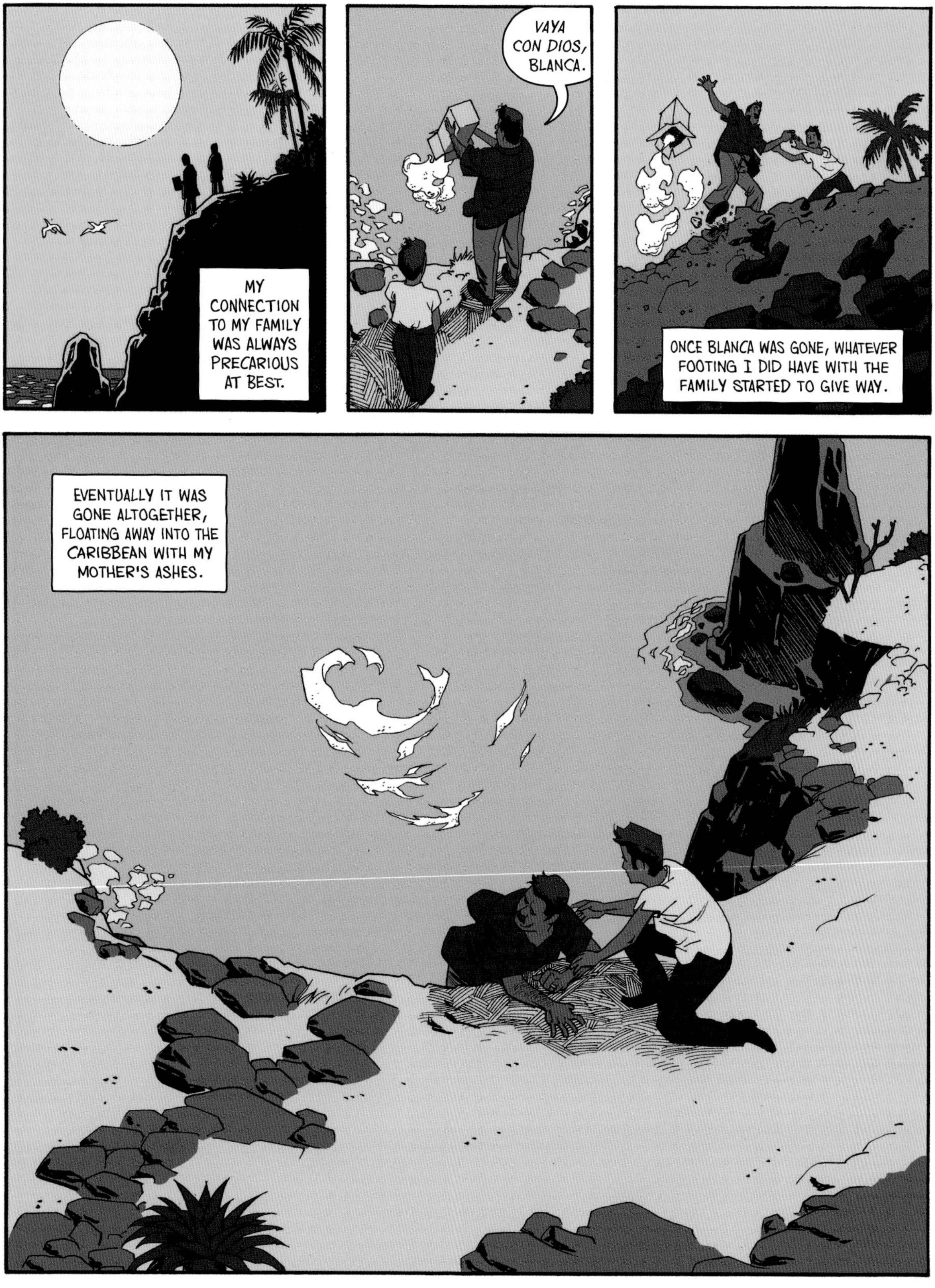
MY CONNECTION TO MY FAMILY WAS ALWAYS PRECARIOUS AT BEST.
VAYA CON DIOS, BLANCA.
ONCE BLANCA WAS GONE, WHATEVER FOOTING I DID HAVE WITH THE FAMILY STARTED TO GIVE WAY.
EVENTUALLY IT WAS GONE ALTOGETHER, FLOATING AWAY INTO THE CARIBBEAN WITH MY MOTHER'S ASHES.

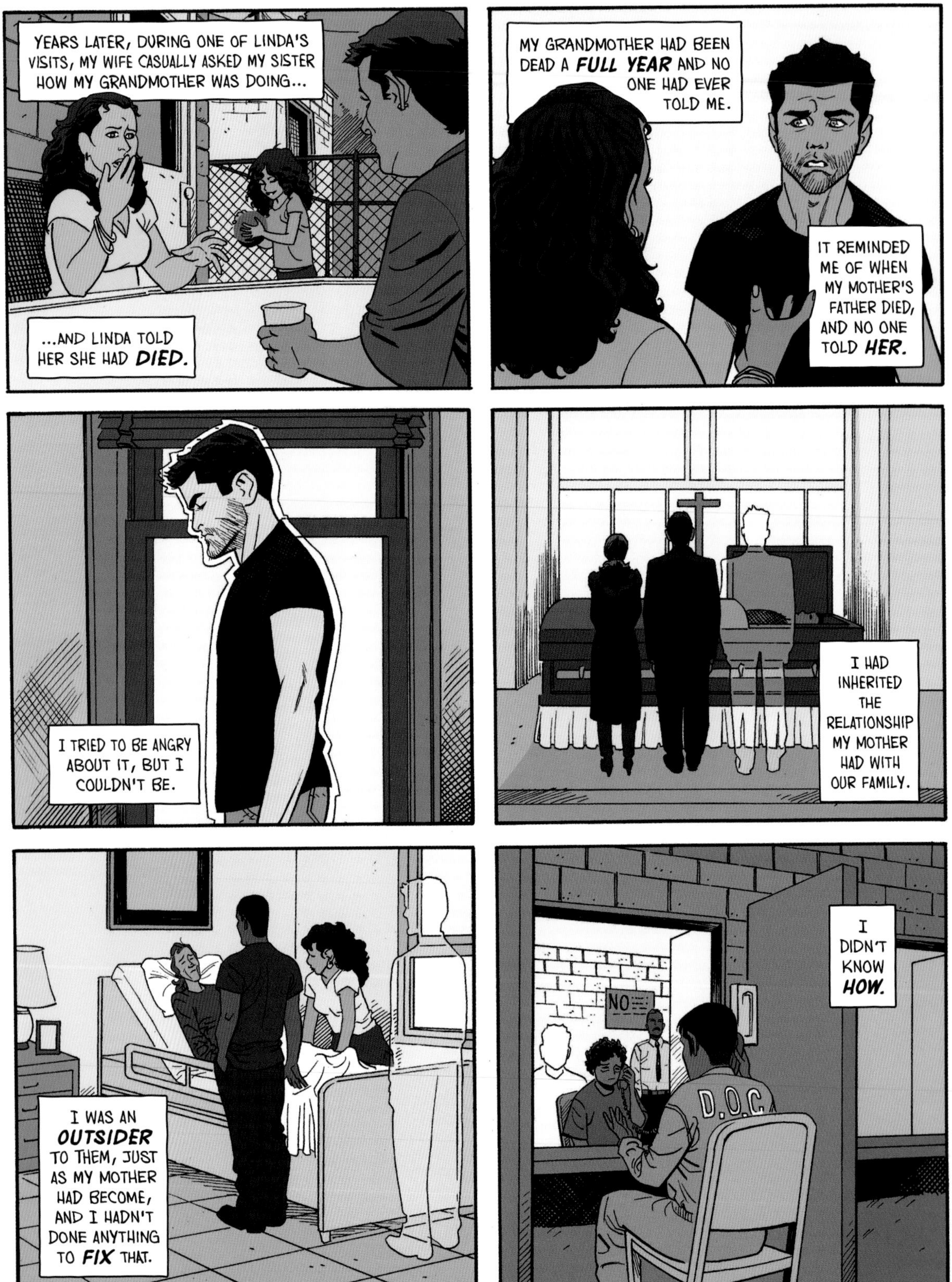
YEARS LATER, DURING ONE OF LINDA'S VISITS, MY WIFE CASUALLY ASKED MY SISTER HOW MY GRANDMOTHER WAS DOING...
...AND LINDA TOLD HER SHE HAD DIED.
MY GRANDMOTHER HAD BEEN DEAD A FULL YEAR AND NO ONE HAD EVER TOLD ME.
IT REMINDED ME OF WHEN MY MOTHER'S FATHER DIED, AND NO ONE TOLD HER.
I TRIED TO BE ANGRY ABOUT IT, BUT I COULDN'T BE.
I HAD INHERITED THE RELATIONSHIP MY MOTHER HAD WITH OUR FAMILY.
I WAS AN OUTSIDER TO THEM, JUST AS MY MOTHER HAD BECOME, AND I HADN'T DONE ANYTHING TO FIX THAT.
I DIDN'T KNOW HOW.
NO
D.O.C.

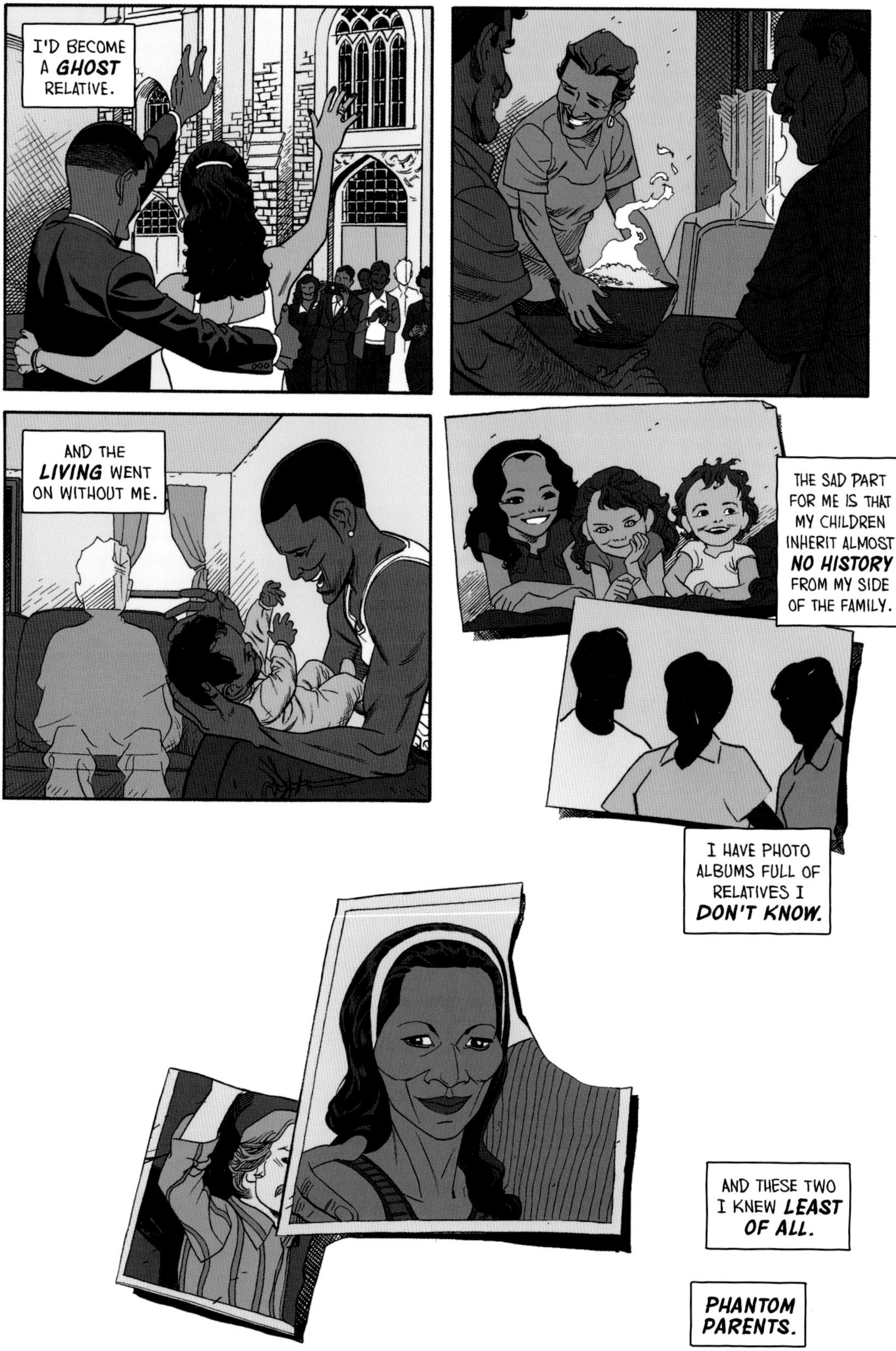
I'D BECOME A GHOST RELATIVE.
AND THE LIVING WENT ON WITHOUT ME.
THE SAD PART FOR ME IS THAT MY CHILDREN INHERIT ALMOST NO HISTORY FROM MY SIDE OF THE FAMILY.
I HAVE PHOTO ALBUMS FULL OF RELATIVES I DON'T KNOW.
AND THESE TWO I KNEW LEAST OF ALL.
PHANTOM PARENTS.

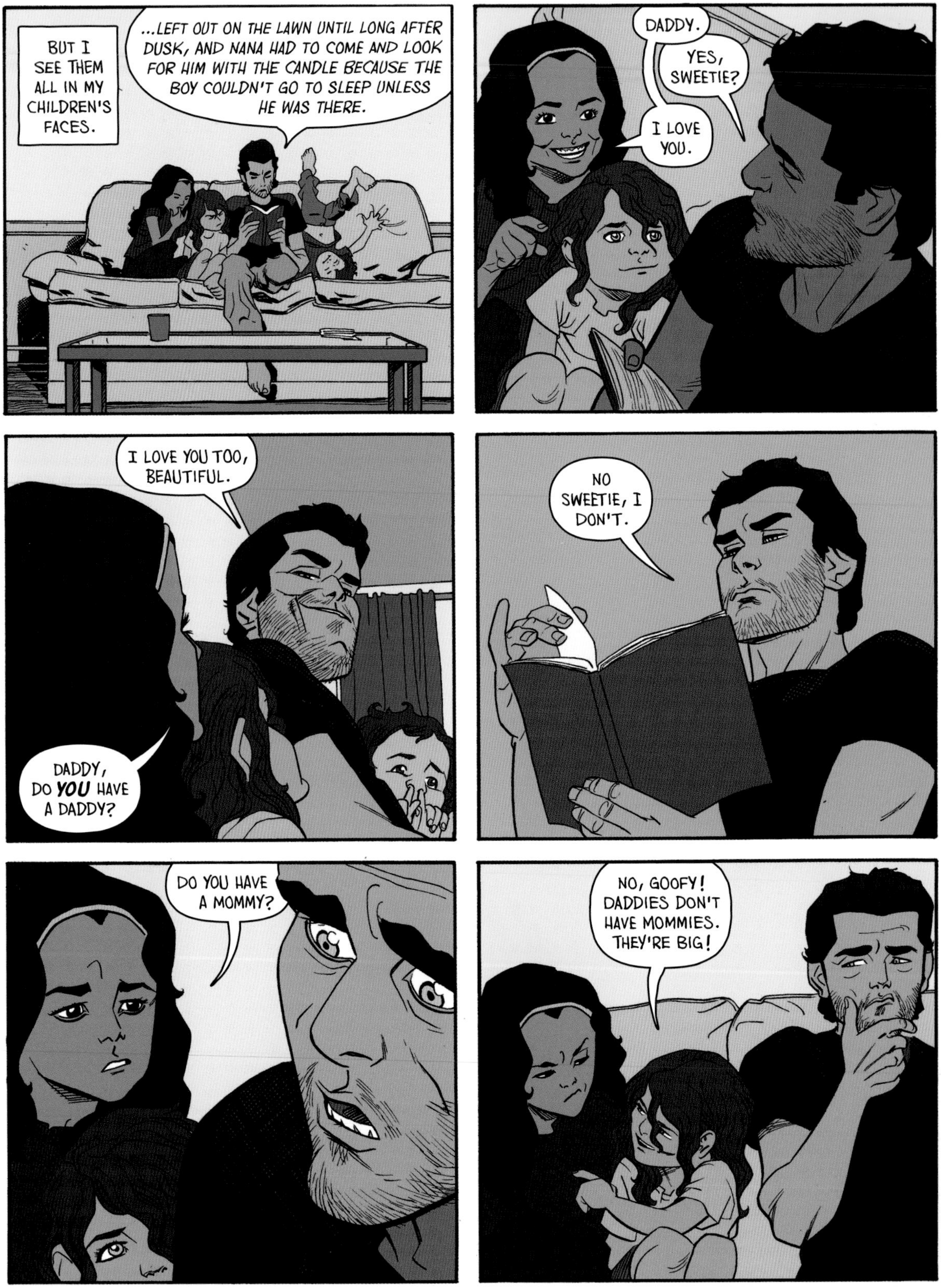
BUT I SEE THEM ALL IN MY CHILDREN'S FACES.
...LEFT OUT ON THE LAWN UNTIL LONG AFTER DUSK, AND NANA HAD TO COME AND LOOK FOR HIM WITH THE CANDLE BECAUSE THE BOY COULDN'T GO TO SLEEP UNLESS HE WAS THERE.
DADDY.
YES, SWEETIE?
I LOVE YOU.
I LOVE YOU TOO, BEAUTIFUL.
DADDY, DO *YOU* HAVE A DADDY?
NO SWEETIE, I DON'T.
DO YOU HAVE A MOMMY?
NO, GOOFY! DADDIES DON'T HAVE MOMMIES. THEY'RE BIG!

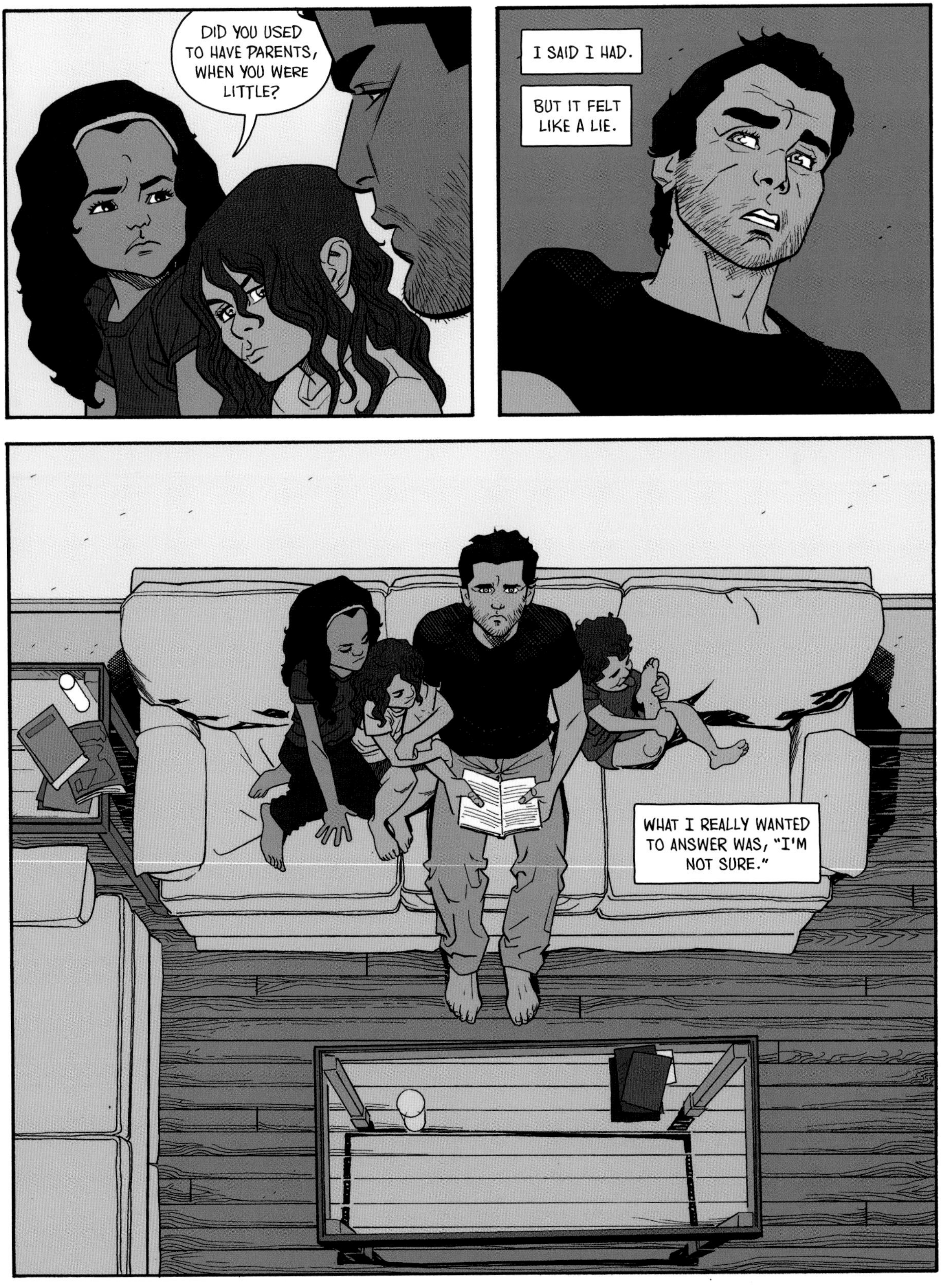
DID YOU USED TO HAVE PARENTS, WHEN YOU WERE LITTLE?
I SAID I HAD.
BUT IT FELT LIKE A LIE.
WHAT I REALLY WANTED TO ANSWER WAS, "I'M NOT SURE."

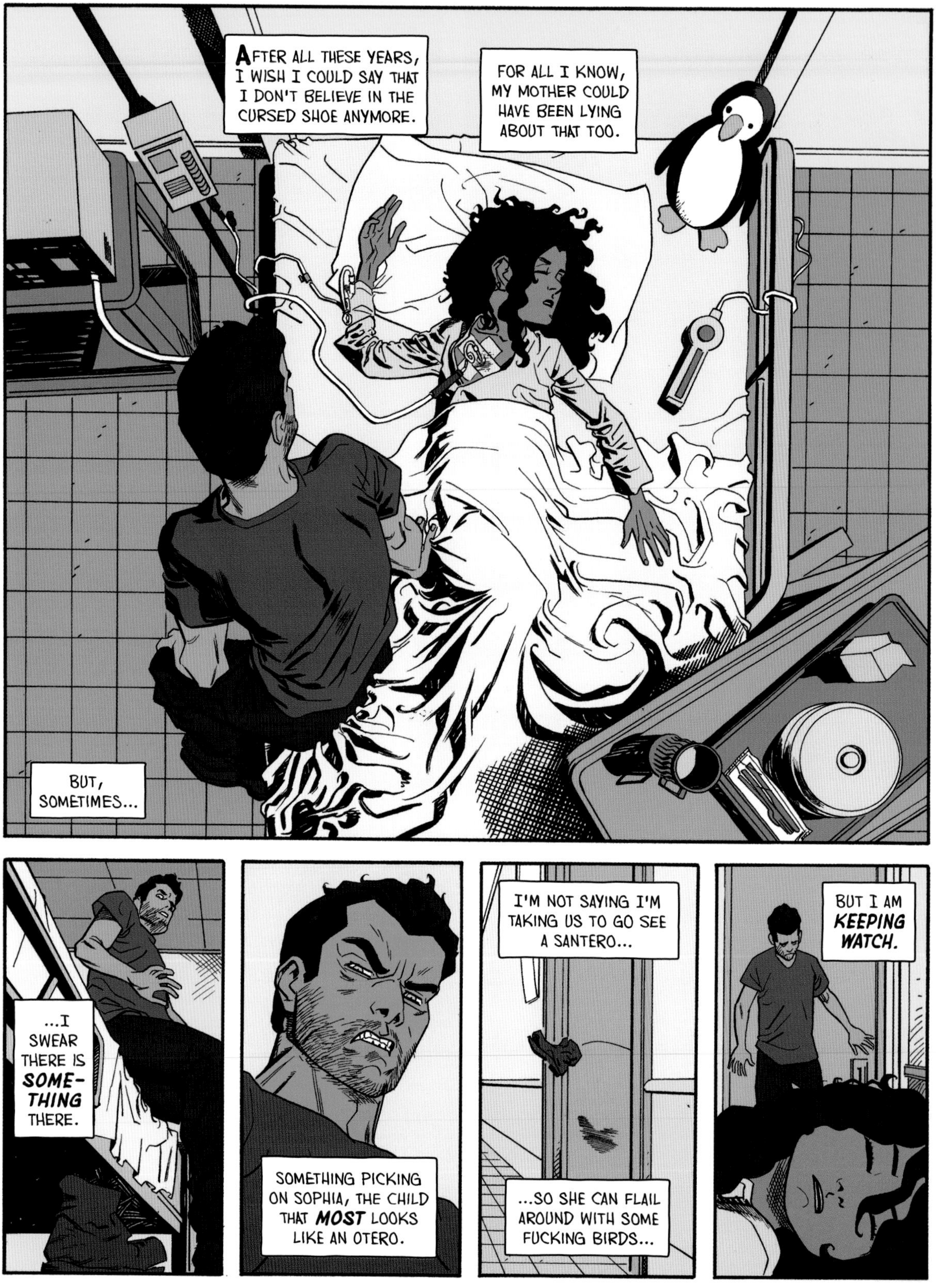
AFTER ALL THESE YEARS, I WISH I COULD SAY THAT I DON'T BELIEVE IN THE CURSED SHOE ANYMORE.
FOR ALL I KNOW, MY MOTHER COULD HAVE BEEN LYING ABOUT THAT TOO.
BUT, SOMETIMES...
...I SWEAR THERE IS SOME-THING THERE.
SOMETHING PICKING ON SOPHIA, THE CHILD THAT MOST LOOKS LIKE AN OTERO.
I'M NOT SAYING I'M TAKING US TO GO SEE A SANTERO...
...SO SHE CAN FLAIL AROUND WITH SOME FUCKING BIRDS...
BUT I AM KEEPING WATCH.

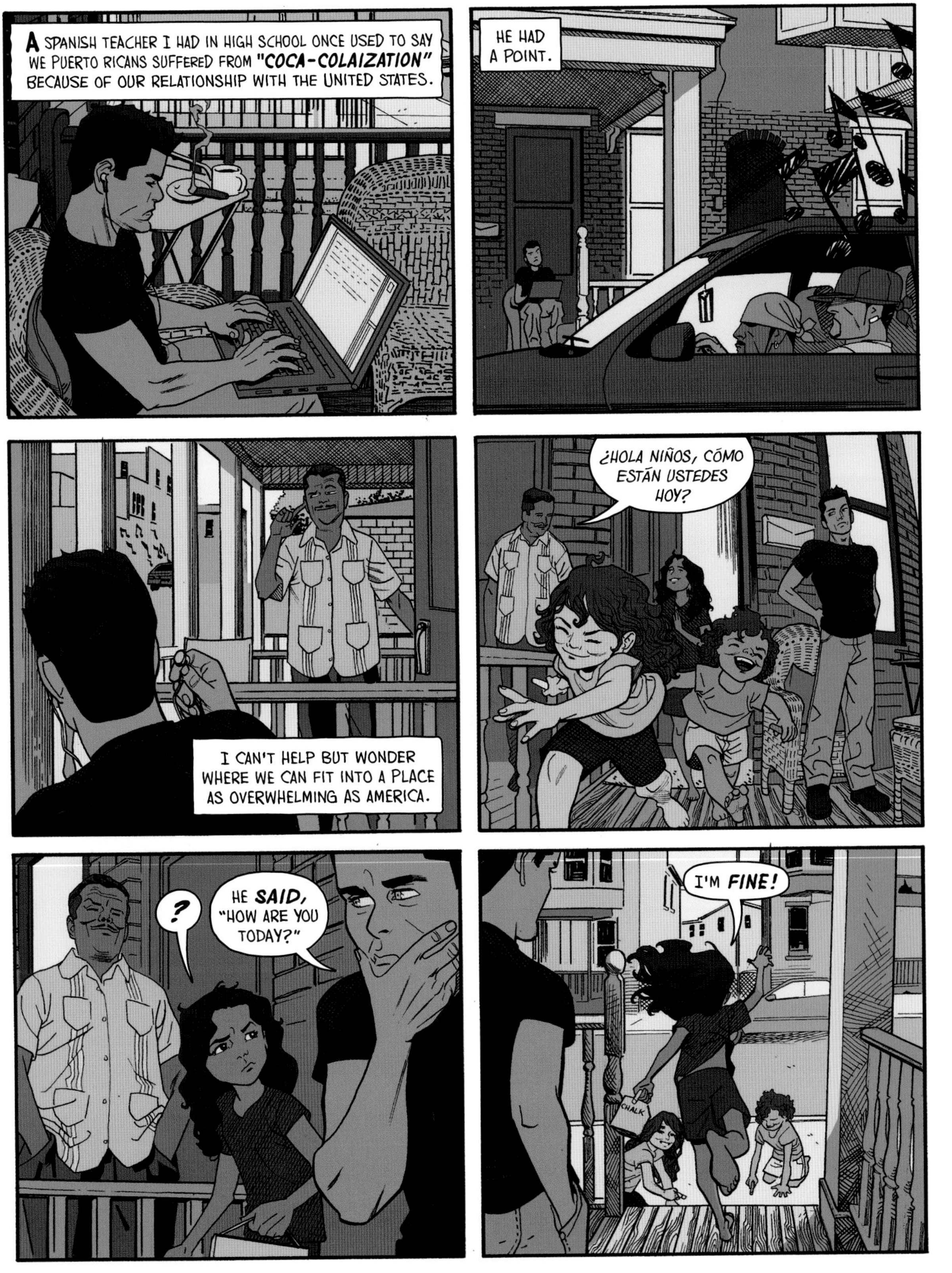
A SPANISH TEACHER I HAD IN HIGH SCHOOL ONCE USED TO SAY WE PUERTO RICANS SUFFERED FROM **"COCA-COLAIZATION"** BECAUSE OF OUR RELATIONSHIP WITH THE UNITED STATES.
HE HAD A POINT.
I CAN'T HELP BUT WONDER WHERE WE CAN FIT INTO A PLACE AS OVERWHELMING AS AMERICA.
¿HOLA NIÑOS, CÓMO ESTÁN USTEDES HOY?
?
HE **SAID,** "HOW ARE YOU TODAY?"
I'M **FINE!**
CHALK

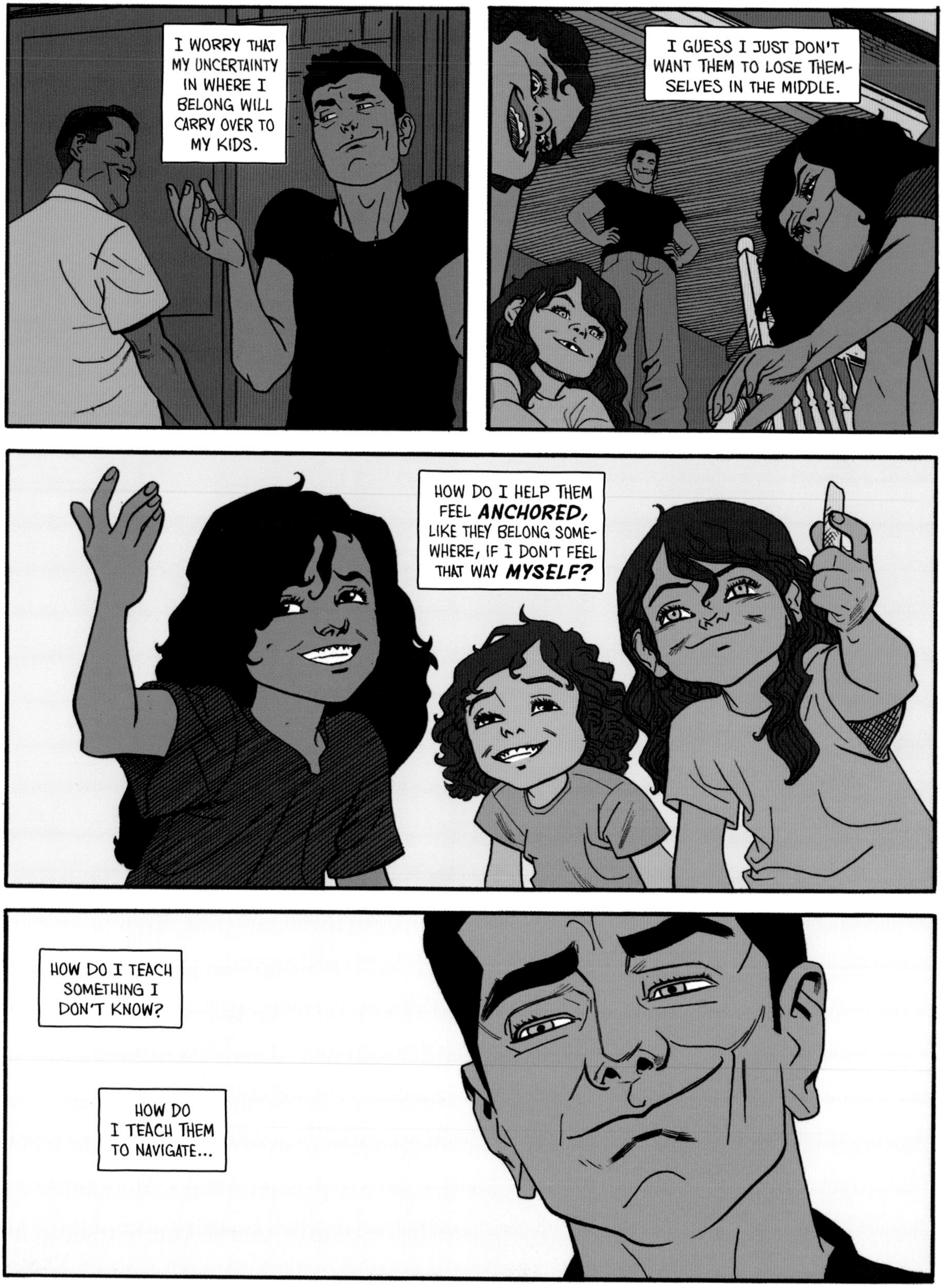
I WORRY THAT MY UNCERTAINTY IN WHERE I BELONG WILL CARRY OVER TO MY KIDS.
I GUESS I JUST DON'T WANT THEM TO LOSE THEMSELVES IN THE MIDDLE.
HOW DO I HELP THEM FEEL ANCHORED, LIKE THEY BELONG SOMEWHERE, IF I DON'T FEEL THAT WAY MYSELF?
HOW DO I TEACH SOMETHING I DON'T KNOW?
HOW DO I TEACH THEM TO NAVIGATE...

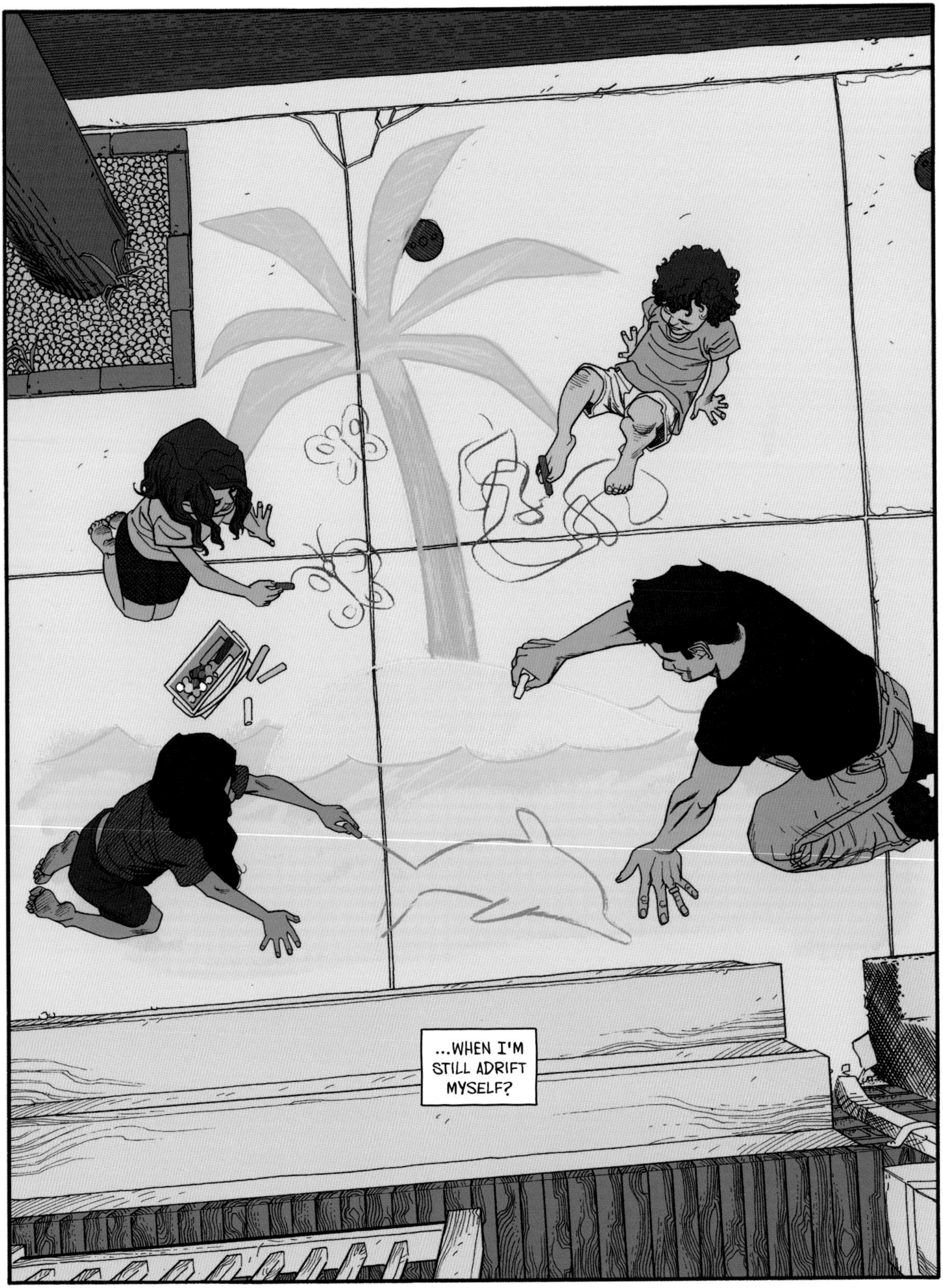
...WHEN I'M STILL ADRIFT MYSELF?

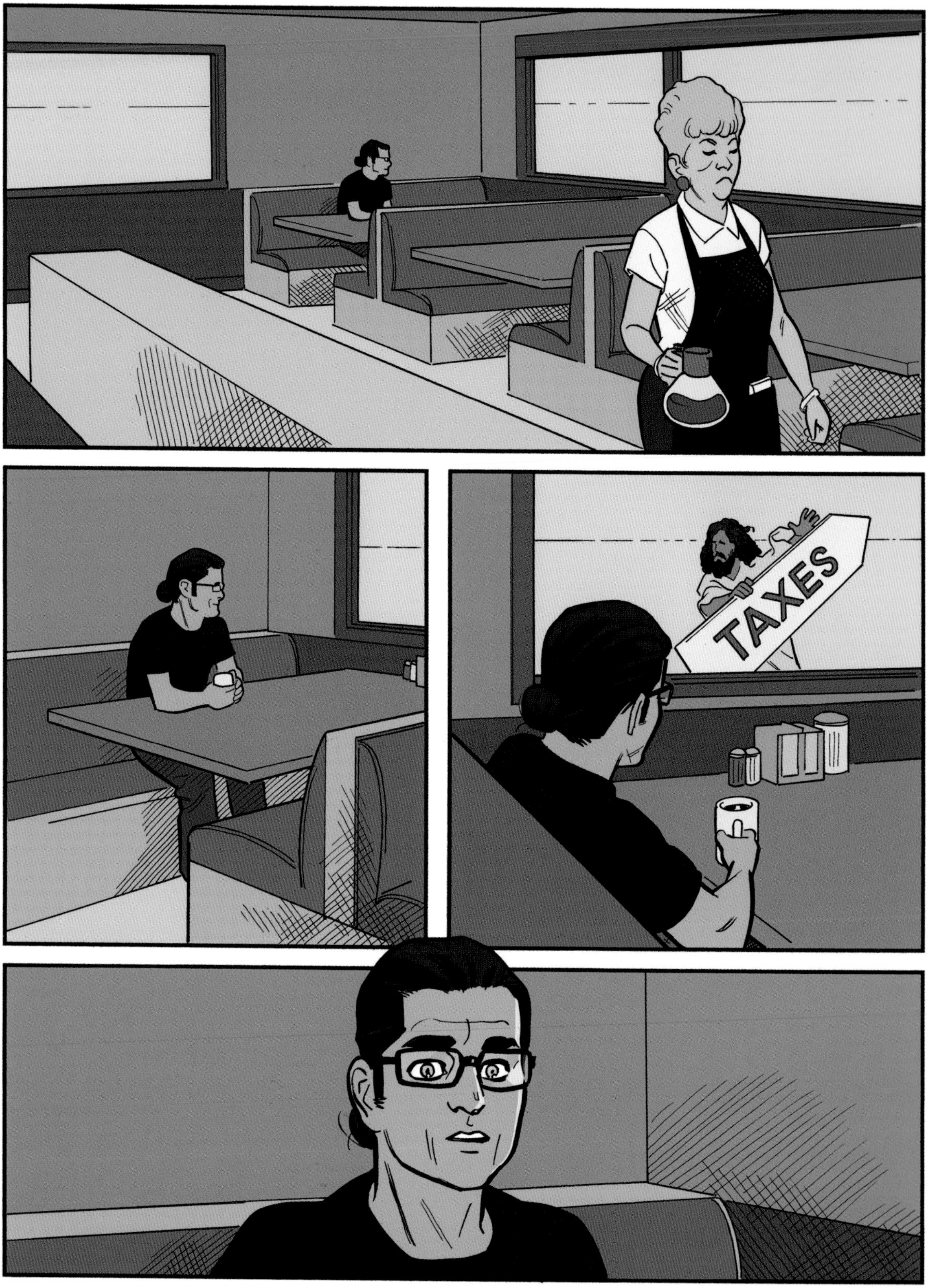
TAXES

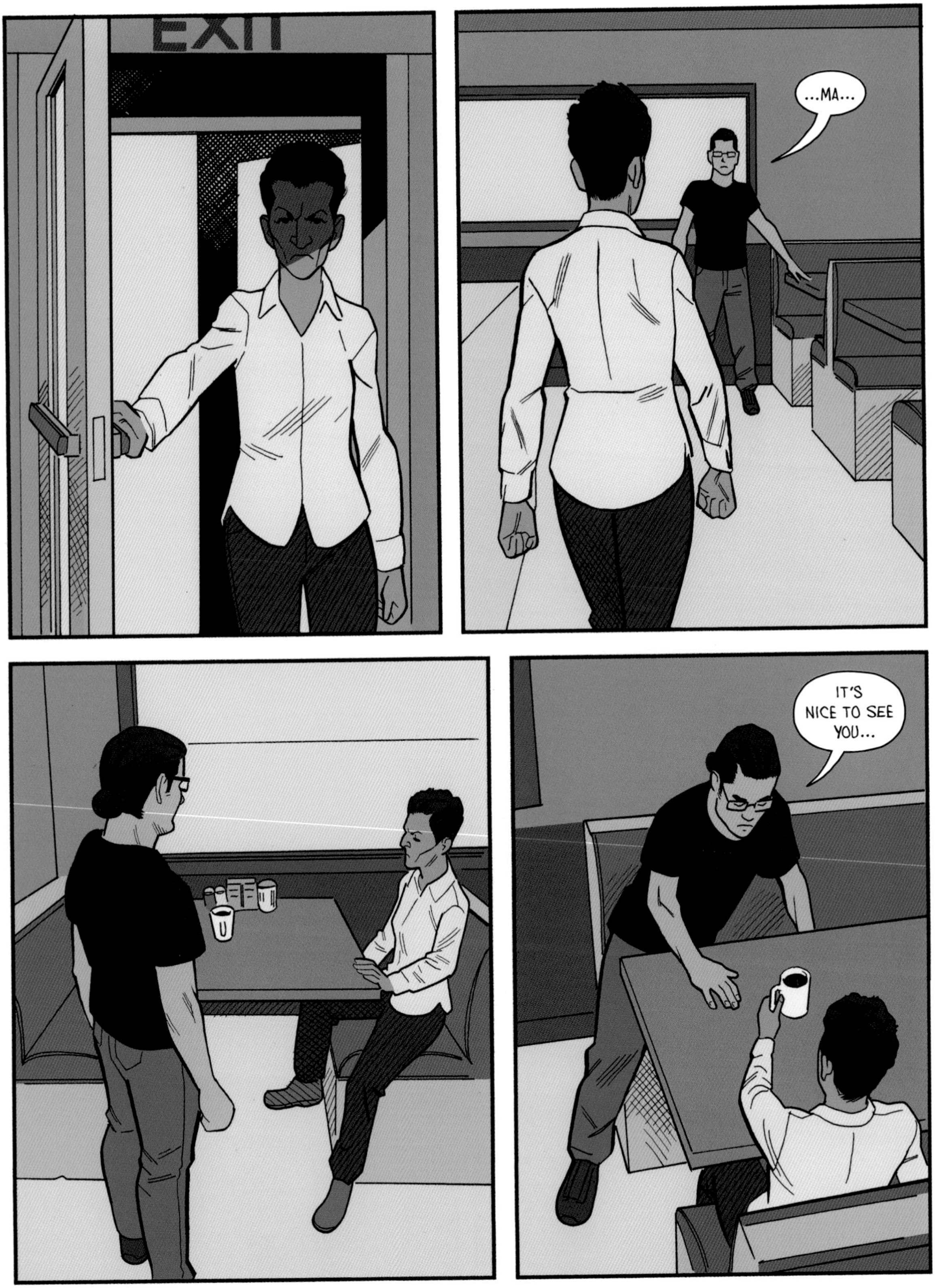
EXIT
...MA...
IT'S NICE TO SEE YOU...

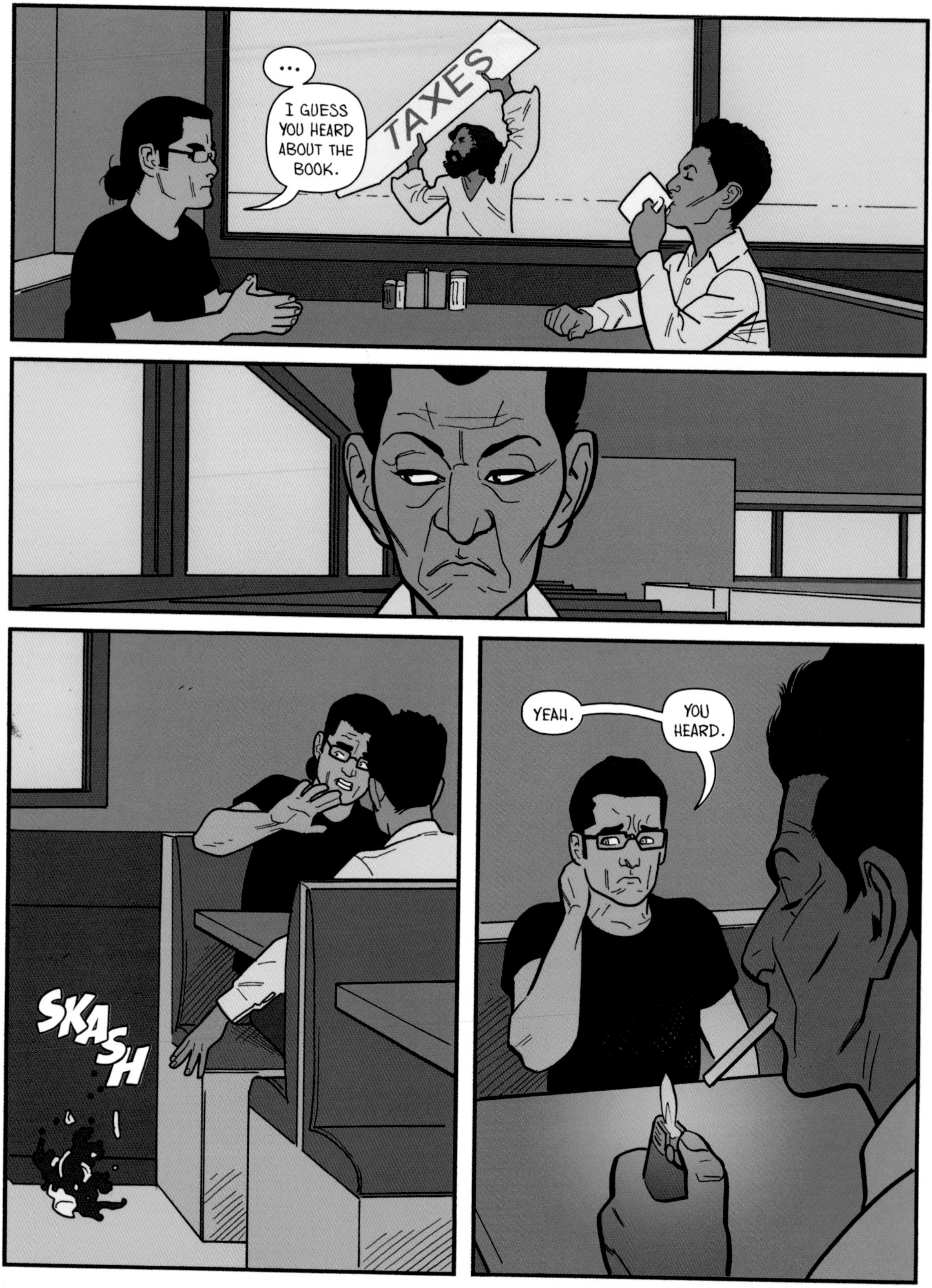
...
I GUESS YOU HEARD ABOUT THE BOOK.
TAXES
SKASH
YEAH.
YOU HEARD.

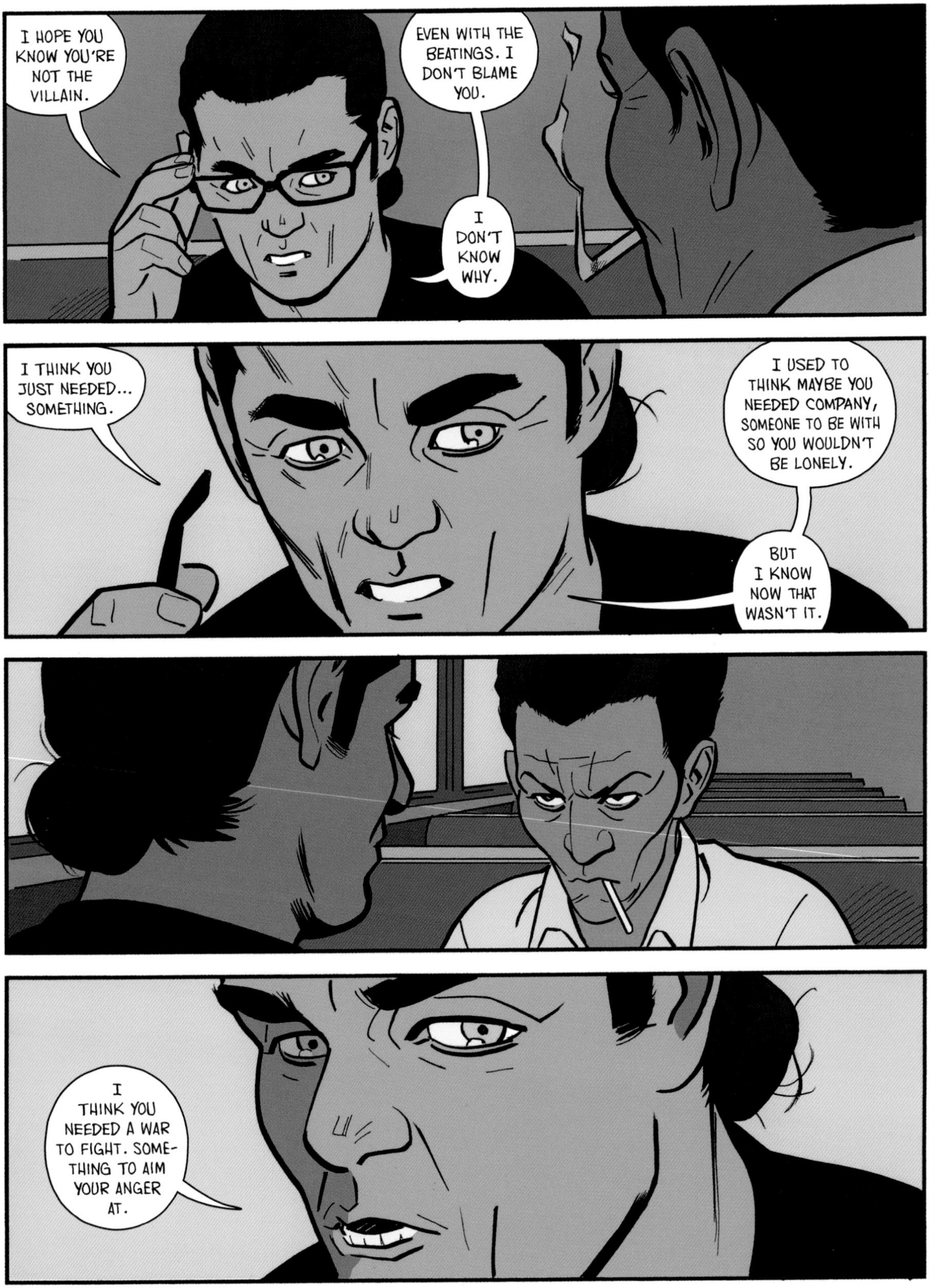
I HOPE YOU KNOW YOU'RE NOT THE VILLAIN.
EVEN WITH THE BEATINGS. I DON'T BLAME YOU.
I DON'T KNOW WHY.
I THINK YOU JUST NEEDED... SOMETHING.
I USED TO THINK MAYBE YOU NEEDED COMPANY, SOMEONE TO BE WITH SO YOU WOULDN'T BE LONELY.
BUT I KNOW NOW THAT WASN'T IT.
I THINK YOU NEEDED A WAR TO FIGHT. SOME-THING TO AIM YOUR ANGER AT.

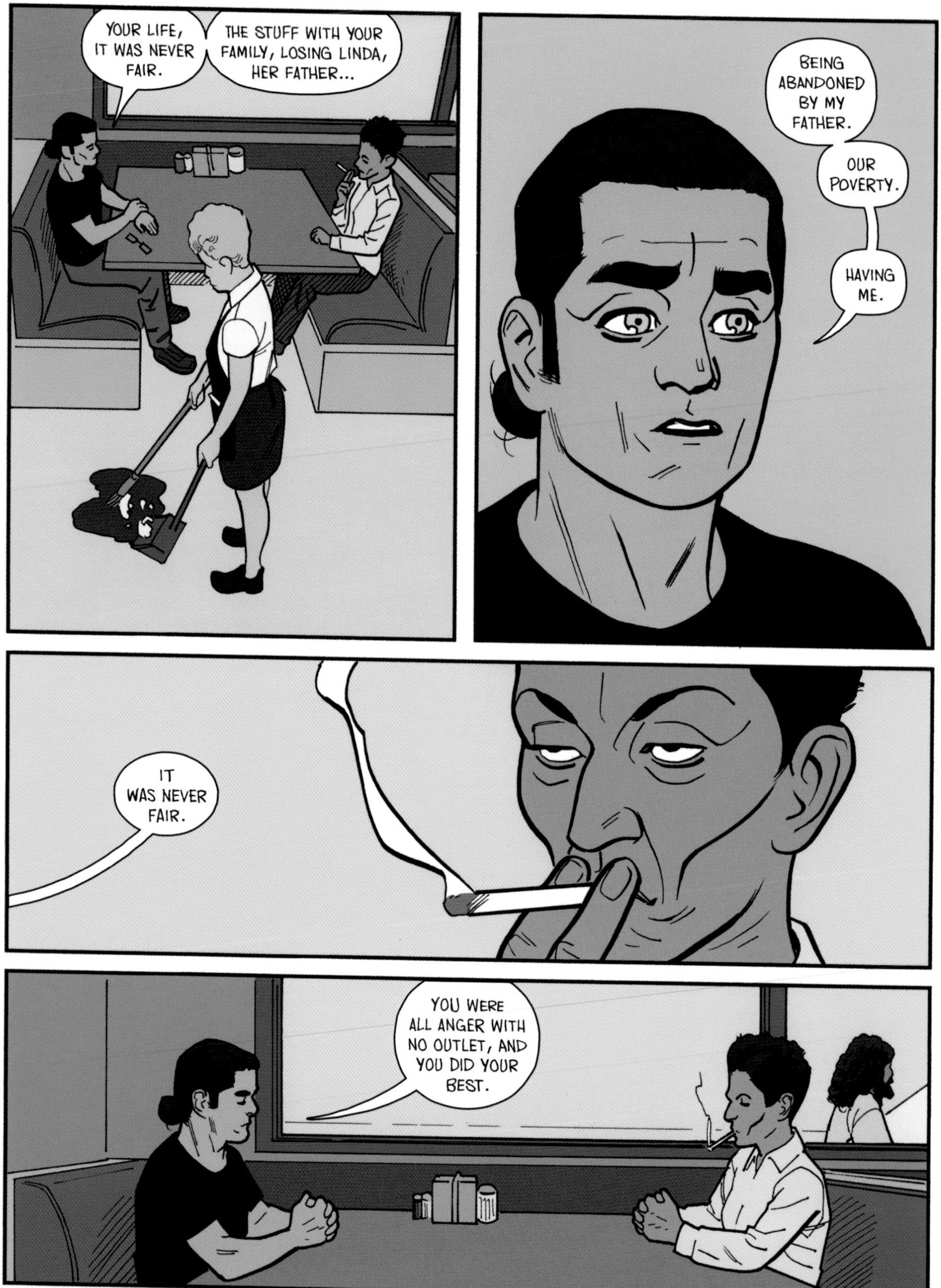
YOUR LIFE, IT WAS NEVER FAIR.
THE STUFF WITH YOUR FAMILY, LOSING LINDA, HER FATHER...
BEING ABANDONED BY MY FATHER.
OUR POVERTY.
HAVING ME.
IT WAS NEVER FAIR.
YOU WERE ALL ANGER WITH NO OUTLET, AND YOU DID YOUR BEST.

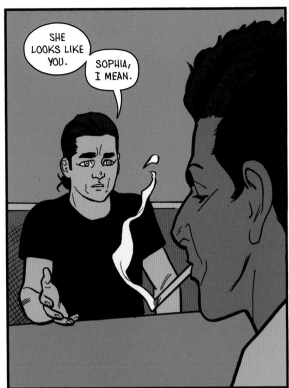

SHE LOOKS LIKE YOU.

SOPHIA, I MEAN.

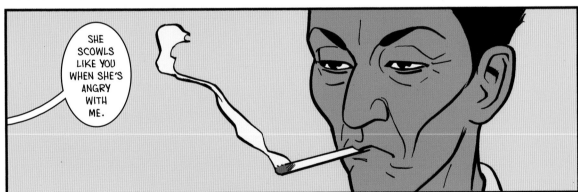

SHE SCOWLS LIKE YOU WHEN SHE'S ANGRY WITH ME.

I WISH YOU COULD HAVE MET THEM. I SEE YOU IN BOTH GIRLS, BUT YOU'RE NOT REAL TO THEM.

THEY KNOW YOU FROM ME, AND I'M NOT SURE I REALLY KNEW YOU.

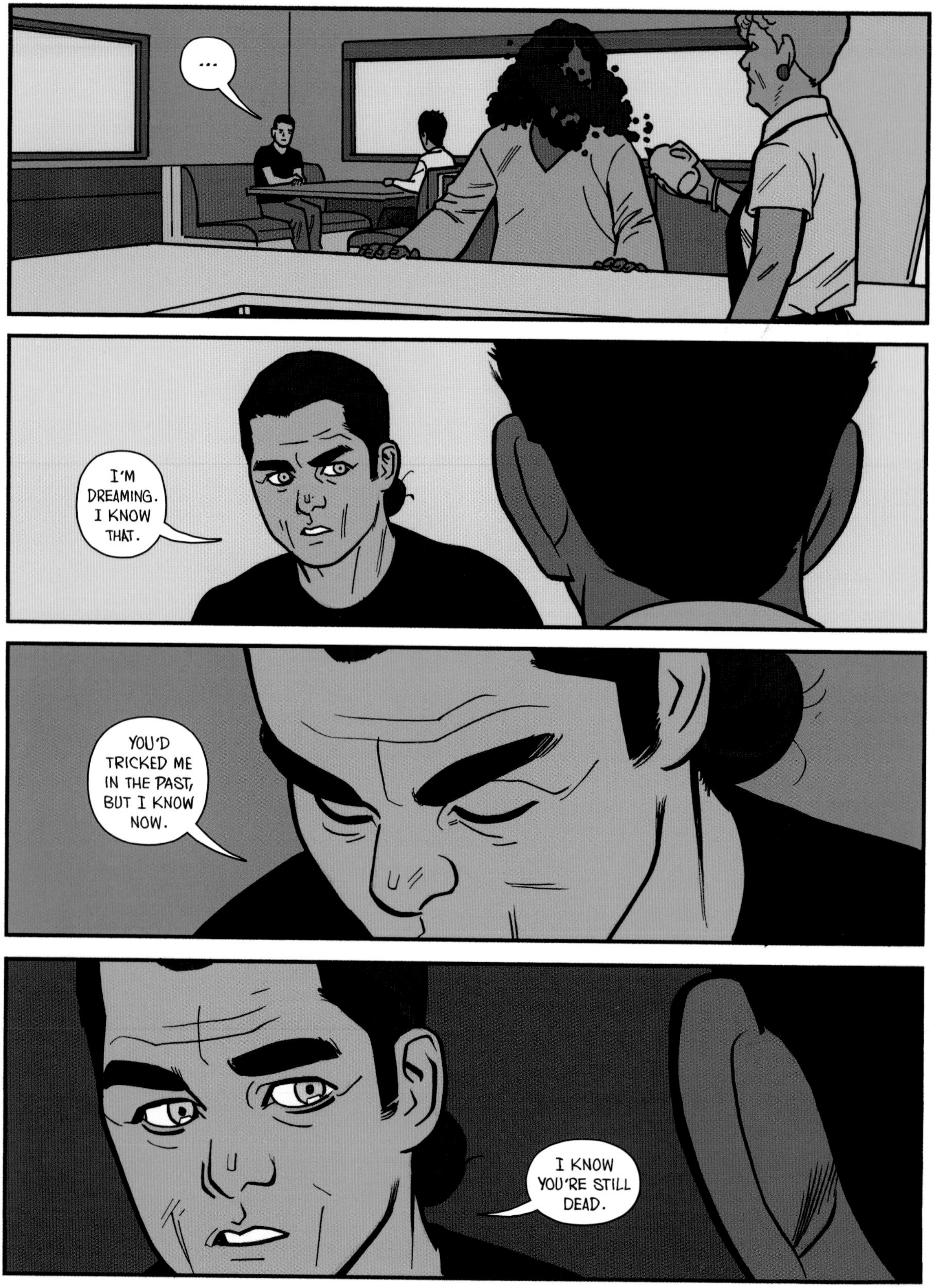
...
I'M DREAMING. I KNOW THAT.
YOU'D TRICKED ME IN THE PAST, BUT I KNOW NOW.
I KNOW YOU'RE STILL DEAD.

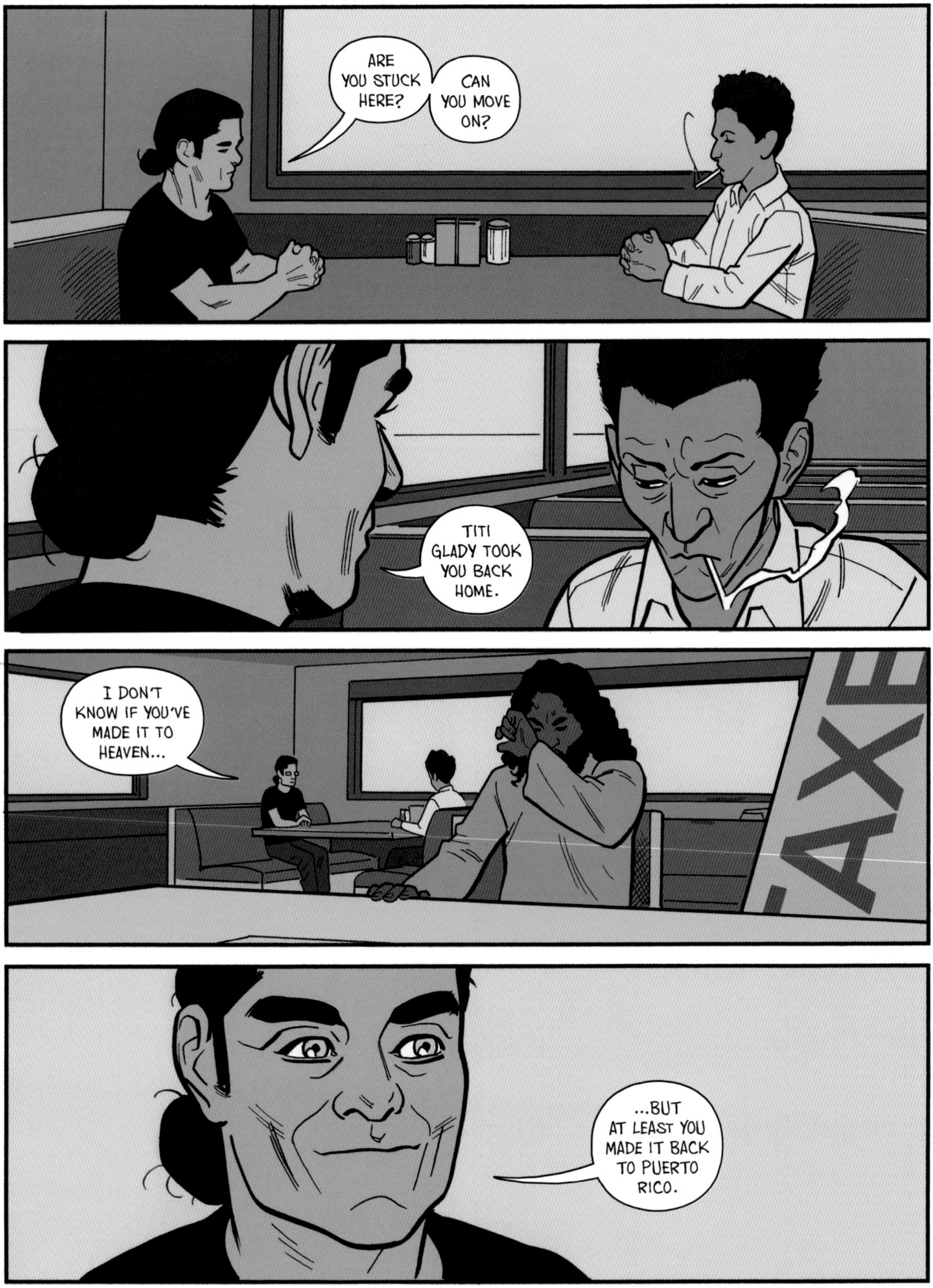
ARE YOU STUCK HERE?
CAN YOU MOVE ON?
TITI GLADY TOOK YOU BACK HOME.
I DON'T KNOW IF YOU'VE MADE IT TO HEAVEN...
AXE
...BUT AT LEAST YOU MADE IT BACK TO PUERTO RICO.

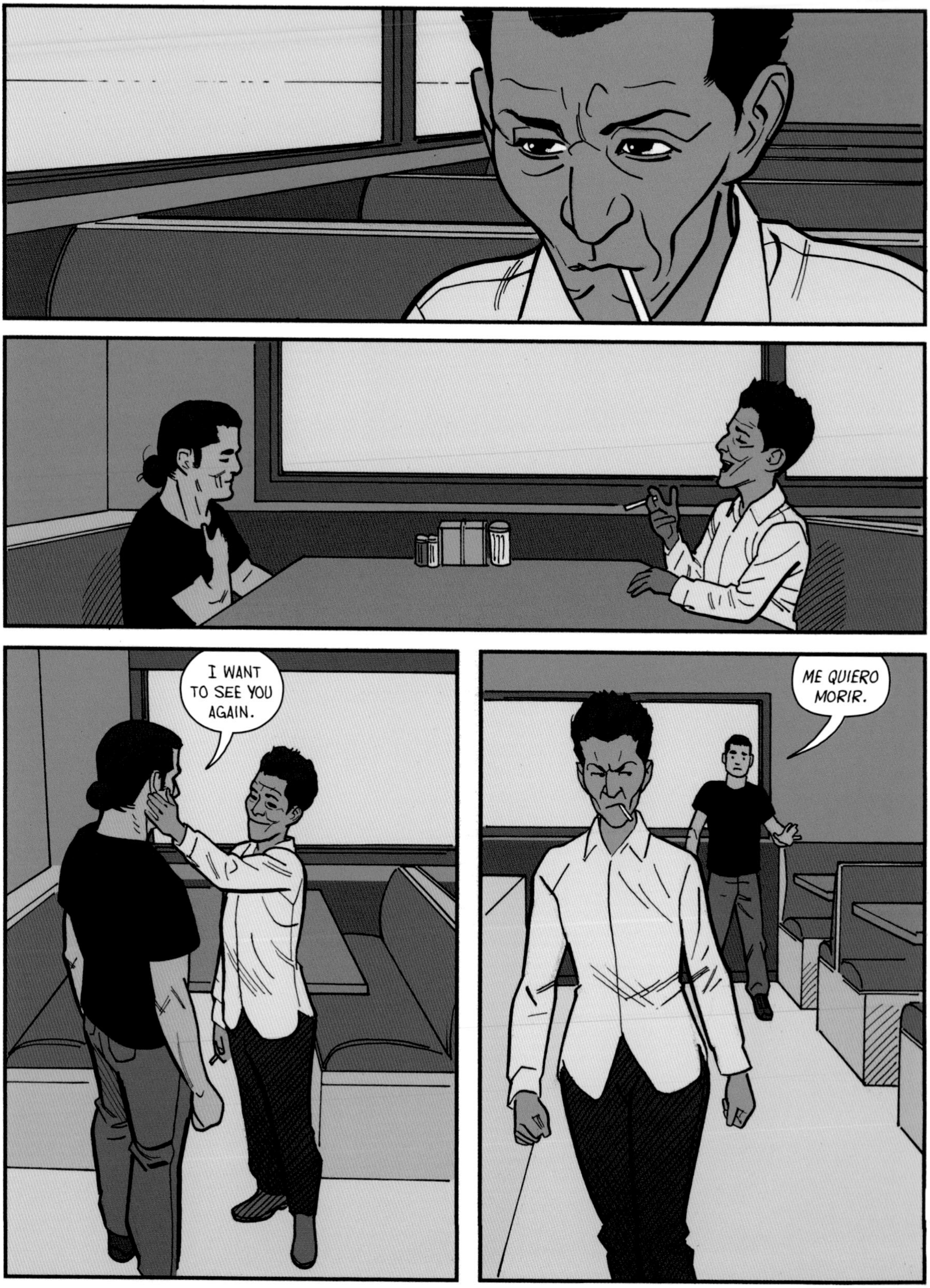
I WANT TO SEE YOU AGAIN.
ME QUIERO MORIR.

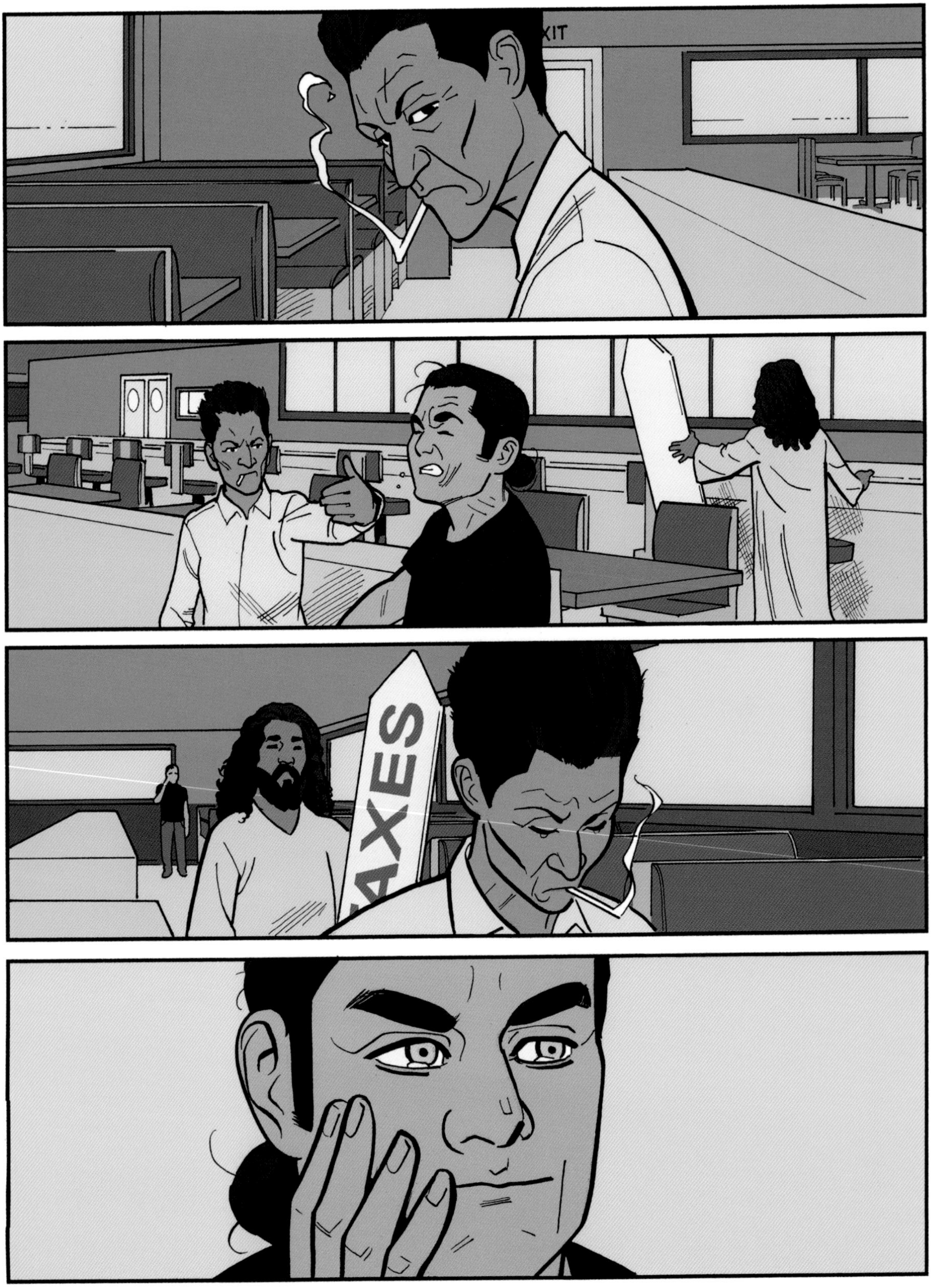
XIT
AXES

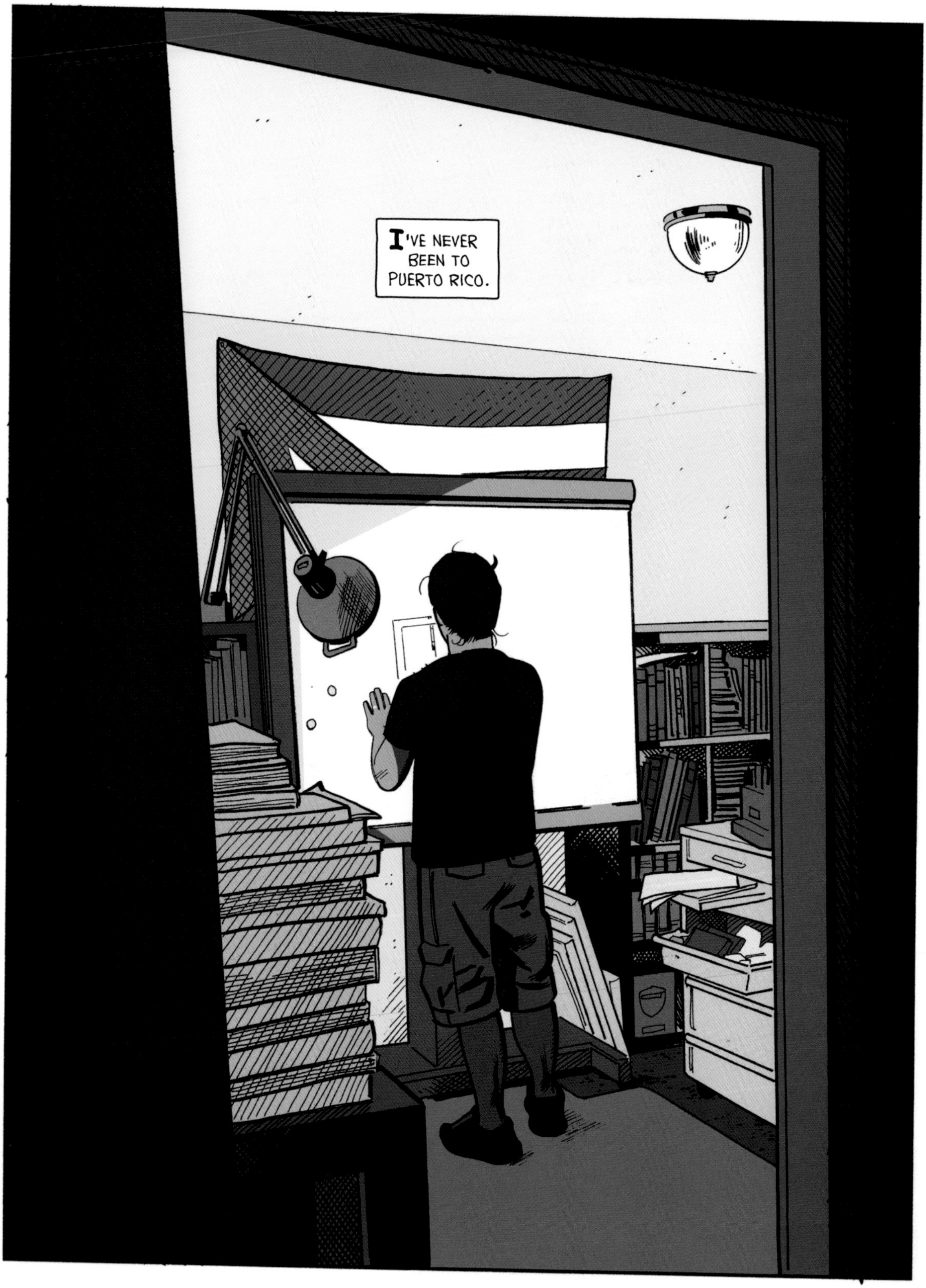
I'VE NEVER BEEN TO PUERTO RICO.

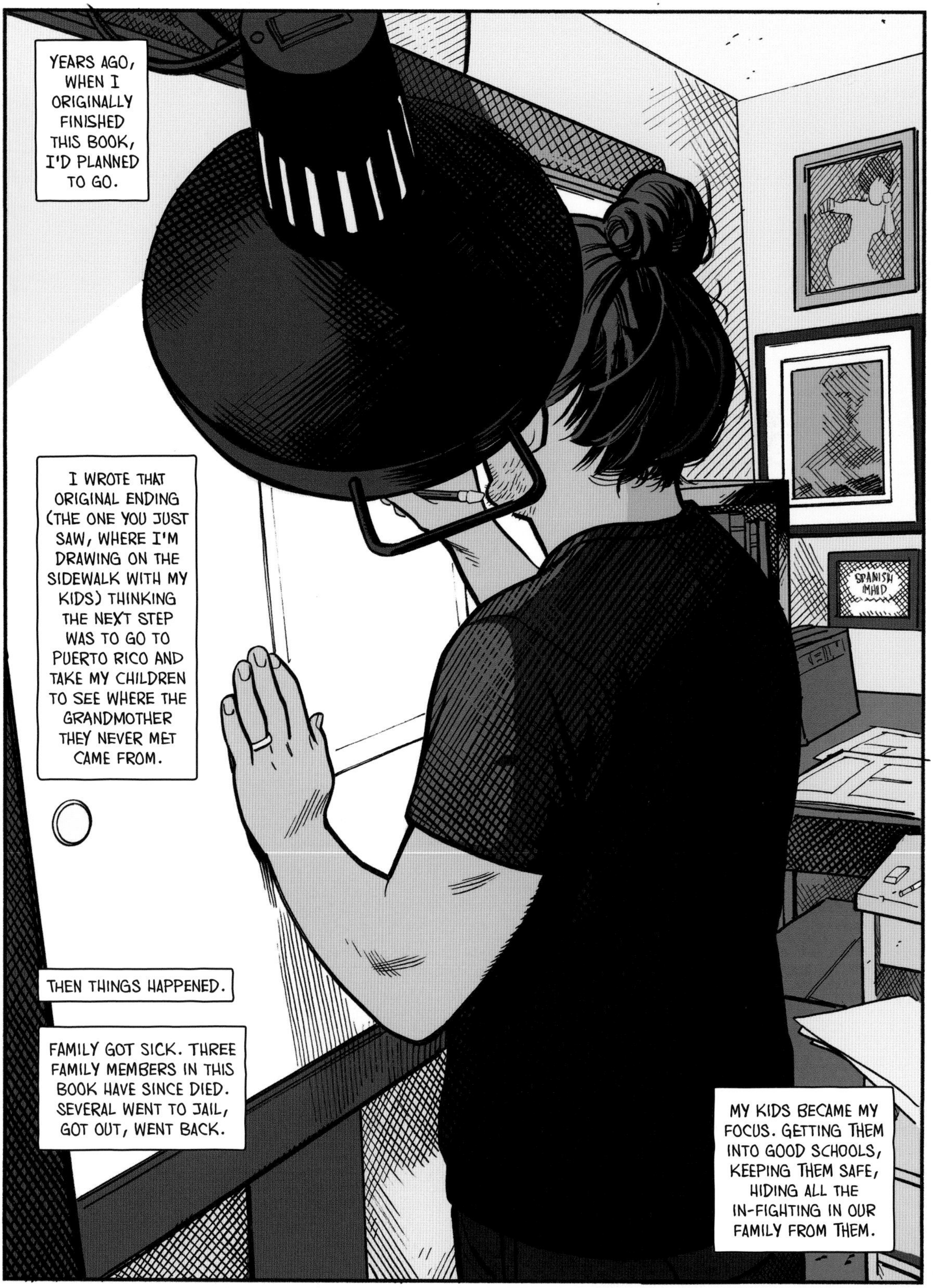
YEARS AGO, WHEN I ORIGINALLY FINISHED THIS BOOK, I'D PLANNED TO GO.
I WROTE THAT ORIGINAL ENDING (THE ONE YOU JUST SAW, WHERE I'M DRAWING ON THE SIDEWALK WITH MY KIDS) THINKING THE NEXT STEP WAS TO GO TO PUERTO RICO AND TAKE MY CHILDREN TO SEE WHERE THE GRANDMOTHER THEY NEVER MET CAME FROM.
SPANISH
THEN THINGS HAPPENED.
FAMILY GOT SICK. THREE FAMILY MEMBERS IN THIS BOOK HAVE SINCE DIED. SEVERAL WENT TO JAIL, GOT OUT, WENT BACK.
MY KIDS BECAME MY FOCUS. GETTING THEM INTO GOOD SCHOOLS, KEEPING THEM SAFE, HIDING ALL THE IN-FIGHTING IN OUR FAMILY FROM THEM.

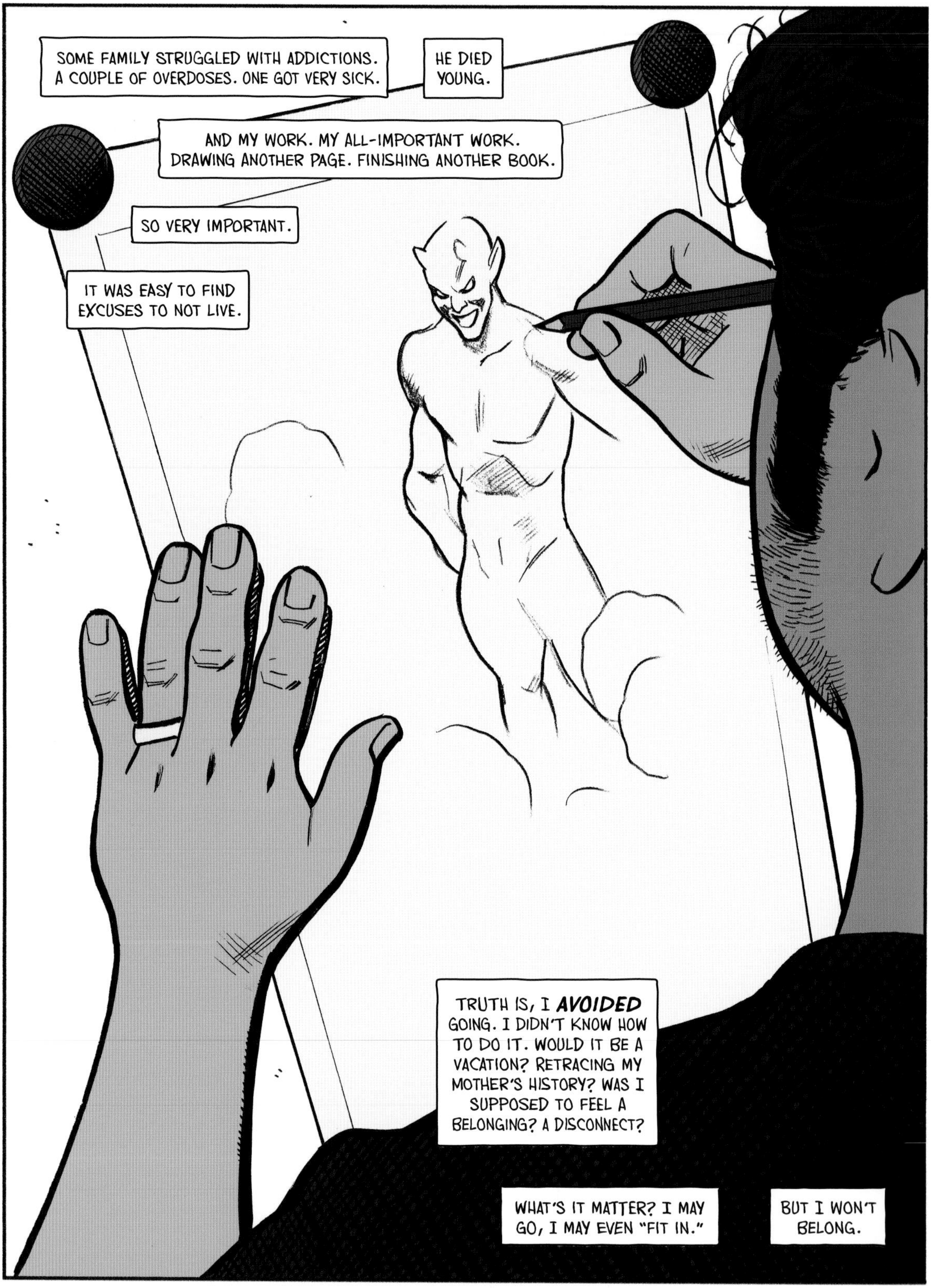
SOME FAMILY STRUGGLED WITH ADDICTIONS. A COUPLE OF OVERDOSES. ONE GOT VERY SICK.
HE DIED YOUNG.
AND MY WORK. MY ALL-IMPORTANT WORK. DRAWING ANOTHER PAGE. FINISHING ANOTHER BOOK.
SO VERY IMPORTANT.
IT WAS EASY TO FIND EXCUSES TO NOT LIVE.
TRUTH IS, I **AVOIDED** GOING. I DIDN'T KNOW HOW TO DO IT. WOULD IT BE A VACATION? RETRACING MY MOTHER'S HISTORY? WAS I SUPPOSED TO FEEL A BELONGING? A DISCONNECT?
WHAT'S IT MATTER? I MAY GO, I MAY EVEN "FIT IN."
BUT I WON'T BELONG.

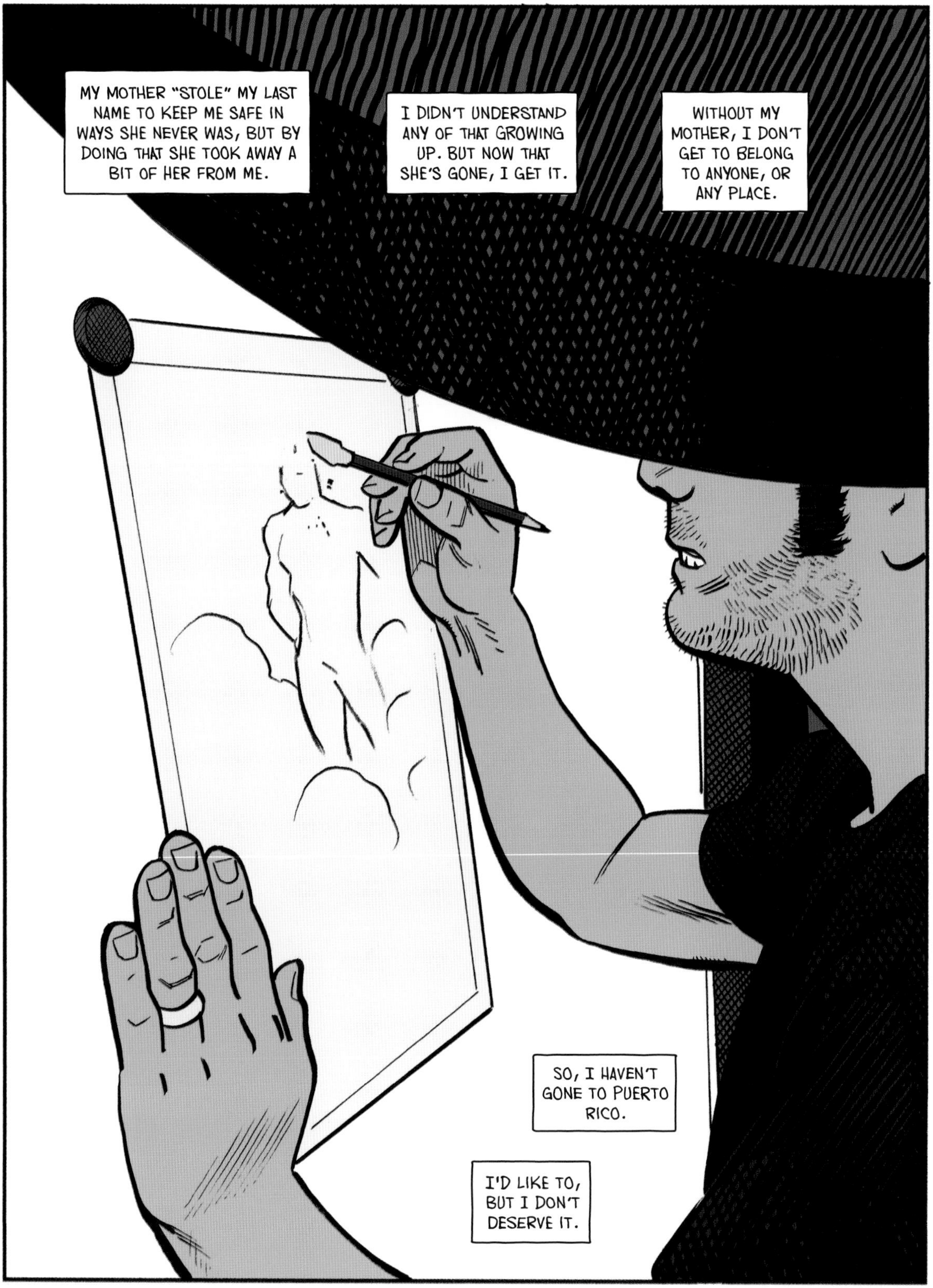
MY MOTHER "STOLE" MY LAST NAME TO KEEP ME SAFE IN WAYS SHE NEVER WAS, BUT BY DOING THAT SHE TOOK AWAY A BIT OF HER FROM ME.
I DIDN'T UNDERSTAND ANY OF THAT GROWING UP. BUT NOW THAT SHE'S GONE, I GET IT.
WITHOUT MY MOTHER, I DON'T GET TO BELONG TO ANYONE, OR ANY PLACE.
SO, I HAVEN'T GONE TO PUERTO RICO.
I'D LIKE TO, BUT I DON'T DESERVE IT.

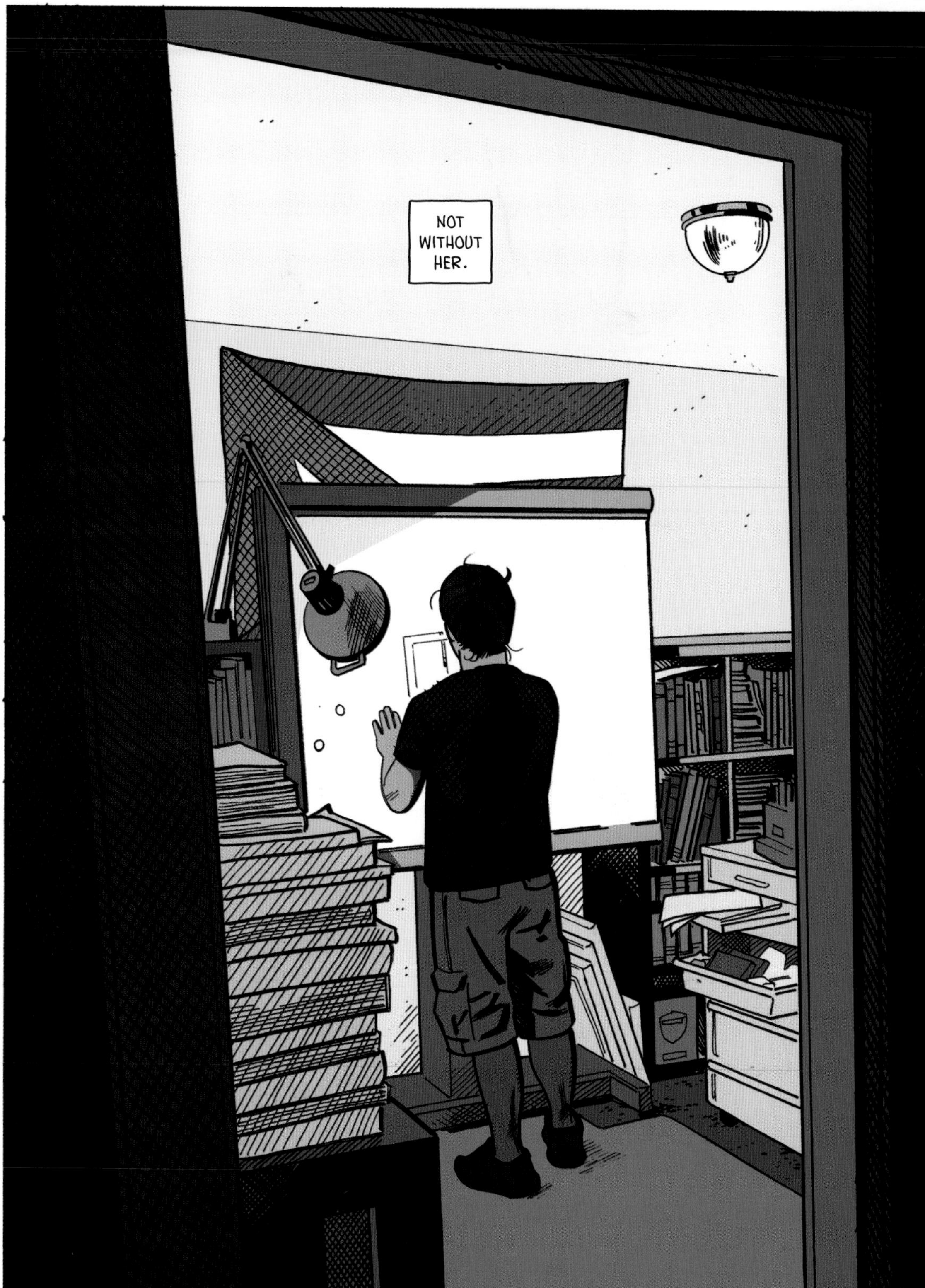
NOT WITHOUT HER.

WHILE IN THE THICK OF MAKING THIS BOOK, I WAS CONSTANTLY WORRIED ABOUT GIVING EACH PERSON DEPTH AND NUANCE. I DID MY BEST...BUT I CAN'T SHAKE THE FEELING THAT AS A READER, YOU MAY COME AWAY THINKING OF FOLKS IN THE STORY AS "GOOD" OR "BAD."

PARTICULARLY WITH BLANCA. SHE COULD BE ABUSIVE, I UNDERSTAND THAT. BUT, THINK SHE'S THE VILLAIN? READ THE BOOK AGAIN, ONLY THIS TIME, SEE IT THROUGH HER EYES.

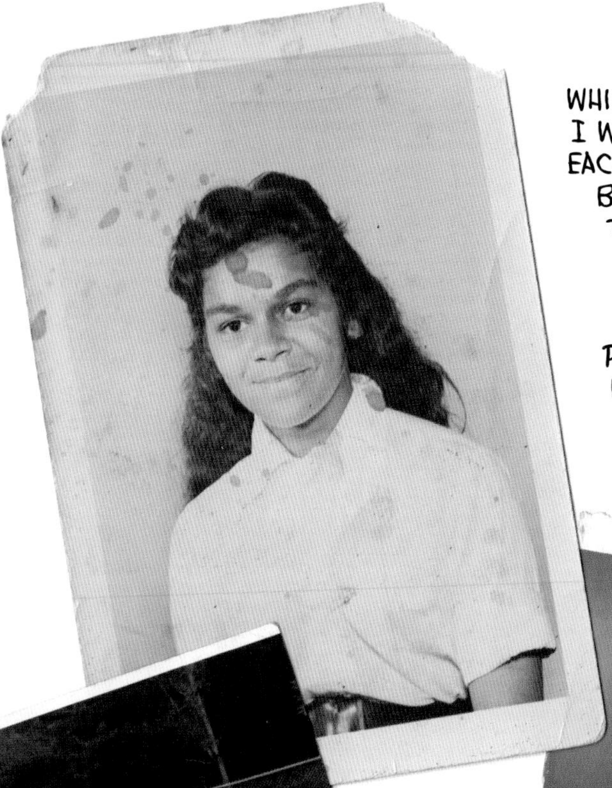

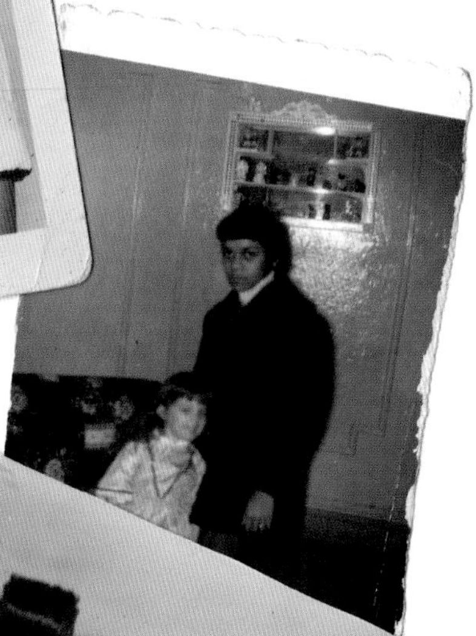

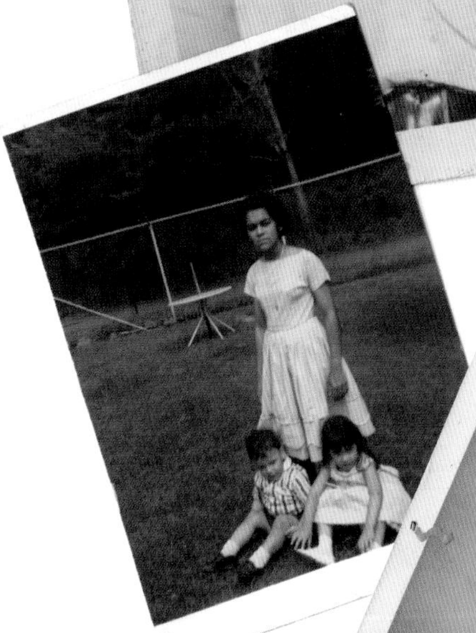

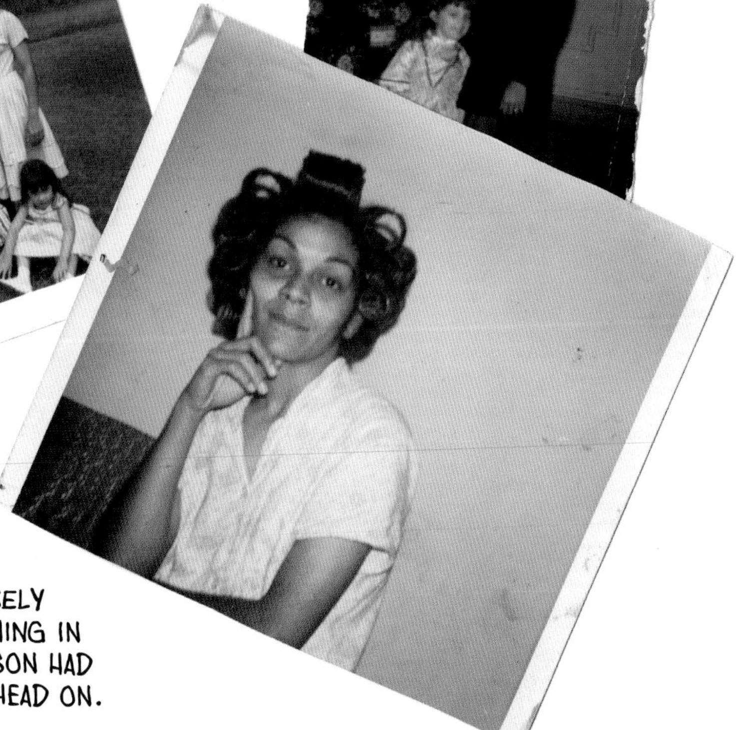

THE CHAPTER WHERE WE WERE HOMELESS? YEAH, READ IT AGAIN.

THAT IS AN INTENSELY PROUD WOMAN CASHING IN HER PRIDE SO HER SON HAD A BED TO REST HIS HEAD ON.

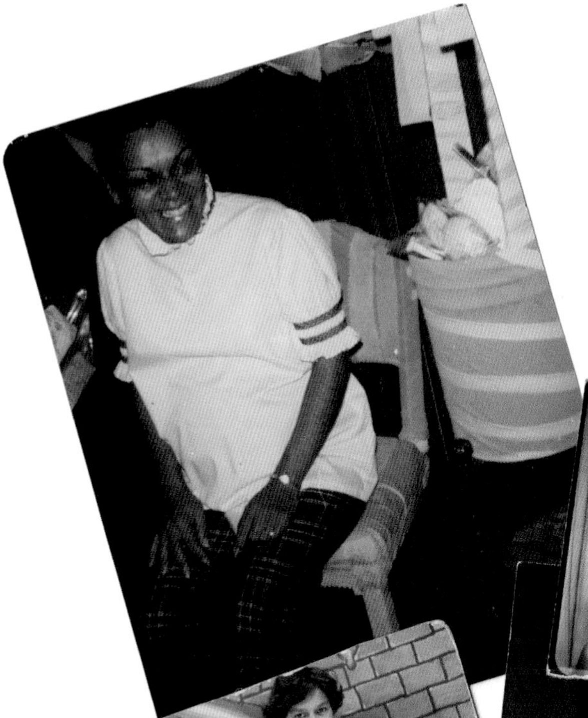

THE CHAPTER WHERE SHE BEAT MY ASS?

IT'S WRONG, I KNOW, I KNOW.

BUT SHE WAS ALONE RAISING A BOY IN THE '80s, WHEN BOYS LIKE ME ENDED UP IN JAIL EVERY DAY.

SHE'D ONLY KNOWN FORCE. IT'S HOW YOU KEPT PEOPLE IN LINE, IN HER MIND.

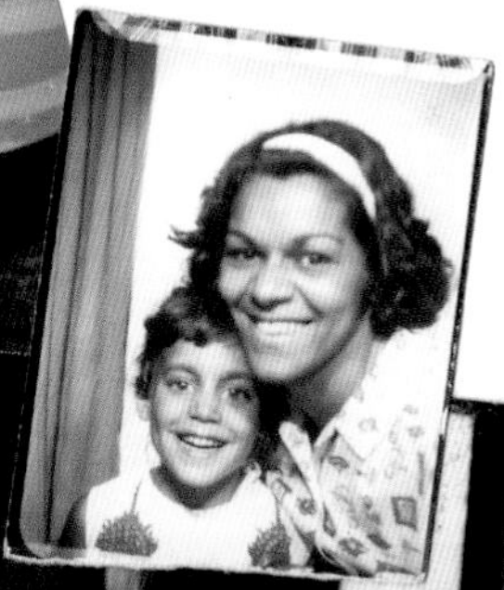

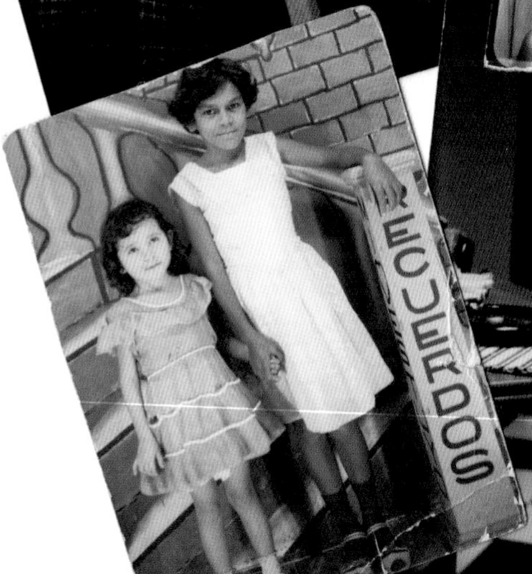
RECUERDOS

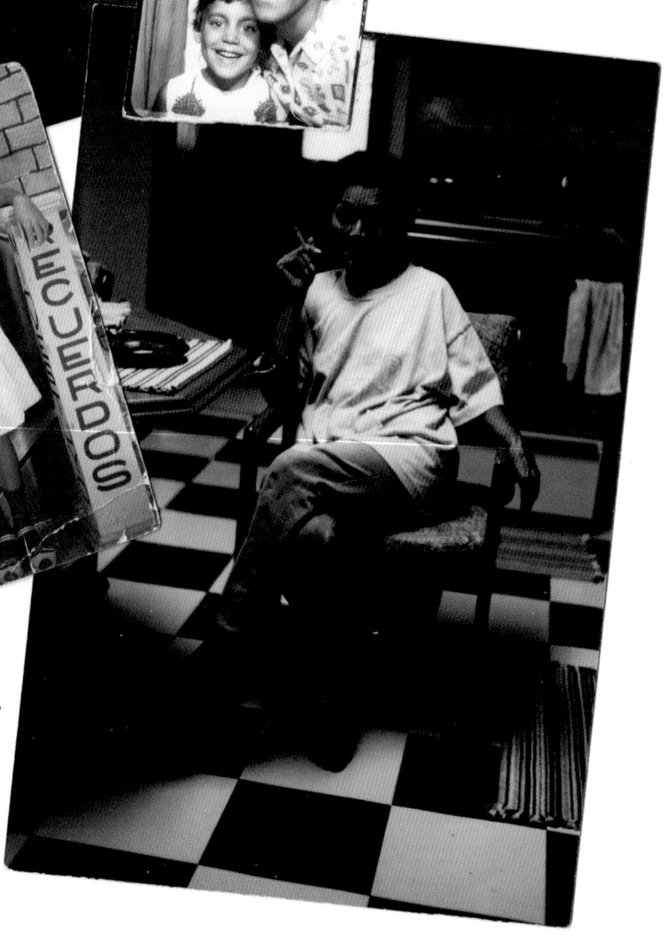

SHE BEAT ME INTO SUBMISSION.

I KNOW THAT.

AND MAYBE YOU'LL SAY I'M RATIONALIZING HER BEHAVIOR, BUT I PRAY YOU SEE HER STRUGGLE.

THAT CHAPTER WHERE SHE SOLD DRUGS?

OKAY. OKAY. IT'S BAD, I KNOW.

BUT I WAS ALWAYS FED.

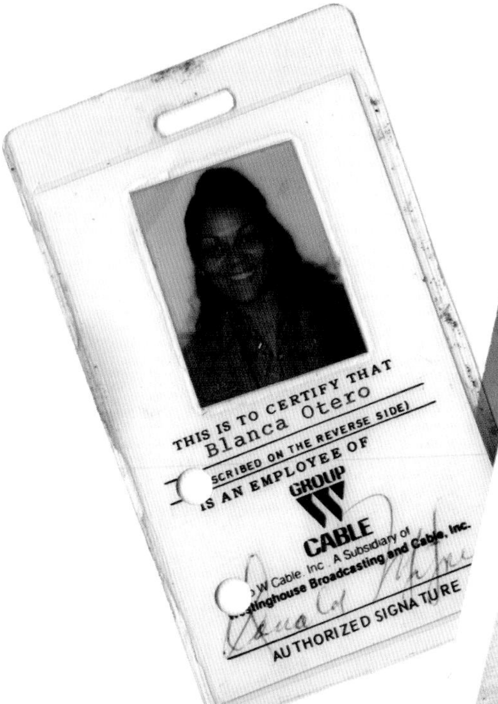
THIS IS TO CERTIFY THAT
Blanca Otero
SCRIBED ON THE REVERSE SIDE)
IS AN EMPLOYEE OF
GROUP W CABLE
W Cable, Inc. A Subsidiary of
Westinghouse Broadcasting and Cable, Inc.
AUTHORIZED SIGNATURE

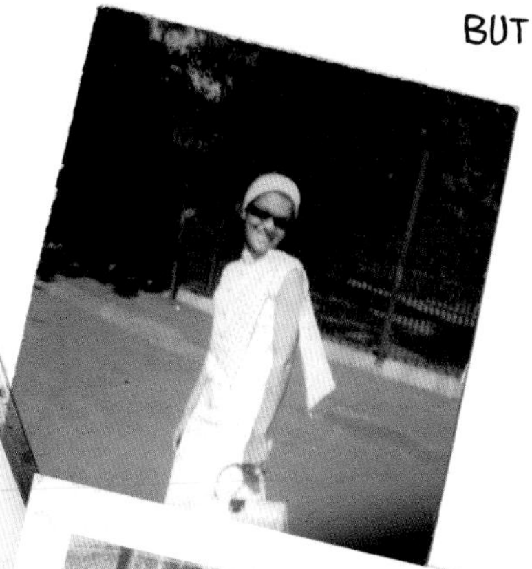

YOU EVER
HAVE TO CHOOSE
BETWEEN MONEY
AND NO MONEY?

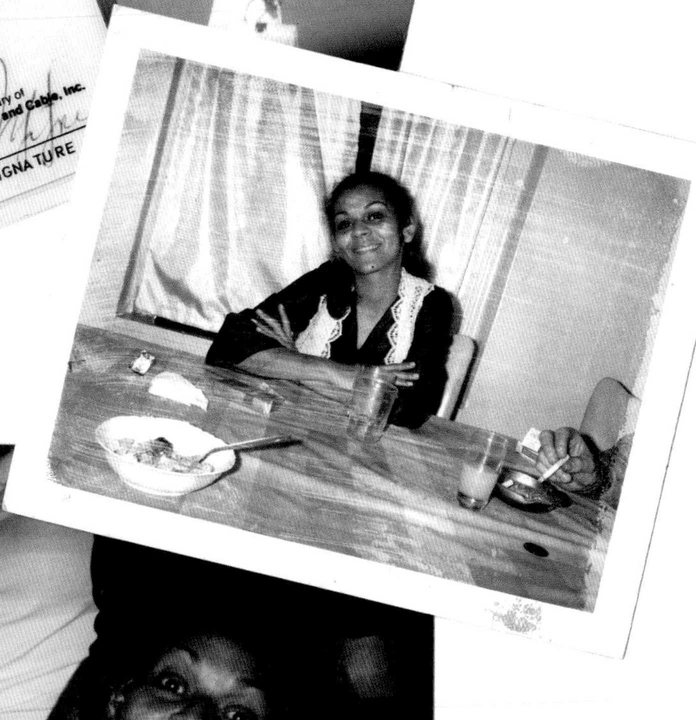

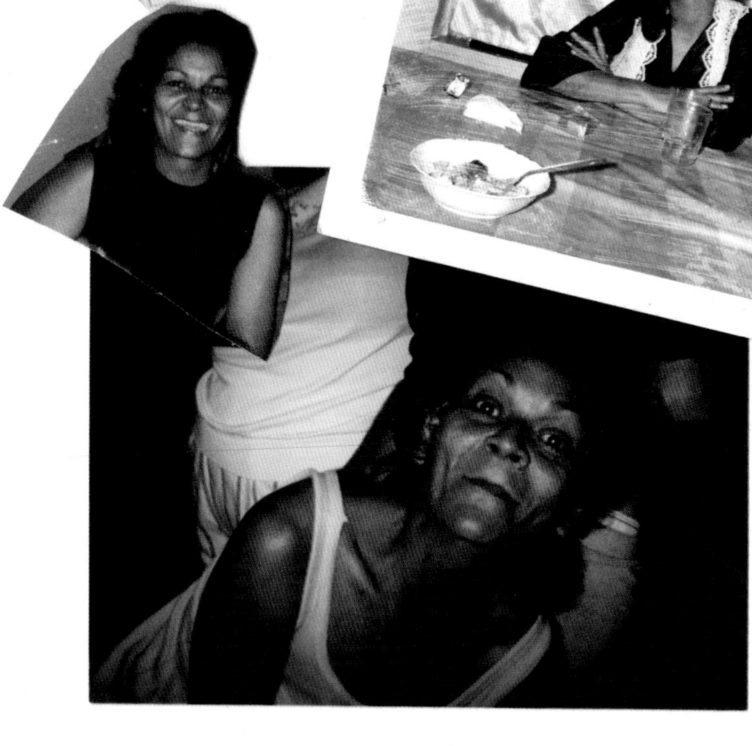

I MEAN,
REALLY
CHOOSE?

IN THE FACE OF
NOT EATING?

WHEN SHE DIED, SHE WAS UNDER FIVE FEET TALL, AND LESS THAN A HUNDRED POUNDS.

SHE SPOKE WITH A HEAVY ACCENT IN A WORLD THAT HELD THAT AGAINST HER.

SHE WAS A SMALL WOMAN WHO HAD TO SURVIVE A LIFE THAT WAS NEVER FAIR TO HER.

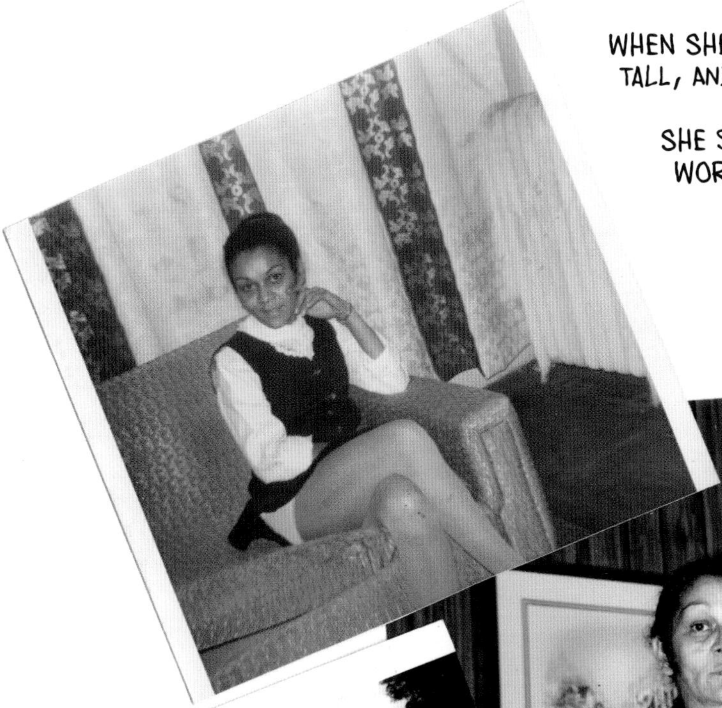

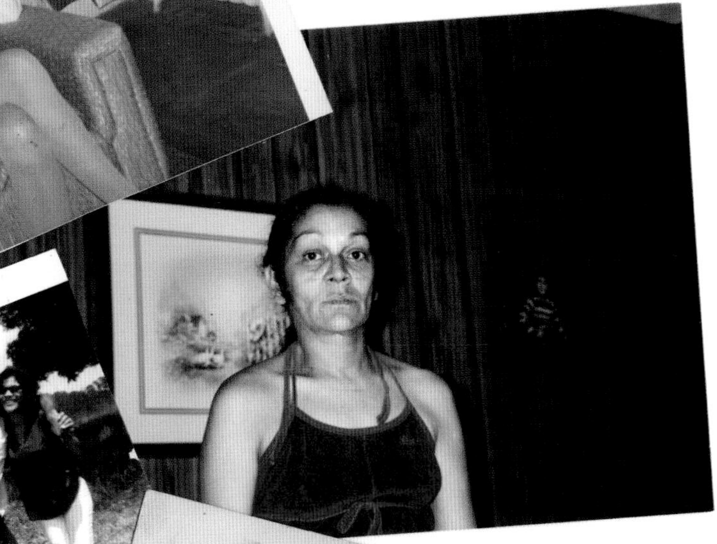

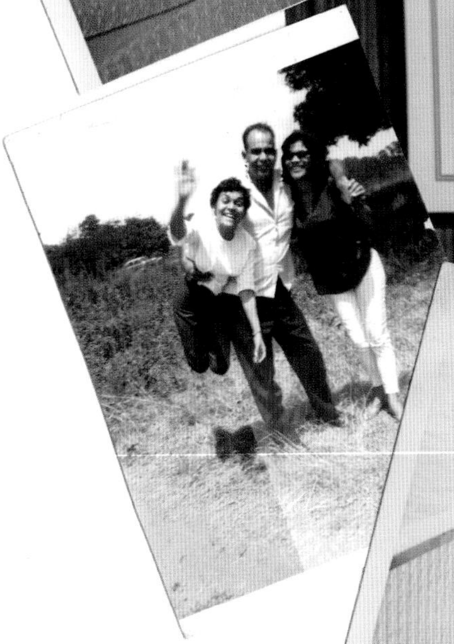

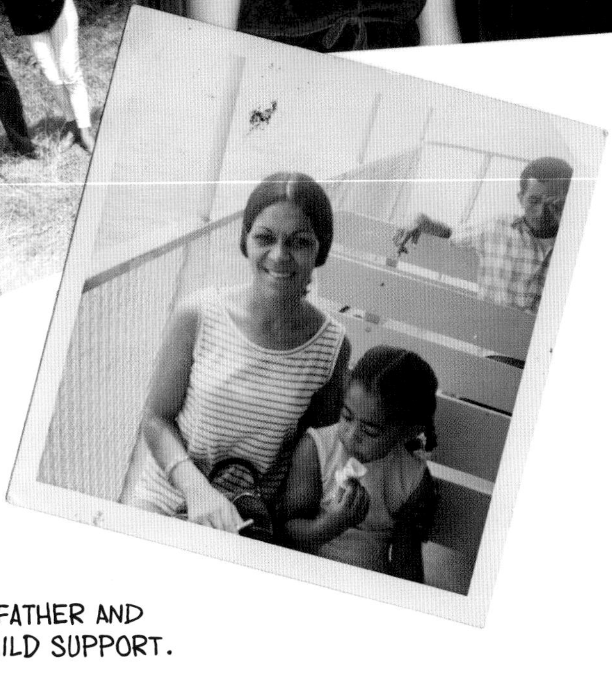

SHE WAS TAKEN ADVANTAGE OF AS A TEEN, LOST HER KID, SENT TO A CONVENT AGAINST HER WILL, THEN HAD TO MAKE IT THROUGH THE WORLD WITHOUT SUPPORT.

SHE WAS ABANDONED BY MY FATHER AND NEVER RECEIVED A CENT IN CHILD SUPPORT.

SHE WAS HURT. AND HURT PEOPLE HURT
PEOPLE. THAT'S NOT AN EXCUSE FOR HOW SHE
TREATED ME, IT'S JUST A FACT.

BUT THROUGH IT ALL, SHE GENUINELY
BELIEVED IN LOVE. I BELIEVE SHE LOVED ME,
DESPITE IT ALL. I THINK SHE DID HER BEST.

MAYBE I AM RATIONALIZING HER ABUSE.

I AM.

I KNOW IT.

I DON'T CARE.

I MISS HER.

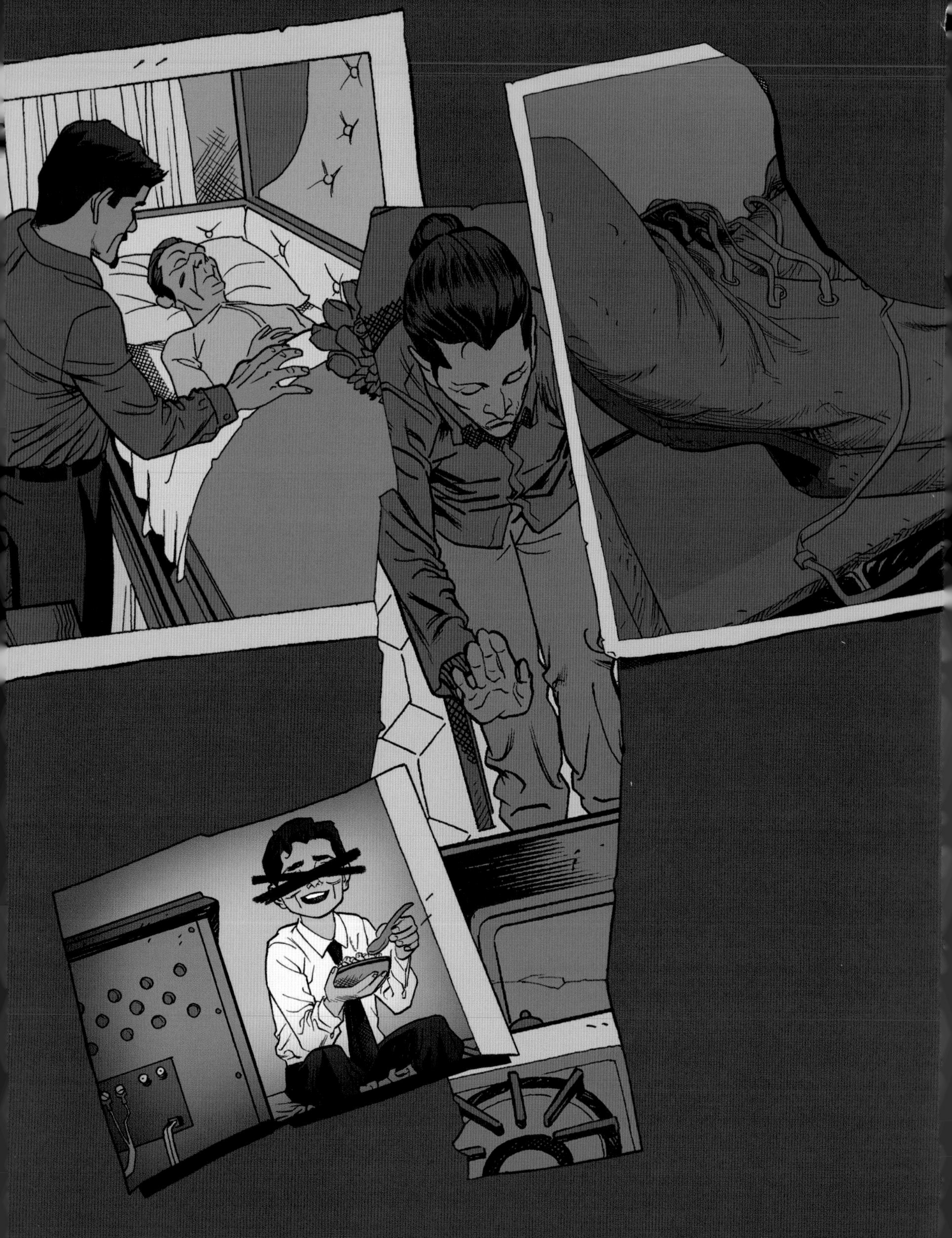

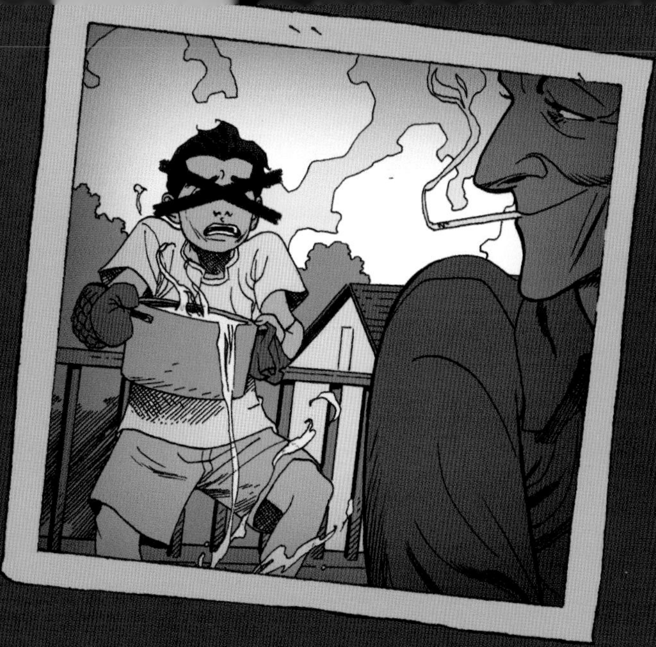

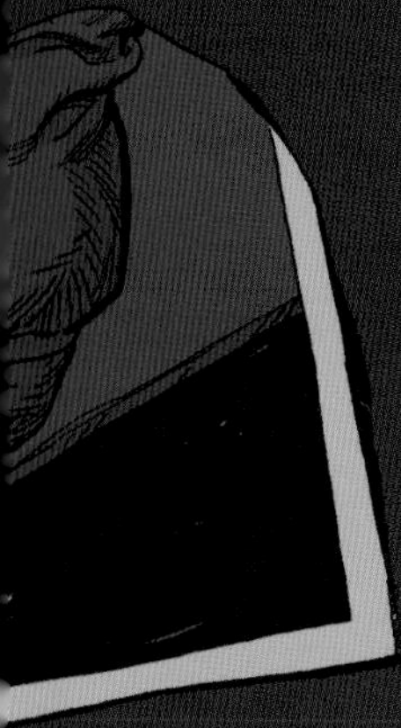

Special thanks to **Linda** for the guidance.

Extra special thanks to **Despina**, **Sophia**, **Maria**, and **Michael** for the love and support.

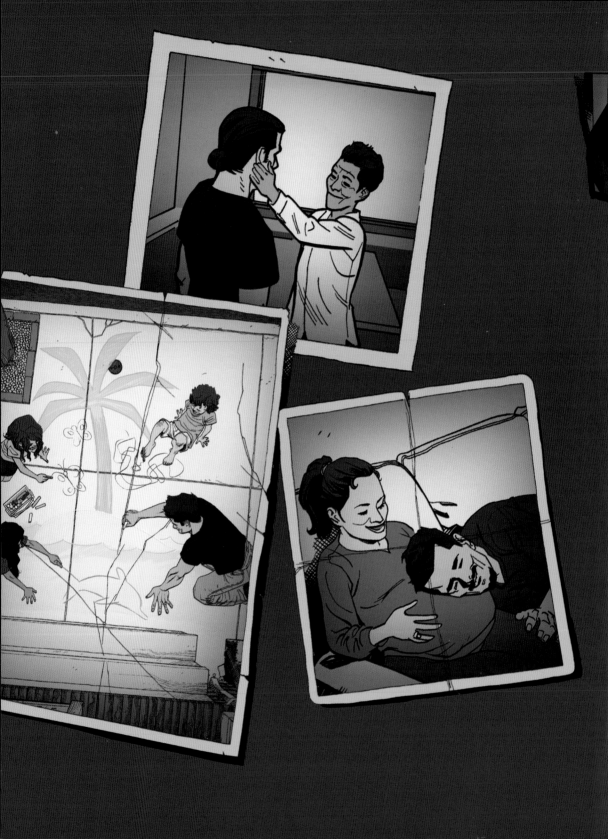

Photo by Despina Hawthorne.

**MIKE HAWTHORNE** is an Eisner and Harvey Award-nominated cartoonist and illustrator best known for his record-setting run of *Deadpool* and his more current work on *Spider-Man*. In addition to his comic work, Hawthorne has served as a story artist and illustrator for Fox, Illumination, Epic Games, and Marvel Entertainment, where he did concept work for the upcoming *Moon Knight* and *Hitmonkey* shows.

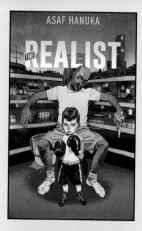

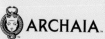